MW01248345

Cap'n Fatty's

Cruising World Yarns

by **Gary "Cap'n Fatty" Goodlander**

Contact: Gary Goodlander at Fatty@fattygoodlander.com
or visit our website at : ***FattyGoodlander.com***

ISBN# 1440447241
EAN 13# 9781440447242

Dedication:

To Herb McCormick

for giving me a second chance

and to John Burnham

for assisting me in deserving it.

My heart-felt thanks to both of you—and to the entire crew of

Cruising World.

Table of Contents

Introduction to Cap'n Fatty's Cruising World Yarns

By John Burnham

Nobody writes the way Cap'n Fatty Goodlander does. Most people sit in a cubical at a proper desk; Fatty writes with his laptop set up in the head. When I'm stretching my legs under my desk, his legs are cramping after spending the morning perched on the throne. While I'm throwing on a sweatshirt because the A.C. is cranked up so high, the humidity aboard the 38-foot *Wild Card* has Fatty dripping sweat onto his keyboard.

Of course, I suspect Fatty barely notices his environment when he's writing—he's never complained about it to me, his editor at *Cruising World* magazine. His focus on his subject is complete, as is his ability to string together a seamless narrative from one end to the other, and his stories reflect that. Reading any of his stories in the pages that follow, you're unlikely to find rigid organization, but you'll have no trouble following the plot. In fact, you probably won't even notice that you're reading—you'll be listening to Fatty's voice, telling you another story laced with insight and humor.

At regular intervals, Fatty e-mails a new story or two for his monthly "On Watch" column in *Cruising World.* Never does he take my acceptance of the story for granted. Typically, my job is to read and enjoy the column, tell him why I love it, and then spend a few minutes minimizing his overenthusiastic punctuation. In the rare instance when I offer a structural or thematic criticism, however, Fatty nearly always loses interest in the story and starts over with a fresh idea—cheerfully. The mere idea of revising a story so I'll think it's good enough to publish doesn't cut it for him. "I want my readers to be wowed," he tells me. "I want them to expect nothing but the best."

Not only does Cap'n Goodlander set high standards for himself, but he also beats his deadlines every month. And that includes delivering photos, usually with help from his wife Carolyn, posting disks with images from remote Pacific islands to Newport, Rhode Island, by Fed Ex or DHL. Some writers complain about the challenges they face; Fatty simply delivers. And the only question I hear consistently from him is "What more can I do for you, John?"

OK, it's true that Fatty has strong opinions. Sometimes he rubs readers the wrong way, and they let me know about it. But I've never printed a critical letter to the editor without receiving several responses from others rising to his defense, which reassures me that my judgment about his value as an important and entertaining voice in *Cruising World* is on target.

Fatty's stories have a lot going for them that easily invites readers along. They're typically set in unique, tropical or sub-tropical locations; they take place on or around sailboats; and they're almost always about people, about making friends, about helping others. And not just other cruisers. More often than not, through Fatty we get to know local people and we gain a sense that they're a lot like us—only sometimes a little better. Not surprisingly, these are the themes that count most to Fatty in his life as well as his writing. He's a sea gypsy, at home wherever he and Carolyn sail and with whomever he meets. He's unfailingly modest ("with much to be modest about," Carolyn often reminds him), and he consistently shows his love and respect for his wife—another thing that *CW* readers love about him.

Throughout his work, Fatty pokes fun at himself first and foremost. Whether he's making us laugh at all the stupid things he's done or seriously addressing the drinking problems he's had in the past, there's no façade. Warts and all, we get to know the man, sailor, and husband, and his candor and imperfection make the lessons he imparts all the more compelling.

My favorite story by Fatty in this book is the profile of his father called "The Guru and His Gospel." It's a tribute to the man, and the family, who made Fatty the person and the sailor he is today: self-reliant, industrious, romantic, and a little bit crazy, not to mention an insightful and entertaining writer. Fatty's recollections of his old man include some of his best storytelling and also say much about his own life story in the process.

"The world is our oyster," his dad always told him. Fatty absorbed that joyful outlook on life, and it can be found it in every story in this book. If you haven't done so already, turn the page: you're in for a treat.

John Burnham
Cruising World Editor

Foreword

I grew up aboard the 52-foot schooner, *Elizabeth.* We were poor and had no television, radio or phonograph. There were few marinas back in the 1950s. If we couldn't anchor out, we'd just tie alongside a fishing boat for free. We spent years aimlessly (and delightfully) wandering between New Orleans and the Florida Keys. Our best friends were Gulf Coast fishermen. They seldom had much but were notoriously generous with what they did have. If we stayed in a harbor for more than a week, they'd all get to know us. Each evening a bunch of them would come over to *Elizabeth*—lugging a huge red snapper or a fat grouper. My mother would cook it up with fried onions and lots of garlic. And we'd all eat and laugh and yell across *Elizabeth's* fist-banged galley table.

Afterward, as the fading sun would hiss into the sea astern, my mother and two sisters would "retire foreward" as was the custom in those days. I'd get to stay up and listen—if I didn't make a sound.

My father would slowly trim the wick to our swaying kerosene cabin lamp. Many of the men would roll cigarettes—Bull Durham and Bugler, mostly. A couple of tobaccy pipes would be thoughtfully gouged and tamped. One or two of the sailors would chew a toothpick with whatever was left of their teeth. A large rum bottle, wrapped in a small paper sack, would appear, and begin to silently circumnavigate the table.

Then it would start—the storytelling.

"...did I ever tell you about the time we brought Cap'n Mackie back—laid out on ice in the hold of *Hard Chance*—after he got his dick caught in that long-liner's spool off Cozumel?" someone would ask. And you could hear a pin drop. "...remember Mackie, with that wild Davey Crocket hair of his—and that ole brass spittoon he always carried? Anyway, we wus fish'n down off Honduras…"

And just as that story would be winding down, another sailor would nervously jump in with, "…that reminds me of the night I was in the wheelhouse—standing right next to Charlie the Whale—when he piled *Lucky Strike* up on the rocks off Campeche…"

Each tale seemed better than the last. A whole new action-packed, word-filled world opened to me. I thrilled to the stories of 60-foot swells, sinking boats and dying men; of loose women, tight rodes and slack tides; of crazily caulking the topsides with socks; of desperately manning the awash deck pumps until dawn; of running her aground in the eye of a hurricane to save the crew.

During a particularly good story I'd have to be careful not to pee my pants.

After a while, I began to study the stories, to carefully dissect them element by element.

The first thing I noticed was that the storytellers were like gunslingers.

You were only as good as your last tale. And some younger, faster gunslinger was always ready to jump in and take away the conversational spotlight with a highly-crafted line like, "…did I ever tell you about the time I was gut-shot in the lobby of a Mexican bank while stark-naked?"

Details were important: They nailed the words to reality. But you couldn't allow 'em to slow down the headlong rush of the story. Plot too, was important; plot was the *boss*. And, the most important part of any story was the lead sentence. It had to grab the listener by the throat, make a promise, *and* show physical action—all at the same time, invisibly.

No wonder the best storyteller was the most respected man in any harbor.

I'd listen all night. I didn't just *like* the stories, I *lived* for the stories. They were magic. They transported me. They intoxicated me. They were my first drug.

Right then and there, I decided to be a storyteller.

I want to thank the crew of *Cruising World* magazine for making that possible—in a manner that far exceeds my wildest boyhood dreams.

Mind the rudder,
Or meet the rock.

Stupid Things I've Done

The mighty short path from Good Samaritan to raving Chicken Man is paved with the best intentions

There are two types of people who can't understand how our shipboard marriage works: people who know us well and people who don't. Carolyn is, well, a very unusual person. She and I have cruised together now for the last 35 years, pausing only to build or rebuild our various boats. Since 1970, she has never had refrigeration, running water or a door to her bedroom. Ditto a telephone, 110 volts or television. I've almost never worked ashore, and we have often gone a year or two between writing assignments.

Once I heard her telling a well-dressed man at a yacht club party, "We don't count my husband's income—because it isn't worth counting!" Another time I caught her telling a girlfriend, "We don't have much money, because they pay my husband what he's worth!"

And I'll admit, there have been times during our cruising life when it wasn't just rice and beans, it was rice and *bean*! "You cut, I'll choose," she'd say grimly.

But we're still together. And I treasure every day and each ocean mile passed in her wonderful, sensuous company.

What's our secret? Well, I think the key to our watery marriage is our shared passions—for sailing, traveling, and each other—and our sense of humor.

"The only reason I'm still with you," she once told me, only half joking, "is because every day you do something stupider than the last, and I can't believe you can continue to top yourself!"

Some days I'm just full of energy. When I am, I like to work on the boat and do all those pesky little jobs I've been putting off. This was one of those days. So I grabbed my tool box and went forward.

"Whoa," Carolyn said. She was in the cockpit, reading a magazine with one eye and the horizon with the other. "Where are you going?"

"Foredeck," I said briskly. "The roller furler has been a tad sticky lately. I'm gonna check it out."

"Now?" she asked. "In the middle of the Indian Ocean? Fatty, it's blowing over 20."

"Why not," I said. "We're off the wind. *Wild Card* is stable. I do it all the time at anchor. What's the dif?"

She shrugged and then tossed up her hands with familiar rueful exasperation.

I went forward and started disassembling my roller-furler housing just as I'd done a dozen times before. The only problem this time was that with the constant "popping" of the jib off the wind, a split retaining ring had finally worn away its aluminum shoulder and slid up. To my utter amazement, bearing balls started slowly spitting out of the gear housing and bouncing down the spray-dampened deck. One by one. Like a bratty kid spitting peas.

I only had nanoseconds to react.

Now, I'm in pretty good shape. I can move fast. And, I'm pretty clever, too. So I decided to leap aft and boldly *smother* all those escaping bearings balls by falling upon them with outstretched, scooping arms. Thus I leapt a mighty leap.

I really thought I was going to do it. There I was: completely horizontal, fully extended, and directly above the bouncing bearings balls. *Yes, I was going to redeem myself right before Carolyn's eyes.*

When— "Boing! Twang!"—my safety harness (clipped to the staysail stay) came up short. And I crashed to the deck, completely stunned, just in time to watch the bearings balls, one by one, disappear into the Indian Ocean. Ugh!

As I struggled with consciousness, I could hear Carolyn laughing in the cockpit. "Oh, my God," she was saying. "That was *so* funny! The look on your face when the harness took up—priceless! Do it again, Fatty, do it again!"

We seldom sail with guests—never, if a potential one has communicated with a previous one. Danny Daly, a Chicago garbage-truck driver, hadn't had that good fortune. We picked him up in Bequia and immediately headed back out to sea. I was exhausted, but we were in a rush to be somewhere for something. The sea was rough; the waves were like square boulders. It was midnight. Danny slept on the cabin sole between Carolyn's bunk and my bunk. Carolyn was on watch. We were hard on the wind, really taking a pounding. I was fast asleep, in a deep, exhausted slumber.

We got nailed by a really large sea. *Bang!* Somehow, the impact from the wave flipped on our bilge-alarm float switch. Now, I hate quiet bilge alarms. This one was an industrial burglar alarm that I'd ripped off the wall of the warehouse where I'd built the boat. It was loud—really loud. It was designed for a huge factory.

The sound of it paralyzed me. I jumped up, totally disoriented, still mostly asleep, and in the middle of a weird aquatic dream.

Well, perhaps I should let Danny tell it: "It was, like, *The Last Bell*," he said afterward. "I was really nauseous, just dropping off to sleep. It was pitch-black in the cabin, I couldn't see my hand in front of my face and I was pretty scared anyway, when I heard *The Last Bell*. The sound was *huge*, like it was right inside my head, man. I didn't have the faintest idea what it was. Just, like, a death knell! Then, before I could do anything about it—*wham*!—all the breath was knocked out of me. Completely. I had no air. I was, like, dying! And then, just as my auto reflexes kicked in and I started to breath in again, gasping in a giant lung full of air, another foot came down and cut off my windpipe."

My perspective was completely different. The bell was so loud it filled my *entire world*. I was still asleep, and I certainly didn't remember we had a guest aboard. I assumed we had a bilge full of water and were sinking. I jumped up, terrified. It was pitch-black. The boat was swaying wildly. Why were we sinking? I'd vaguely remembered a large impact before the bell went off.

Suddenly, I froze. "Oh, no!" I groaned. I was standing on something—something alive! What could it be?

"A whale!" I thought groggily. "We've hit a whale so hard that it's holed us and I'm standing on its back."

What should I do first, I wondered. SSB? EPIRB? Liferaft?

Suddenly, the cabin light came on. Carolyn poked her head into the cabin. She looked at me completely perplexed, "Why is he blue?" She pointed at Danny, writhing beneath my feet.

"I'll never forget *The Last Bell*," said a hastily departing Danny as he leapt ashore in Fort-de-France, Martinique.

Yes, I've done some stupid things. I suppose we've all done this one: The outboard won't start. You get frustrated. You give it a *really* savage tug, and then, when it's finally started, you calmly turn to your wife in the dinghy and ask, "What happened to your nose? Why are you bleeding?"

I try to not get into trouble. I honestly do. But it isn't easy because trouble often finds me. Once, in the early 1980s, Carolyn and I were dinghying through Cruz Bay harbor in St. John, U.S.V.I., when we come upon a scene of absolute bedlam.

A bareboat was anchored right in the middle of the crowded harbor. It was in gear and running at full throttle. Because its anchor was down, it was scribing a giant arc at the end of its anchor rode and hitting the moored boats again and again and again.

Its crew, all six of them, were in their lifejackets. Huddled around the mast. Screaming. Total panic prevailed.

"Oh, no," Carolyn said. "Don't even think about it, Fatty!"

"Come on," I told her. "Don't be so hard, honey! Let's help them out. It'll just take a second. Swing me alongside."

With a grimace, Carolyn momentarily rammed the offending vessel and I leapt aboard. The crew didn't even notice. I strolled to the cockpit, and pushed the electric kill switch on the diesel. It didn't stop. I grabbed the throttle, and pulled it aft. The engine didn't slow down.

Hmmm.

Meanwhile, we were still hitting the other boats. Repeatedly. I mean, really ramming into them. It was difficult to think. People were screaming. It was a fiberglass repairman's wet dream. I forced myself to be calm and to think logically.

I grabbed the shifter and attempted to pull it aft. It wouldn't budge. I really yanked at it. Nothing. I cursed it. Nada.

I grabbed a winch handle. I hit it. Its handle fell to the cockpit floor.

Oops.

The diesel was still running. In gear. At top speed.

"Oh, darn!" I muttered, knowing I'd have to chance tactics. I grabbed the wheel and straighten it. This caused us to pull straight on our anchor line and stop spinning circles. I temporarily lashed the wheel with a sheet end.

"Don't worry," I said to the startled bareboaters, as I nonchalantly strolled passed them, "I do this all the time!"

I went up the bow, waited until she clocked into a hole between vessels, whipped out my Buck knife, and cleanly sliced the anchor line. We went shooting out of Cruz Bay like a scalded cat. To me the sea is safety. Now I had all the time in the world. Nothing was being damaged. There was far less chance of anyone being hurt. Things were starting to look up. But not everyone felt this way.

"Oh, my God," screamed one of the ladies, "he's taking us out to sea! Harry! Harry! He's taking us to sea!"

It was difficult to communicate. I'd never dealt with a demonically possessed diesel before. But, boy, are they *loud*! I decided I'd stop the engine first, then explain what a nice guy I was later.

"Steer," I commanded one of the men and went below.

It was a brand-new, pristine 48-foot bareboat. The engine was under the aft cabin bunk. I could smell the motor, and it was hot, hot, hot. I decided I'd better shut it off quick or it might explode or shoot a piston through its block. I yanked up the plywood under the mattress. There it was, even louder. I could smell the rubber and plastic melting. It was giving off heat like a coal stove. It was leaking oil, too. Worse, the oil was getting on the fan belt and it was winging all over the ceiling, upholstery, mattress, and curtains of the plush cabin.

Oh, well.

The first thing I tried to do was shut off the fuel to the engine. I could see where the fuel line went into the fuel pump but I saw no shut off.

I didn't want to just cut the copper tubing for fear the cherry-hot engine would ignite the diesel. I looked around the engine compartment and spotted a short stainless-steel pipe—maybe a pump handle?—and used it to flatten the tubing so that no fuel could get through.

The engine revved on. Next, I attempted to short-out its electric kill switch. Nada. In frustration, I brutally yanked out both wires going to the kill switch. Still the engine screamed.

The third thing I tried to do was to throttle it back. On top of the fuel pump I could see the throttle-cable end. I removed it by sliding its spring-loaded Morse swivel connecter aft and lifting the cable completely off the engine. Then I flipped the lever back and forth. Nothing. Either that wasn't the throttle or, for some reason, it was useless.

The engine started to sound a lower note, which seemed meaner, somehow.

I spotted a battery switch, and dashed to shut it off. I slipped and fell during this mad dash, shattering a mirror and heavily crushing a lamp shade.

"Damn it!" I screamed.

As near as I could tell, there was neither electricity nor fuel getting to the engine. And the throttle was in the idle position. And yet still it ran. By this point, I was starting to whimper. "Die, you sumbitch, die!"

I grabbed a large piece of varnished interior wood, wrenched it free, and used it as a lever on the tranny. Suddenly there was a horrible noise, a *very* expensive grinding sound, and the boat was shooting backward. I heard people falling on deck, the rudder slamming hard over, the wheel spinning.

"Not a good idea, Fatty," I said as I jammed it back into forward again. More screaming, falling on deck.

All this takes longer to tell then do.

I decided that I'd either kill the engine or it would kill me. I found something large and heavy to use as a club, and savagely beat the air cleaner off it. I knew now there was only one way to kill it: Cut off its air supply. Once the air cleaner was gone, there was a hole. I thought, "Gee, what should I toss in there?" It was difficult to move because I was covered in hot, black oil and I was very slippery. I grabbed the pillows—and instantly beheld the results of another classically stupid Fatty idea. Suddenly, the air was filled with feathers, millions of them: oily, hot, stained feathers everywhere!

And the engine kept running.

By now, I admit, almost all rational thought had fled my overheated brain. It was just *me* and that *f'n* engine. A classic fight to the death! I knew what I had to find: something to seal off the air, something hard enough *and* soft enough. There was a woman's purse on the floor. I emptied it. Inside was a compact, with a makeup mirror. It was dished. I put it on the air-intake hole in the middle of the head of the diesel and pressed down as hard as I could. The engine slowed. I shifted position, pressed harder, cursed louder—and finally it shut off.

Silence has never sounded better. I stumbled back on deck, bleeding from every knuckle, covered in oil and sweat and fear, and completely basted with feathers. I looked like a nautical Chicken Man. I could see Carolyn speeding towards us in the dinghy, attempting to swing alongside, a big frown on her face.

"I think," I said calmly to the still-quivering but obviously relieved crew, "that you might want to have someone check that engine. Some of the... er, parts... might have jiggled loose."

They thanked me and assured me that they could sail their vessel back into Cruz Bay by themselves.

"We were just sitting there charging our batteries," said one of the bewildered men, "when the engine sped up. It ran at full rpm for a couple of minutes, and then must have sort of jiggled into gear. That's when we starting hitting things. Do you want some cash for your troubles?"

"No, thanks!" I said, "All the money in the world wouldn't be enough."

"What's with the feathers," Carolyn asked as she swung alongside. "Did you, like, destroy the entire interior?"

"Don't be silly," I said. "I didn't do anything that, well, 20 grand or so won't fix."

"What's your name?" one of the bareboaters asked as we pulled away.

I thought about that for a moment. I knew that I had the Good Samaritan law on my side. I also knew the Virgin Islands is a small place and the bareboat company wasn't going to be exactly pleased when they saw the boat—or what was left of it by now.

"Tarr," I said. "Cap'n Tarr. But you can call me Jack."

The Sea Gypsy's Guide to the Oceans

Congratulations! You have a well-found craft that you've outfitted for offshore sailing. You're ready to sail around the world. But, alas, you have one small problem: You don't have much money—only $5,000. Would it be foolish to set off with such a piddling balance in the account?

No. Foolish would be *not* to set off. You've got the boat; you're worked hard outfitting it; you're ready to quit your job. Go for it! Just because you don't have as much money as the other guys doesn't mean you can't have *more* fun than they do—and be safer and more seamanlike as you go.

Here are some simple suggestions on how to circumnavigate inexpensively with the vessel you have now.

The first thing you have to realize is that if you don't have much money, you can't spend it like people who do. That seems self-evident in principal; in practice, it's rather hard to grasp. The problem is that you'll find yourself in constant contact with wealthy retired cruisers spending $50,000 a year while circumnavigating—and you have to steel yourself not to succumb to the "I deserve it too" temptation.

Think of it as a challenge: Sailing around the world on peanuts takes far more effort, determination and intelligence than doing so while well funded. Are you up to the task? Of course you are—because you are willing to work longer, harder and smarter to accomplish your goals.

One thing you don't want if you are on a limited budget offshore, is old shoreside bills. My wife, Carolyn, and I have only one annual bill: That's the $250 for SailMail (our shipboard SSB e-mail provider), which we need so that I can market my writing.

We don't have a house or a storage shed or a car back "home" in the States—nor do we bet against ourselves by buying insurance. For us, this makes sense. Freedom is our drug, and we mainline it—we don't need or want most of what Middle American considers "the necessities of life." That's why we think of ourselves as sea gypsies—not yachtsman or cruisers or circumnavigators.

OK, let's get down to the nitty-gritty. To voyage cheaply, you need a relatively modest boat without a lot of toys. That's logical. But you also need to sail a slightly different route and schedule from those of many other voyagers. For instance, almost all circumnavigators want to spend three months in French Polynesia. It is far, far more economical to spend 11 of those weeks in the pristine Marquises and Tuamotus and only one week in metropolitan and ultraexpensive Papeete, than it would be to do the opposite.

If you don't have much money, then you have to visit inexpensive countries more often and longer, spent less time in cities, almost never go to marinas, become knowledgeable about clearance and visa fees, limit your shore side activities to those that are free, and walk and take local buses.

How do you learn about the actual costs of one destination versus another? The logical ways: by reading the guidebooks, doing internet research, and, most important, attending to the word of mouth of fellow cruisers. Chances are, many of the people you meet while circumnavigating know a hell of a lot more about where you are and where you are going than you do. They've been there longer. Use their expertise to cruise both smarter and cheaper.

Not everyone sails east to west, A few lovable fools always go the other way; they're also invaluable sources of accurate, current knowledge. Example: While circumnavigating from 2000 to2004 aboard our extremely modest Hughes 38, *Wild Card*, Carolyn and I weren't flabbergasted by the astronomical prices in Tahiti. We expected them. We spent almost no money while there, because we knew that a day ashore in Papeete would cost the equivalent of a month ashore in Southeast Asia.

We also knew that while our circumnavigation would take approximately four years, it was up to us how much of that time we spent in the Papeetes, the New Caledonias, and the Singapores of the world. Instead, we concentrated on the less visited, "storeless" islands of Oceania; Indonesia, Southeast Asia, India, Chagos, Madagascar, and Africa—places where our dollars went a delightfully long way. We dipped down to New Zealand and Oz only when the U.S. dollar became extremely strong, and we left when it corrected itself six months later. As it worked out, those were glorious months of very cheap First World living!

Buy Low, Eat High

The trick, of course, is to buy stuff where it is dirt cheap—and then consume it in expensive places. We usually carry between 50 and 100 pounds of Thai jasmine rice, and 20 pounds of dry beans. Basically, these two staple items mean we'll never starve, even if we're marooned on a deserted island or adrift at sea for many months.

We're also avid carnivores, so we can our own meat in half pint and pint glass jars. This is fun, inexpensive and delicious. We usually carry 100 jars of pork, chicken and beef that we can use to cook in a variety of ways. In addition, we occasionally can fish, heart-of-palm, beans and veggies. Many of our Australian and South African cruising friends, air dry their fruits and veggies as well as their fish and meat. We're currently experimenting in this area, with widely mixed results. (Saltfish: yeck!)

Paper products are a problem. They are expensive, easily damaged by dampness, and very bulky. Sometimes we re-cut our paper towels, and use washable rags when possible. But we like paper towels and soft toilet paper, so we consider them one of our extravagances.

We eat well while watching our pennies; wherever we go, we eat locally grown products. If sailing offshore is an adventure, so, too, are the markets of Southeast Asia. Just leave your Western food prejudices behind: Those roasted sewer-pipe bugs in Thailand are tastier than you might think.

Many of our cruising friends "sail the farm" and "live off the land" to a far greater extent than we do. But you have to be really into it; it takes a lot of time to be a hunter/gatherer. It's possible, and a growing number of sea gypsies find it highly fulfilling, to be as independent from land and civilization as possible. But it *is* a lot of work.

Still, it's certainly possible while on passage to easily catch enough fish to dramatically stretch your ship's stores and vastly improve your protein diet—and have a lot of fun doing it along the way

Maintaining the Craft

A frugal sea gypsy pays to haul his or her boat only if there is major work to be done. Otherwise, the gypsy merely scrapes the bottom, hoists the anchors, and sails to somewhere warm with big tides. Once there, the sailor lays the boat against the wall to paint the bottom and replace the zincs. It's absolutely free. If, while out on the tide, the discovery is made that the prop shaft is bent or the rudder is starting to delaminate, the gypsy removes the offending item, leisurely fixes it ashore, then remounts it on a later tide. No surcharge.

What's the exact procedure for laying against the wall? Simple: Sail your boat to a place where it's a regular practice, then ask the guy on the boat next to you.

Of course, careening—heeling your boat down with the aid of lines—is also still possible. If the rum-soaked pirates of yore regularly did it, then surely you can figure it out. It's almost (but not quite) impossible to paint your entire boat in this manner. However, you have all the time in the world, unlike when using the tide, and it's amazing how much of one side you can cover at a time.

Pulling the mast? I never hire a crane for this. I just wait until two of my "big-boat" friends, aboard craft of 50 feet or more are rafted together in a calm anchorage. Then I wiggle *Wild Card* in between. I attach their spinnaker halyards to my mast just below the spreaders, then ask them both to winch at the same time. Thus, with perfect control, I pull out my stick as if it were a Fabergé egg! Again, no charge.

Ditto for restepping.

I hate working on the masthead from a bosun's chair, especially if I am mounting a new tricolor, antenna, or wind-instrument array. Instead, if I'm in or near a city, I motor over to a city bridge of approximately the correct height, then maneuver with dock lines until my masthead lies within easy reach of the railings. I've done this a dozen times in Chicago without a problem—although, I must admit, I don't stay around too long afterward to discuss the process with city officials. I find such officials to be, well, humorless.

On the topic of fuel and lube oil, you can save money by running your engine less often, purchasing your petroleum products in cheap places like Venezuela, India, and the Mideast, buying your fuel at duty-free prices after you've cleared out, jugging your fuel from a service station rather than buying from a marina, and buying your lube oil at auto-parts stores rather than marine chandleries.

I buy my diesel fuel filters by the carton, wholesale, before I leave the States, then store each one in an individual resealable bag. I no longer carry an extensive inventory of spare parts for my diesel engine. I used to carry a spare starter motor, alternator, voltage regulator and a complete set of gaskets and spare injectors. Now I just air-freight in what I need when I need it—which is ultimately far less expensive. The salt air gets to stuff whether you use it or not, and the boat is happier without the extra weight.

I've never understood the "fancy yacht" syndrome. I mean, what kind of a sicko wants to spend millions of dollars on a pristine gold-plater—and then sail it to Hispaniola and anchor it off Cap-Hatien? It just doesn't make sense to me.

I don't believe in spending a lot of money to cosmetically maintain my vessel. I'd rather spend it on what I call "strength and safety" issues. Or

actually cruising. But not on varnish or topside wax or brass polish. The result is, of course, that my boat looks like crap. But it does so while averaging about 10,000 ocean miles a year. It's your choice. I've made mine.

Of course, all boats require *some* money to maintain. But not too much, if you are careful and do your own work. Sails and running rigging last many years if you guard against UV damage and chafe—or only a few weeks if you don't. A spool of polyester line is laughably cheap from its manufacturer in Durban, South Africa. When I sailed across the Pacific, my goal wasn't to go fast, but to make the passage as comfortably as possible, while loading up the rig as little as possible. Thus we broke nothing during that 8,000-mile stretch of trade-wind sailing, neither gear nor records. Still, we averaged 128 miles a day. Not fast, but not slow either.

Good antifouling paint is cheap in Asia. There are large tides in many parts of the world, and as I've mentioned, many yacht clubs and marinas will allow you to go against the wall for free.

We only hauled out once during our circumnavigation—when we had to replace our cutlass bearing and patch some fiberglass. This occurred after I, ahem, smashed into the Great Barrier Reef! (Yeah, I knew it was there. Stop laughing, OK?)

What to Bring, What to Leave behind

Don't bring dogs, cats or birds if you expect to stop in NZ, Oz or any Muslim country. Some countries and small islands have a foolproof method of preventing the spread of rabies; they shoot any dog that shows up. Our friend Pauline aboard *Summer Breeze* had to hastily flee the Maldives before they plugged Charlie, her beloved fish-catching poodle.

SSB radio: You don't have to have one of these—just a VHF will do. But we were lucky, and the wonderful people of St. John, U.S.V.I., collectively purchased an ICOM M710 SSB for us just before we set off on our first circumnavigation; we've since got our ham licenses to maximize its benefit.

A SSB radio can save you a lot of money, time and trouble. Most important, you can learn from the mistakes of cruisers ahead. Just a few of the benefits: You can avoid paying bribes to corrupt officials, avoid ports with expensive user fees, and learn which boat boy is a thief or a rip-off.

Visas and harbor fees: Most countries welcome cruising boats, and charge them only modest fees. But not all. At one point, the Seychelles wanted $100 a day from visiting boats—very few of which showed up once the word spread. The country quickly changed its policy when they realized that it was far better to collect a couple of dollars a day from a lot of boats versus $100 a day from no boats.

Australia, Indonesia, and India all require that visa fees be paid before arrival—often not an easy or inexpensive thing to arrange.

Charts and guidebooks: The bad news is that traditional charts are horribly expensive; the good news is you probably don't need to buy many. Before I left the United States, I purchased $200 worth of privately printed charts and a couple of Pacific guidebooks. After that, I only purchased two additional charts in New Zealand. The rest we copied by hand or machine, others were given to us or we traded for them.

In a pinch, we borrow a chart and laboriously hand copy it in pencil. Sure it takes a lot of time, and I don't necessarily recommend this. It's just a possible last resort.

If we don't want to take the time to hand draw a whole new chart, we just tick off (and numerically record) a series of carefully considered GPS waypoints. After all, something is better than nothing. This isn't a perfect solution and can get you into serious trouble, but we have occasionally been forced to do so, without problem. Rationalization: There's about 3,000 miles of empty water between the Galápagos and Fatu Hiva. Do you really need an expensive chart when a sheet of graph paper will do nearly as well? Needless to say, if you have to change course because of a dismasting or health emergency, a piece of graph paper without the needed GPS points ain't gonna help much!

As an absolutely last resort, I take a series of digital photos of the chart with my camera, provided the chart isn't copyrighted.

Batteries: I believe in carrying good batteries—and maintaining them well. Stateside batteries aren't cheap, but they're well-made. Asian batteries are *very* cheap, but have a shorter life span and lower at-rest voltage.

Solar cells can be purchased very cheaply in Malaysia; the very nice BP panels are manufactured in Kuala Lumpur.

Travel inland: Carolyn and I would like to do more inland travel as we cruise, but it is relatively expensive. Often we "help somebody out" by traveling long distances to get his or her boat or car back to them—getting an all-expenses-paid shore trip in exchange for our time. It works for everyone.

The bottom line to all of this is that with a little ingenuity and a lot of hard work, you can sail around the world for *far less* than it costs to live and work in the good ol' USA.

It's Already Beer Time in Tonga

Cruising through the world's time zones sets this sailor back—way back

Sailing around the world is confusing—at least to a sun-drenched, rum-soaked guy like me. The sad fact is, I can't seem to keep track of where I am, or even *when* I am. Time zones make me zone right out. A few days into our circumnavigation, soon after St. Thomas was astern, the sun started setting later and later. "Gee, and I thought things happened slowly in the Virgins," I told my wife, Carolyn.

"Don't be silly," she scolded. "We've sailed into a new time zone, that's all."

"I musta missed the sign."

"It's simple, really," Carolyn said. "Every 15 degrees of longitude is a new time zone."

"No problem," I said. "I don't care if the sun sets later here."

"Actually," Carolyn said, with a wicked grin, "it sets earlier."

"Huh?"

"We have to set our clock an hour back."

"Let me get this straight," I said. "We're going about 150 nautical miles forward every day, so we have to set our clock back."

"Exactly!" said Carolyn. "See how easy it is once you understand."

Not that easy. There's more than one clock aboard *Wild Card,* our S&S Hughes 38. In fact, there are about a dozen clocks, watches, and timers. That's not to mention our computers, digital radios, and camera/video machines. We finally managed to get all of them reset, just as we sailed into another time zone.

"I guess we'll have to start all over again," said Carolyn, "unless, of course, you want to use Greenwich and keep the same time all the time."

"OK," I said. "Which reminds me—I'm hungry. When's dinner?"

"The same time as always," she said. "About an hour after midnight."

"Huh?"

Now turns out—and this is really strange—that Greenwich Mean Time (GMT) doesn't exist anymore. It's now called Coordinated Universal Time (UTC), and many old salts, some of whom are still tottering around the tropics, are used to referring to GMT/UTC as Zulu. Just after we'd managed to (yet again) switch all the clocks and timers over to it, I told Carolyn that I didn't think using GMT/UTC/Zulu would work.

"OK," she said. "You wanna use ship's time?"

"What the hell is that?" I asked.

"It's whatever you say it is," Carolyn said. "You're the captain—you can marry people, and you can set your own ship's time."

"You mean I can just say, 'Time for dinner!' or 'Time for sex!' and it happens?"

"Not exactly, Carolyn said. "But sorta."

"In that case," I said, "it's time to party!"

About a month later, I thought I finally understood it: Every 15 degrees of longitude is an hour.

"Except for the Marquesas," Carolyn said. "They're a half hour different."

"Why?" I immediately regretted asking.

"Because they don't like being governed by Tahiti, so they use a different time."

"I'm gonna cry," I said.

The breaking point came as we sailed into the Kingdom of Tonga in the western Pacific. One minute it was Wednesday, then the next moment it was Friday.

"What the *hell* happened to Thursday??" I demanded, rudely shaking Carolyn awake in her off-watch bunk. "They've gone too far this time."

"Don't get so excited," she said sleepily. "It's the International Date Line."

"You mean to say I don't get it back until the other side of the world, when we pass through the Prime Meridian?"

"Actually," Carolyn said, "you never get it back, Fatty. It's gone."

"They can't do this to me," I wailed. "I was planning to win the lottery on Thursday! Sleep with Madonna! Understand Bob Dylan's lyrics!"

"Don't have a cow," she said. "Besides, we really didn't cross the International Date Line yet—it's just that the king of Tonga wanted to be the first on the planet to see each new day, so he had them jog the Date Line around the kingdom."

"You're making this up!" I cried, holding my hands over my ears.

"I'm not," she said. "In fact the motto of the local royal beer is "The First Beer of the Day for the Whole World!"

At last, I thought, cracking a cold one: Now that makes sense.

Single Female Solo Sailor Seeks…

It's an old familiar story: Sailor meets a member of opposite sex, starts to flirt, falls in love, sails across ocean.

"I was sitting in a bar in La Paz, Mexico," said Jennifer Scheifla, "when this cute little Italian guy with bluish-green eyes said to me, 'You and your boat are just rusting here, Jennifer. You are either going to learn to play the offshore sailing game or not, eh? Why don't you and *Vigilant* cruise to the South Pacific in company with me and *Ghibli* instead of wasting away in Margaritaville?'"

"I thought about it for ten seconds or so," recalls Jennifer, "and then asked the guy on the other side of me if he'd be my crew. 'Sure,' he said. So I told the Italian guy, 'OK, why not?'"

"Of course," said Jennifer, "the crew-guy crapped out at the last minute, and I was about a thousand miles off the coast of Mexico before it truly dawned on me that I was all alone in the middle of the Pacific with only a cat and a dog for crew—and neither of them could steer worth a darn!"

Jennifer Scheifla, 25, is not your average woman—not by any measure.

There are times when she appears incredibly macho. For instance, she was recently paying out her anchor chain in a deep water anchorage in the Marquesas, French Polynesia, when it jumped out of her anchor windlass gypsy head. Faster and faster it paid out, until Jennifer literally leapt upon it with her entire body and somehow managed to slow it down enough to grab it with her bare hands.

"Gee, I think I just broke a couple of my fingers!" she laughed, as she watched them swelling and turning black and blue. "That was *exciting*, huh?" An admiring German sailor saw the same incident from a slightly different perspective. "She smothered the escaping chain with her iron bosom!"

Jennifer isn't an easy person to pin down. Is she joking? Utterly serious? Hopelessly naive? All of the above? She flip-flops between Captain Macho and Miss Manners personae; and the words on her favorite T-shirt reveal the strange dichotomy within: *Ladies Sewing Circle and Terrorist Society*. "Don't paint me as some super-macho singlehander. I'm not. I just recently learned how to sail. There is much about seamanship I don't know, and I'm still learning new stuff every day. I don't care about setting records or sailing into the history books. I'm really just searching for love—in all the wrong places, evidently! I'd love a quote-man-unquote to fix all the stuff that isn't working on my boat."

Jennifer hated her Pittsburgh, Pennsylvania high school. "I told everyone I could—my parents, teachers and counselors—I was dropping out. My big passion in life has always been the sea, above or below its surface. So I wrote to six dive resorts around the world offering to work for "air and food." All six responded positively, and I soon discovered myself working in Belize, and the following year studying dolphins in the Bahamas."

In the Bahamas, she first encountered sea gypsies and was seduced by the cruising lifestyle. "I worked for seven months on a pinky schooner that was going cruising in the Pacific, but they tossed me off within weeks of departure—just as all the hard work was over and the fun was about to begin."

"So I next attended Evergreen State College in Washington State, and managed to spend most of my time working on their 38-foot Brewer cutter, *Sea Wolf*, or their Luhrs 44 yawl, *Resolute*. Then I met a guy who was a shipwright, and the next thing I knew I was a student at the Northwest School of Wooden Boat Building."

But the academic life seemed so tame, so removed from the realities of offshore voyaging that Jennifer decided to jibe yet again, and chart a more pro-active course in her quest to become an offshore voyager.

"At that low point in my life, I realized that the person who owns the boat ultimately calls the shots." she says. "So I cashed in the rest of my college money and bought my own boat."

Vigilant is a 1981 steel, Ted Brewer-designed Verity 40 sloop. "I'll never forget launching her in San Diego," says Jennifer. "The boat was floating there in the slings and the guy running the Travelift was like, 'Well?' and I was like, 'Gee, what do I do now?' and he said gently, 'You gotta move it, skipper!' So I finally worked up my courage, climbed aboard, cranked the diesel, and backed it up—utterly terrified the whole time."

"I don't find the sailing daunting at all," she said. "It's keeping all the onboard systems running that's a challenge. Sometimes the mechanical complexity of the vessel sort of overwhelms me.

But gradually Jennifer's confidence grew with her accumulated sea miles. "There's no substitute for experience," she says. "I learn by doing. I make mistakes and I learn from them. If I can't figure it out myself, I ask somebody. Eventually, I get it together—sort of!"

After the first year of cruising Mexico, she hauled the boat back in San Diego and went through it with a fine-toothed comb. "I knew that eventually I was going to sail offshore," she says, "and so I prepared the vessel as best I could with the knowledge that I had. I installed back-ups for my back-ups, and purchased an extensive list of offshore safety equipment. So, when I finally did head offshore 'on the spur of the moment,' I felt I was as prepared as I possibly could be. But, yeah, it did take a sweet-talking Italian fella to nudge me out of safe harbor."

Jennifer is an incurable romantic. "I was around 125 degrees west as I approached the equator," she says, "and I knew that my Italian friend and his crew were only three degrees or so behind me. I was kinda sad because it's traditional to have a party when you cross the Line. So I turned back, and after a couple of days of searching, managed to sight my friend's sail on the horizon." They sailed across the equator together, their vessels majestically charging along within yards of each other.

"We were grinning like fools at each other—just these huge stupid smiles plastered on our faces. We were so close, yet so very far apart in so many ways. It was blowin' about 24 knots from the southeast and we could not stop or transfer. I sailed ahead and duct-taped a bottle of champagne to one fender and a can of smoked oysters and some water-proofed girly pictures to another, and then tied them together with a long piece of poly line. I jibed back and tossed the whole mess overboard as I cut across his bow. He snagged it with his boat hook."

"It was romantic, kind of," she says.

But such bliss can't last, especially offshore. Jennifer soon found herself alone again. "After almost four weeks at sea," Jenny says, "the boat was getting a little tired. The heavy reinforced hose that connects the stuffing box to the propeller tube split, and my boat started taking on water. I managed to affect temporary repairs within the day, but it took a lot of time upside down in the bilge. Then the engine quit and refused to start. The autopilot packed it in, all my lights went out, and my steering cables started to stiffen."

By this point, many seasoned sailors would be feeling quite grim. Jennifer, however, found this the most enjoyable part of her 3,000 mile passage. "I hand-steered the last 500 miles into Fatu Hiva," said Jennifer. "It was a wonderful experience. The stars filled the sky from horizon to horizon. I had a fair wind, my boat was handling beautifully, and I felt good, really good. And free. It was as if I had no connection whatsoever to land, as if the boat was my whole world. In fact I began to think of my boat as my kingdom and my seat behind the wheel as my throne. I know it sounds silly now, but at the time it was utterly beautiful."

What's next for Jennifer? "A pina colada, I guess," she jokes. "No, seriously, sailing is my life now. I'm looking forward to the next few months of leisurely cruising in the South Seas. I'm vaguely heading for Tahiti to get my engine and autopilot fixed. Then I guess I'll continue westward for a while—unless, of course, Mister-Right the Fix-It Man sweeps me off my deck shoes before I can get squared away for sea again."

Visiting the Grave

An unexpected encounter with a ghost from the past poses 16 years' worth of difficult questions.

I was having a great week end. We were in Culebra, Puerto Rico. *Wild Card*, our S&S-designed 38-foot sloop, nestled her anchor in Ensenada Honda. I was just sort of joyriding around in my dinghy. I felt happy, free, complete. I'd just spend a couple of days with *Cruising World*'s Herb McCormick. He'd laughed at my jokes, didn't laugh at my boat, and failed miserably at seducing my wife, Carolyn.

Like I said, I was in a good mood. It was a fine day. The wind felt nice as it ruffled what is left of my hair. My new outboard engine purred. I scribed a large looping arc in the spacious bay and headed up the southeastern mangrove slough. Suddenly, I stood up—then sat down abruptly, as I almost tipped the dinghy. I throttled back and killed the engine.

For awhile, I was unable to look. Then I regained control and glanced back. Cringed. An obscenity ripped out of me. Startled birds within the mangroves noisily took to the sky, and I started to hyperventilate.

The last time I'd hyperventilated on Culebra was a couple of days after Hurricane Hugo in 1989. I was striping *Carlotta*, the 36-foot ketch I'd built in Boston, when St. John sailors Jody Culbert and Elaine Simmons strolled up. What I was trying to say wasn't complicated. I was trying to say, "A man who builds a vessel should never have to take a crowbar to it," but I couldn't say it. Someone nearby was crying. Loud. It annoyed me. There was much work to do. I had to stay focused. This was no time for crybabies. Good Grief! Jody and Elaine were looking at me sadly. Elaine was reaching out her arms. I still didn't know who was crying.

I am not hung-up on material possessions. I have little and want less. However, there are some things made of "sticks and stones" that I do care about. I am still, to some degree, a caveman. For comfort, I want to believe that God lives in certain inanimate objects. Thus, I personalize them. I dress them in human clothes, paste on personalities, and overlook their flaws. During this process they become more than the sum of their parts. They become, by divine spark, somehow cosmic, mythic and oh-so-large. I pray to them unabashed.

I don't care what the dirt dwellers who write the *AP Stylebook* say this week: My vessel is a "she." I think of her as... well, her.

When I decided to built Carlotta I was 19 years old and had $600. I drew her—first on a napkin and then life-size—with the infinite confidence of untested youth. I didn't *merely* build her; I breathed life into her. First she didn't exist, than she did. She became herself, with her own history, foibles and strengths. I was, ultimately, reduced in rank to her captain. But it was as if we'd once been lovers, and, thus, would be forever joined by our respective remembrances. I massaged her into existence. She owed me. I owed her. She was my miracle of mind over matter—all 36 feet and 20,000 pounds of her.

As Hurricane Hugo approached Culebra back in 1989, our daughter Roma Orion and I were on *Carlotta's* cabin top playing "fat bellies." Roma was 8 years old at the time, and we were lying there allowing the gusty winds to fill our billowing T-shirts. It was fun. We were giggling. It had been 50 years since a major hurricane had hit this area. I'd prepared for hurricanes dozens of time, always in vain. Seven anchors were down and I was ready.

"What was that?" Carolyn asked, washing dishes below.

"What?" I asked still fat-bellying topside with Roma.

"That sound," Carolyn said.

We didn't know it at the time but it was the sound of the barometer dropping—like, into the bilge.

I'll never forget launching *Carlotta* in Boston: how she "floated like a swan," to borrow the words of my hero, Josh Slocum. How she sat so perfectly on her preordained lines. How her bow dipped and curtsied to that first ocean swell, the feeling of her heeling under sail for the first time, the sweet chuckling sound she made as she sliced through tens of thousands of ocean miles.

For over a decade, she was our seashell, our floating safe harbor, our watery home. Watching her gallantly riding the seas while hove to in a gale brought one word to mind: noble.

She was noble. She was strong. She was—forever.

But nothing is forever.

"Don't worry," Carolyn told Roma as she rushed forward through the middle cabin to get more chafe gear. A few minutes later, as I dashed through for the vice-grips, water dripping from my foulies, I hastily sang Roma the same song, "Don't worry."

The wind howled and shrieked and moaned outside, shaking *Carlotta* like a limp rag in an angry dog's mouth. Roma Orion sat stiffly, like a wooden Indian, on the port bunk. She couldn't lie back. She was wearing a buckled life jacket, a safety harness, and reef-walkers. There was a long coil of heaving line in her lap. In one of her hands was a life-boat whistle; in the other hand was a waterproof personal strobe. Worst of all: Beneath her PFD and her clown blouse there was her passport, sealed in a plastic bag, duct-taped around her stomach. Just in case.

The wall of the eye of Hugo, Category Four, approached. We were in 120 knots, and it was going to get worse. "Don't worry, don't worry, don't worry," we chanted to Roma as airborne trees tore off our spreaders, a flying dinghy smacked the mizzen, and as sheets of roofing tin became gigantic, rotating razor blades. The wind increased, and increased some more, and increased yet again. It shrieked like the tormented souls of a thousand drowned sailors.

Then *Fly Away*, a 68-foot Alden schooner, did just that. I watched her dragging, catching, and dragging down on us for a long time. It was agonizing. Even before she hit us, I knew it was over for *Carlotta*. Her bowsprit jammed aft of *Fly Away's* shrouds. They became entangled. We began smashing each other into eternity.

The noise was awful. So loud. I'll never forget the sound two well-built vessels make as they slowly demolish each other in that kind of wind. Our hull/deck joint suddenly gaped open. A stanchion, complete with base, got sucker punched clean through the deck. It wiggled and waggled and rattled sadistically over the port bunk. Water poured in—cold, evil, hurricane-driven water—right on top of Roma Orion. She tried not to, but she couldn't help it: She screamed, *"Can I worry now?"* as *Carlotta* began to founder.

That was 17 years ago. We survived; *Carlotta* didn't. I sold her salvage rights to a local fellow. I later heard he'd refloated her, got her engine running and moved his family aboard.

A friend reported he'd seen her sailing off Vieques. Another said he'd seen her powering along off of Fajardo, pretty as you please. A happy ending, right?

That's what I wanted to believe and, thus, it's what I *did* believe. I dismissed the stories of him selling her piece-by-piece and callously running her up on a sandbar when there was nothing left to sell. Now I was sitting in my dinghy right next her, right next to the Horrible Wreck That Had Once Been the Noble Ketch *Carlotta*—and I was feeling both angry and sad. Why was I angry? I'd sold her. I'd abandoned her first. What right did I have to feel violated? I had none.

The sadness was harder. I couldn't so easily rationalize it. I swung alongside *Carlotta*. I reached out, hesitated, and finally worked up the courage to touch her. "I am *so* sorry," I whispered into her dark, water-sloshed interior. Crabs scurried. Water bugs crawled. Snakes slithered. Death and decay were everywhere. I couldn't decide who I was feeling so sorry for: her or me. Me, I guess.

I felt like a traitor. Here were the broken bones of *her*, the lovely vessel I'd created to sail me around the world. And I'd just done it—but within the embrace of another. What's the modern buzzword: conflicted? Yeah. I was feeling conflicted. To the point of throwing up.

I'm an optimist. My glass is always half full. I tried to look on the bright side. I'd built *Carlotta* to sail around the world, and she'd helped me to do so in many diverse and unexpected ways: the experience of building her, the experience of sailing her, the experience of—loving her.

Even in the end she came through. The money I received from selling her carcass to the butcher went directly into the purchase of *Wild Card*. I wanted to figure out a way, a clever story line, in which all this made some delightful, cosmic sense. One in which I was a hero and *Carlotta* had eventually become something more than—well, ugly litter.

But I couldn't. I just stared at her. Appalled. Sad. Guilty. Finally, I couldn't take it anymore. I could almost smell my brain cells frying. So I cranked up my outboard and went back to *Wild Card*. Carolyn was just finishing up her yoga. She was all sweetness and light, all peaches and cream. "Want some tea," she asked me brightly. "I've got Red Zinger."

"Sure," I said.

"How was your dinghy ride," she asked. I must have hesitated. She turned toward me and arched an eyebrow.

"Stressful," I said.

It's the People You Meet

For salt-stained sea gypsies like us, the world is a place full of wonderful wackos.

We have friends all over the world—both sailors and dirt dwellers—whom we've met in the most unexpected, bizarre ways. Take India. When we pulled into Kerala, our ICOM 710 SSB wasn't working. There wasn't a local dealer, and I was worried about sending it off to the States. So Carolyn contacted a local amateur radio club and asked them if any of their members might be able to fix it.

Immediately, the ham club sprang into action. They e-mailed all their national members: "Emergency! The American yacht *Wild Card* is in trouble. Their SSB radio isn't working and they've asked us to fix it. The honor of India is at stake! We *must* help them!"

A few thousand miles away, Sandeep (VU2MUE) heard of our plight. He contacted his friend Balsun (VU2UYC) in Kuwait, who had once met the renowned Professor Mani (VU2ITI) of Kerala.

The following day, a small brown fellow in a dress trotted up to *Wild Card.* "I am busy-busy," he panted. "Much work to do I have! But, for the honor of India, do you need your radio fixed tonight? Or could I bring back to you the following day?"

I explained to him that we'd been hit by lightening, that I didn't know what was wrong with the radio, and that I didn't have any spare parts or even a schematic.

"Day after tomorrow OK?" he cried. "Yes? No?"

"Yes," I said.

He grinned. "How you say… 'No Problem!'" He quickly uncoupled the radio, tossed it on his head, and trotted off into the teeming crowd.

Carolyn was just arriving. "That isn't—?" she began.

"Yes!" I said. "That was our radio, and that guy is going to take a look at it and see if he can fix it."

"What company is he with?" Carolyn asked. "Did you get his business card?"

"Well," I said, "I don't think he's got a business, per se."

"What's his name, then?" Carolyn asked.

"Well," I said, "in the rush to uncouple the radio and all, it seemed rather rude to—"

"Don't tell me you gave our $2,000 SSB radio to a little man in a dress—without getting his name!"

"That's *exactly* what I'm trying not to tell you!" I blurted.

But the following day he showed up with the repaired radio as promised, then spent the entire day tuning up my SSB rig, from grounding plane to antenna top, until *Wild Card* was transmitting louder and farther than ever.

India is a poor country. In the States, I'd been mentally prepared to spend at least $500 having the radio repaired.

"How much do I owe you?" I asked.

"Big price," he said, and then nodded at Carolyn. "I respectfully request the honor of your company."

The following weekend we went to his home for a traditional Kerala feast. It took him and his lovely wife a couple of days to prepare it and almost an entire day to eat it.

He turned out to be Professor T. K. Mani, a renowned physicist, inventor of the acoustical rain gauge (which measures rainfall at sea), and one of the most intellectually stimulating people whom I've ever encountered.

Through "our friend, the Professor" we were immediately welcomed into the heart of India's scientific community. I gave lectures on marine electronics at Cochin University; we attended various weddings, fancy dinners and exotic cultural events. In essence, because of our ever deepening friendship with Professor Mani, we had the time of our lives in tradition-rich India. And the price for his labor. "No charge," he grinned, "Friends are friends, eh?"

On one of our many jaunts together, we happened to visit the special needs school his autistic daughter attends. It was a marvelous place, brimming with love, compassion and patience. Each year since, we've sponsored the annual tuition of a student there.

Yes, the best part of cruising is the people you meet. On the other side of the world and many years earlier, we came to know Bait Broad. She sold worms. ("Want 'em to go or you gonna eat 'em here," she'd ask the local New England fishermen.)

While we scrimped and saved in the 1970s to outfit *Carlotta* for ocean sailing, she helped us in a million ways. Basically, she just gave us use of everything in her life: store, car, freezer, water, telephone, tools. She fed us, nurtured us, encouraged us, believed in us. For years, she kissed away our tears until the day we sailed away from Boston.

Fate is a funny thing. Three years later, I'd made a writing windfall while we were cruising in the Bahamas. So we flew Bait Broad in for a wild weekend of degenerate gambling and utter decadence in Nassau. We had a great time together. Bait Broad was happier than I'd ever seen her. "I've had the time of my life," she said as I poured her back on the plane. And a couple of weeks later, we heard she'd been killed in a tragic gun accident. "I'm so glad she came to the Bahamas," said Carolyn, her eyes red with crying. "It's the best money we've ever spent."

I'm always amazed at how good can come from the oddest of occurrences. I couldn't afford a Chicago mooring for my first boat, a 22-foot Atkin double-ender named *Corina*. However, a friend of mine allowed me to use his mooring, in exclusive Jackson Park Harbor—an arrangement that was as illegal as it was convenient. Within days of shifting *Corina* onto the mooring, the harbormaster, who lived in a house next to the yacht club, put a dreaded notice on it "See me immediately." And so we began a summer long game of cat and mouse.

One late night, I staggered down to my boat and discovered that *Fame*, the lovely schooner moored beside me, was rapidly taking on water. I zoomed over in the dinghy and seeing the vertical geysers from the cockpit scuppers, I knew she'd sink within minutes if I didn't do something fast. I knew the harbormaster had a big gasoline pump, so I raced to his house, woke him up, helped him lug it frantically into my dinghy, and, well, we saved the lovely ol' vessel from sinking.

"Are you the guy I've been chasing after for half the damn summer?" the harbormaster asked me afterward.

"I am," I said.

"Well, I ain't no more," he smiled.

Yeah, a cruiser never knows when or where they'll meet some wonderful or interesting folks.

My father tied our 52-foot Alden schooner *Elizabeth* up behind the Me-Oh-My Club in New Orleans. And soon *Elizabeth* was a floating magnet for wonderful waterfront wackos; the costumed transvestites lounged on deck between acts like they owned her. To this day, if I meet a really stunning, statuesque woman, my first reaction is to look at her hands, then for an Adam's apple.

That was years ago, but there's still a colorful cast of characters out there. Bernie the Cowboy is a perfect example. He's an ol' cowpoke through and through, and he looks (and sounds) exactly like he stepped out of *Rawhide*. He's sort of a manure-crazed seagoing horse whisperer—who sails around the world attracting poor lame horses and very rich women wherever he goes.

Bernie's easy to spot. We first met him sailing into a harbor in the Galápagos. He was sitting in a saddle lashed to the bow rail of his steel boat, *Seabird*, twirling a lasso and yelling "Here, little doggies!" at the top of his lungs.

"I was rubbing horses and listening to Lyle Lovett in St. Thomas when I decided to sail around the world," he says. "Yee-haw!"

Does he have any advice for, well, future sailing cowpokes?

"Nope," he says, being a man of few words. When pressed hard, he adds, "I'll admit, though, the spurs are hell on teak!" Bernie extensively rebuilt *Seabird* in Whangarei, New Zealand, and sailed her straight across the Indian and Atlantic oceans, back to his North Carolina horse farm—to build another vessel, buy another saddle, and do it all over again.

The weirdest episode that I still smile about (albeit ruefully) took place as we were powering down the Intracoastal Waterway. A pristine yacht ahead of us, crewed by a distinguished-looking but befuddled elderly couple, had run aground near an inlet. They hadn't accounted for the fast side-slipping current.

The tide was dropping. Seconds counted. I knew I'd only have one chance. The swift current complicated things. I swung carefully alongside while watching my depth meter, tossed them a long anchor line and yanked them back into deep water the moment they belayed it.

It gave Carolyn and me a warm feeling to have helped, especially so stylishly and without being asked. Later that evening, as luck would have it, the two boats anchored together. Since I had to row ashore for baby food and other supplies, I stopped by their expensive vessel and asked if they needed anything. "Yes," quivered the old man, "could you pick us up a quart of milk?"

He disappeared below, presumably for the money. But then I heard a small argument ensue, and the wife popped her blue-rinsed head up. She looked disapproving of my torn T-shirt, shaggy beard and beat-up boat. "Bring us the milk *first*," she said suspiciously, "*Then* we'll reimburse you!"

What a long, long way from India.

The Royal Treatment, Kosrae Style!

The monarchy is dormant now, but the queen and her sons can still throw a feast fit for a king.

The island of Kosrae peaked as a world power around the year 1200. True, Micronesia is a small world by today's standards—it's the size of the continental United States but with a land mass less than half of Rhode Island—but it constituted the entire known world to the Kosraens and they dominated it. The other islands, to the west and to the north, were forced to pay tribute. The king of Kosrae was the King of Kings and lived in a fabulous fortress with 20 foot high stone walls, while other island rulers lived in mud huts. The canoe-borne sailors of Kosrae roamed thousands of sea miles during their trading forays, using crude but effective stick charts to navigate their way back home. Their medicines, their magic, their courage, and their stamina led the way. They were always first: first to build a major defensible city, first to carve basalt stone, first to dig canals.

Their social customs were equally elaborate: their city—Insaru, where Lelu stands today—had separate areas for sleeping, worshiping, public gathering, and cooking, with special focus on the preparation of the sacred kava. When a beloved king died, the rituals were especially complex. His body would be publicly displayed for a time, then entombed under a mountain of rocks until his dried bones were reverently deposited into a nearby blue hole.

Ultimately the king became so powerful and his fortress so impenetrable that his job was largely ceremonial. To maintain his power, he'd merely host the leaders of other islands to elaborate magnificent feasts on a regular basis and act as a gracious goodwill ambassador for his people.

Yes, the people of the Pacific are deservedly world-famous hosts because they believe that the more they give, the more prestige they earn. Thus lavish fetes became a large part of Kosrae's society.

But the fortunes of men and nations wax and wane. European ships began to visit Kosrae, first in peace and then in profit. Change was in the air. The kings of Kosrae were fearless—they killed the entire crews of two foreign ships who'd kidnapped and raped their women—but they were also wise. They could sense the pendulum of history swinging—away from them.

In 1852, according to local legend, an apparition of the Sinlaku, the goddess of breadfruit, appeared on the beach of Lelu and said, "I see a white light coming over the eastern horizon to conquer us. Thus I leave tomorrow for Yap." Hearing these words, the reigning king quickly braced for war. The following day, as the canoe-borne apparition sailed out of the harbor in retreat, a gleaming ship named the *SS Morning Star* sailed in to offload its cargo of smiling missionaries.

The king and his warriors were prepared to die in battle, but this field of combat was, alas, completely beyond them. Instead of killing the invaders, they ended up welcoming them into their hearts. Their mighty stone fortress was breached, and their nation of thousands-who-ruled-tens-of-thousands shrank to a mere 200 souls, ravaged by disease, cultural chaos and, ultimately, the agonies of World War II.

Of course, Western historians debate whether it happened *exactly* like this or not, but this is what many educated, socially-prominent Kosraens believe today.

The last king of Kosrae, King John, died in the early 1900s and the island, one of the Caroline Islands, is now part of the Federated States of Micronesia. But his family lives on, and son after son have assumed his duty as a royal host. In recent history, this duty has fallen to three of his great-great-grandsons, John, Smith, and Glen. Their domain is much smaller now—they own the local Ace Hardware—but they're still proud of their rich past, their colorful history, and their royal blood.

They are, above all, dutiful sons. So when their mother, Satako Sigrah, recently looked southward out her kitchen window and saw the fleet of cruising boats anchored in the harbor had unusually swelled to five, she gathered her sons together, pointed to the boats, and said, in Kosraen, "Kill a pig, boys. It's party time!"

It took a while to get the grand dinner together, and by then, one of the boats, a 60-foot wooden ketch named *Roselina* of Denmark, had sailed to a different harbor at Utwe. No matter, Satako merely called the chief of that village—now called the mayor, alas—and invited the crew back to Lelu for the party.

It's difficult to describe the boat-long table they set for us of more than 50 dishes of breadfruit, taro, yams, tapioca, etc. There were mounds of fruits, piles of coconuts—not to mention the mountain of pork, chicken and fish.

And, our money wasn't any good. Yes, it was offered, but, it was politely refused. This wasn't about money or profit; it was about tradition and royalty. It was about history and reverence and love.

It was, as one member of the Sigrah family whispered to me with a hug, about friendship and family. "We are brothers now, Fatty! You are family. In this house, you are home! You help us build it. It is your house, too. You welcome! You sleep here anytime. You are home, brother, home from the sea!"

Yachties of yesteryear including Mike and Susan McKim of the Waterline 44, *Susan Bright*, delivered materials and helped build the house in four main stages over the course of many cyclone seasons. Thanks to them, we didn't just eat; we *feasted*—like the Kosraen kings of yore.

The best part for me was the music. I played country song after country song. Many of the Kosraens knew the lyrics as well as I did to "Please Release Me,""Your Cheatin' Heart," and "Help Me Make It Through the Night."

Late in the evening as the food, the liquor, the smoke from the fire, and the betel nuts all worked their magic; the Kosraens started singing their traditional folk songs.

I'd sing "Blowin' in the Wind" or "Michael Rowed the Boat Ashore" or "500 Miles" and they'd immediately respond with a group tune so beautiful in harmony and so well-sung that my eyes would water.

Satako, the mother of seven sons and three daughters, never said a single word all night. She didn't have to. She was the queen. Her bearing was so regal that her mere wish was everyone's command.

There was one moment when I almost wept. Smith, the son who was most active in the party's preparation, was chewing betel nut and shouting into my ear, "Thank you, thank you for coming, Fatty! It is you folks, the sailor guys, who make the party, not us. We're just the hosts. Thank you!"

I wanted to tell him that I, that we, weren't worthy of such niceness. But how could I? What words could I say? How do you tell a man you're not as good as he is?

I am unable to comprehend the warmth and generosity of these sun-kissed Pacific islanders. I can't quite get my mind around it. It doesn't seem possible. It doesn't make rational sense from any Western perspective. They aren't hustling you for a buck; they are genuinely showing off their culture with pride, dignity and style.

Oh, what a party! It was the party of the year, the party of the decade—perhaps the definitive party of my cruising life. I took little sips of air. I was so happy I was scared of hyperventilating.

I looked across the room, filled with 50 laughing people, and there was Alvah Simon, the author of *North to the Night* and a *CW* contributing editor. His left arm was around his wife Diana, also a *CW* contributing editor. They sail the steel sloop *Roger Henry*. His eyes were closed. There was a secret smile plastered to his drunk-with-happiness face. He seemed to be in a trance. He was swaying awkwardly to the music. His right arm was raised in excited exuberance and frozen there, as if he'd lost his train of thought in some interior explosion of Pacific bliss.

Alvah likes to wrestle polar bears, surf Cape Horn and stare down the Grim Reaper, but he was a teddy bear on that night.

Olivier, who sails the French sloop *Neos,* was drinking cognac and smoking fat Cuban cigars with one of the brothers, John, who was named after King John, of course. They were laughing hard, hugging hard, and singing loud.

The Aussie couple off the 40-foot sloop *Wiikiri* seemed stunned. "Are you *sure* we don't have to pay?" they kept asking.

Towards the end of the evening, even the straight-laced Danes were grinning like children at Christmas. At one point near midnight, I just wheeled out towards the dinghy dock while still playing my guitar. I'd just had yet another perfect moment, and wanted to keep it within me to sparkle forever. Carolyn, my wife, somehow intuitively realized I'd had enough and joined me with her usual post-festivity sack of dirty pots, baking tins and cooking pans.

"Oh, god," she said and took a deep breath. Above us, stars crowded the sky. The smell of night-blossoming flowers filled the air. The palms rubbed and rustled their fronds in contented delight.

"Yeah," I said a long time later. "Wow!"

The following day was Sunday. Everyone—all the boaters and all the villagers—trouped off to church and raised our collective voices together in Christian fellowship. It was a strange moment for me: to be publicly giving thanks to same social institution which had so thoroughly destroyed all of theirs.

I glanced over at Carolyn. She looked so lovely as she sang, she *was* lovely as she sang. Our eyes locked with intensity. She was beaming at me, lasering me with her dark Italian eyes, "Yes, yes, yes!" she was telling me,urging me, thanking me. "These are the moments we live for, sail for, are willing to work our entire lives to be part of."

I stared across the church. One of the local fellows who had been at the party last night—he'd told me, completely without rancor, "I wished we'd killed you all when we had the chance!"—was grinning back at me, our heavenly voices intertwining amid the white-washed church rafters.

It was a hot walk back to the boats. Alvah, Diana, Carolyn, and I stopped to rest midway on the dusty path. We must have looked thirsty because a local woman immediately dashed out of her house with a heaping plate of dripping watermelon slices.

When I took one, she proudly said "Thank you," and it echoed down the eons of her culture. "Thank you," I, too, said, and heard the words echo down mine as well.

The Fat Man Cometh

Reared on sea lore in the hard-knocks school of hands-on cruising, a Caribbean character takes on the big world.

"Land ho," Carolyn says, and purposely doesn't look at me. I glance up. The island of Fatu Hiva seemed to fast-forward toward me: first a faint grey smudge on the distant horizon, then an added hint of verdant green, and finally, an impossible Polynesian lushness.

Carolyn and I have cruised together now for over 30 years and 30,000 ocean miles. We've built a boat, a home, a romance, a family and a life together. She knows me so well that she instinctively pretends that this is just another landfall.

I turn away from both her and the island. I blinked a few times to windward—rub the back of my calloused hand across a damp cheek. It's difficult to catch my breath. I feel so full of joy and love and happiness that I might burst. So it kind of rushes out of me unexpectedly: "We're here, Dad," I gasped. "We're finally here!"

In 1953, my father purchased *Elizabeth,* a sunken 52-foot Alden schooner. He paid $100 for her. I was one year old. I think it's fair to say that this had a rather significant effect on my life. I'm now 48 years old, and I've lived aboard various sailing craft for over 40 of those years. My earliest recollection is of my father standing on the rough-hewn pine deck of the *Elizabeth* in a howling snowstorm in Chicago. He was dressed inappropriately in a colorful floral pareu, a Polynesian wraparound dress ranting at some startled dockmaster, "We'll be sailing to Tahiti and the

South Seas soon," he cried. "Just to get away from fun cops, dream crushers and bean counters like you!"

Looking back, the guy probably just wanted the dockage fee.

Yes, my father was a bit of a nonconformist. A commercial artist by trade, he'd recently been fired from the Bull Durham account for drawing a certain part of the bull's anatomy with ever greater proportions. Disillusioned by his experiences in World War II, he hated authority in any form. "Just because everyone tells you that you're wrong doesn't mean you're right—but it's usually a good indication," was one of his favorite sayings, customized, as were most of his adages, from folklore. The grandness of his pronouncements always made his words, and the man himself, loom larger than life in my young mind.

I was raised, along with my two sisters and my younger brother, to be a sea gypsy. "Men and ships rot in port," he used to say to us. "Beware of the 'dirt dwellers' ashore." And, most of all, he'd say, "Be sure to stay away from Christians and all other religious cultists!"

I was brought up to think that Christians were like members of the Klu Klux Klan or supporters of the American Nazi Party—they existed, but one hoped you'd never have to deal with one. "And watch out for so-called do-gooders," my father would counsel. "They're the worst!"

Once I was forced to hide belowdecks while my father angrily rebuffed a group of well-dressed do-gooders attempting to wrestle me away from my parents (via a local court's custody ruling.)

"The child doesn't go to school or church—just runs wild around the waterfront all day!" I heard someone say. I wondered, what's wrong with that? It was scary. They were going to kidnap me and force me into Protestantism. I'd seen the promotional church stuff and wanted no part of it. I remember looking out a porthole, seeing a man's polished black wingtip shoes, and thinking, "That's a *do-gooder*!" Ever since, I've mistrusted anyone with polished leather shoes.

But the childhood memories that are clearest for me are of the lure of the South Seas. "We're going to Tahiti because they glorify love and procreation there—not greed and violence," my father said. "And because the fruits fall off the trees into your lap and the fish jump into your dinghy."

An ever-evolving mountain of books about French Polynesia written by Robert Louis Stevenson, Joshua Slocum and Harry Pidgeon helped send me down this path. We sang Tahitian songs as we sailed and beat time with our

Tahitian drum. We dressed in pareus. *"Mauruuru roa,"* we'd say in thanks for a gift. Our family motto was *Aita pe'ape'a paya:* No problem!

It was, for all of its salt-stained oddness, a great way to grow up. Our family was a joyous, watery tribe, always one step ahead of the dream crushers and fun cops. We were sea gypsies in every way, totally apart from the dreary landlubbers, rat racers and shore huggers who inhabited terra firma. Freedom was our family's drug, we mainlined it, and it turned me into the man I am today. Each day of my life, I believe, is totally, uniquely my own. I consider myself wealthy beyond measure: rich in time, challenge, satisfaction, and love. People ask me, "How can you keep going?" My instant response: "How could I ever stop?"

As children, our collective job was to "chase the horizon" eternally; to arrive at that philosophy by the time we were adults. Aboard *Elizabeth*, our lovely "seashell," it all came together: My father was the intrepid captain, my mother his spatula-waving life/sailing-mate, we kids the court jesters doing dangerous gymnastic tricks from the mainmast spreaders as we sailed gallantly into yet another unsuspecting port.

But reality reared its ugly head in the end. *Elizabeth* began to rot faster than we could sail her, my mother had my younger brother in her mid-40s, and Parkinson's disease crippled my father—first his dignity, which it shattered, and then his trembling body—until he died. ("Who is skipper here?" were his last words.) Thus I discovered myself, at the ripe old age of 15, "back on the beach" in Chicago. People laughed at my pareu, refused to dance to my Tahitian drumming. The dream began to fade.

But dreams die hard, and occasionally, I'd catch a faint whiff of familial failure. I did not like it, not at all. But the facts were the facts: We'd set off for Tahiti and never made it. So that same year—1967; I was 15—I purchased my first boat for $200. *Corina*, a 22-foot Atkin double-ender built in 1932, which had been abandoned for years while moored in the Chicago River, and used as a gang hangout. She'd been completely stripped and was covered in graffiti. A year later, I took off on my first Great Lakes cruise, with Lusty Laura, a prison-escapee with a tattoo on her butt. (She was a fox, but that's another story.) Once I held my own tiller, I was changed forever.

"That's where we're going, right there—just over the horizon," I told Lusty Laura while attempting to remember the exact phrasing my father had used, "Because, just over the horizon is something so beautiful and so pure that it is worth of a lifetime of traveling just to see it."

"When do you think we'll arrive?" she asked me, not understanding a word I was saying.

"Never," I said. "If we're lucky." The lusty one didn't last long, but the general notion did.

Buying *Corina* is also how I ended up with the name "Fatty," even though at the time I weighed 116 pounds soaking wet and could hide behind a parking meter.

I was working as an actor for the Robin Hood Players, wore fancy "Carnaby Street" clothes from London, and by then had a French girlfriend. The guys on the street corner used to rag on me by saying stuff like, "He's fat! The man is fat!" By this they meant that I was lucky. (If you inherited a million bucks or robbed a bank and didn't get caught, they'd say, "Yo' fat, man!")

When the guys on the corner found out that I'd bought the boat, they were blown away by the fact that anyone in the hood would just… buy his own yacht.

"He's not just fat," one of them sang out the next time I strolled by. "He's Cap'n Fat now!"

By the age of 18, I'd carried my wife, Carolyn, over the companionway threshold of *Corina*. But that same year, 1970, we were hit by a severe gale in the Gulf of Mexico. Our garboard plank opened up, and we were forced to bail for our lives. At the height of the storm, we were steering for half an hour, bailing for 15 minutes, and sleeping for 15 minutes. This gets old after a couple of days, trust me.

"Why do they call this *pleasure* boating," Carolyn asked pointedly; sadly, I couldn't think of a snappy answer.

So the following year, Carolyn and I decided to build our ultimate dream boat from scratch—in Boston, because that was the hailing port of Joshua Slocum's *Spray*. In 1974, we launched the 36-foot Peter Ibold-designed ketch *Carlotta* in the Fort Point Channel of Boston Harbor. We wore our pareus, of course. *Carlotta* was built of ferro-cement, and constructed at a very minimal cost by using salvaged materials. We purchased used lumber from a barn being torn down, mild steel from a warehouse that had caught fire, and even plundered sunken fishing draggers for gear. She wasn't much of a yacht, but she was a simple, strong and utterly dependable cruising vessel that I had built with my bare hands. We immediately decided to take her on a little shakedown cruise to the Caribbean. Seven years into that cruise, Carolyn suggested that I rip out the "tool room" in the forepeak and put a small bunk on one side and a tiny built-in padded chair on the other.

"But the bunk could only be five feet seven inches max," I protested. "Perfect!" she said. And our daughter, Roma Orion, was born nine months later. She didn't slow us down in the least. In fact, she renewed our interest in cruising because we could now see things utterly fresh, through her young eyes. By her first birthday, she had 20 stamps in her passport.

We sailed repeatedly up and down the U.S. East Coast, wherever wind, whim, and wanderlust carried us. We spend a summer in the Gulf of

Mexico, and then cruised Central and South America. Most of the time, we spent in the Caribbean, headquartering out of St. John, in the U.S. Virgin Islands.

Roma Orion was eight years old on September 17, 1989, as the barometer dropped toward the keel and Hurricane Hugo hit us in Culebra, Puerto Rico. We held on without much damage for the first 12 hours of 130-plus knots—until *Fly Away,* a 68-foot schooner, dragged into us. Swimming ashore during a Category Four hurricane with your terrified child in your arms, her passport in a Ziploc bag duct-taped to her soft belly, is no fun. "*Aita pe'ape'a,*" I said as serenely as I could manage. "No problem!"

But I must admit I was taken aback. Losing the boat was like losing a 10-ton portion of ourselves. Yet, though I was 37 years old, long married, a father, and now suddenly penniless, homeless, and jobless, I could still hear that Tahitian drum banging away faintly in the back of my mind. Sure, everything around me was muddy and waterlogged, but it would dry out. It made me realize that I might have been *penniless*, but I wasn't *hopeless*. I firmly believe that I am in charge of my happiness and that my personal destiny lies within my own calloused hands. Hard work is usually the cure for most problems, and this one was no exception. I'd always worked—my childhood was a happy, but poor one—and I've done everything. I've painted fishing-boat transoms for $5 a pop, dug ditches, made crude jewelry, managed marine-supply stores, owned my own businesses. Since the 1970s, I've written for Caribbean-based and other sailing publications, produced three books and edited others. For the last 11 years I've hosted a weekly radio show.

So I rolled up my sleeves, and made a rough survey of all the other vessels that sank in the Caribbean during Hurricane Hugo. There were over a thousand vessels totaled during the storm, and I soon purchased, for $3,000, a wrecked S&S-designed Hughes 38 with a large hole in her port side.

Within days, I had her refloated. I immediately brought her to the Independent Boat Yard on St. Thomas, borrowed a grinder, and relaunched her 21 days later, finishing second in class during that weekend's Coral Bay Thanksgiving Regatta.

Ten years later Roma rowed up to *Wild Card*, carefully tied up her seven-foot sailing dinghy, and happily announced she'd won a scholarship

to Brandeis University. I counter-announced that her mother and I were sailing to Tahiti.

"What about allowance, Dad," she queried.

"Hey," I said, "if you can send us $25 a week, do it. If not, don't sweat it!" At this writing, Roma Orion is on the dean's list at Brandeis. She works two jobs while carrying a double-major. Carolyn and I, and Roma, too, know this: You can't lose if you don't give up.

Cruising without Roma, after 18 years of her cheery presence, was a bit of a change. However, Carolyn and I soon adjusted. I realize it isn't cool to wear your heart on your sleeve, but I must reveal that I'm still head over heels in love with Carolyn, still romantically infatuated after 30 years and 30,000 ocean miles of cruising together. I literally couldn't have become what I am without her constant help and support. She is, at least to my appreciative eye, a delightful cross between Sophia Lauren; Anne Bonny, the pirate; and Joshua Slocum's feminine side. To say that I value her companionship is to make a vast understatement. The bottom line is this: There's no person in the world I'd rather be offshore with. And yes, I lust after her. I mean, a vessel in midocean is the perfect place for romance, isn't it? I'm not ashamed of this. We'll be staring at a chart, our eyes meet, sparks fly—and the self-steering gets the deck watch for the next half hour. "How do you like your Monitor windvane?" some dock lounger recently asked me.

"It's a sex machine," I said

The passage from St. Thomas to the Panama Canal was a rough one. Along the north coast of Columbia, we were forced twice to run off under bare poles. The heavy weather was uncomfortable, sure, but it had its advantages: I was delighted to give the boat a good thrashing before heading across the wide Pacific.

The muggers of Colón didn't manage to maim us, and our Panama Canal transit was stressful but without mishap. The 1,000 mile passage to the Galápagos was utterly delightful, with light but steady breezes the entire way. We were thrilled with the Galápagos, and immediately felt at home with the sea lions, blue-footed boobies, frigate birds, marine iguanas and giant tortoises. Puerto Ayora on Isla Santa Cruz was like an 1800s western town, populated by friendly, peaceful *mestizos* and filled with inexpensive Ecuadorian restaurants. "Gee," Carolyn said, "This is like discovering that the world's largest and most exclusive open-air zoo has cheap catering throughout!"

Perhaps the strangest moment ashore was meeting with the solitary (and understandably pensive) Lonesome George. He's a giant land tortoise, and the last of his particular species. When he dies, that's it. Fini. George has contemporaries of other species, and there's evidence to suggest that many of these were around during Darwin's time. I don't mean their *species,* I mean the same, actual animal. If such things turn you on—petting an animal Darwin may have petted—you'll love cruising the Galápagos.

Our 3,200-mile passage from the Galápagos to the Marquesas and French Polynesia was a relatively uneventful one. However, there were a few odd moments worth mentioning. One took place toward the end.

We were about 18 days out, when we got hit by a squall. It wasn't a particularly violent one, only 35 knots or so, and it didn't last long. But it was midnight, moonless, and darker than a politician's heart. I wasn't really worried because I'd dropped the mainsail in plenty of time. But the squall had to be dealt with, and despite its lack of longevity, it rapidly kicked up a bit of sea.

Wild Card soon fell off a wave rather awkwardly—but it was no big deal. "Hit a pothole!" I thought to myself. Then the boat fell into another hole in the ocean, an even deeper one, and I heard a sickening thud of soft flesh striking something hard, and then Carolyn screaming belowdecks.

I jumped below and flicked on my flashlight. Carolyn was rolling around on the cabin sole, holding both her hands to her nose, and screaming "Is it broken?"

She and her mattress had been launched across the entire width of the boat, and they landed rudely. Blood was everywhere, a truly astounding amount of it. I felt ill.

But I also knew this was no time to panic. "Steady as she goes," I thought to myself. We'd already laughed our way through many emergencies at sea, and now was no time to stop. So I allowed my flashlight to wander over to the blood-smeared bulkhead where her face had impacted.

"No, I think the bulkhead will be fine!"

"My nose, you idiot!" she shrieked. "Gimme a paper towel."

I gave her one, then another, and then yet another. "Er," I said shyly. "These paper towels are kinda expensive...."

She glared at me. I smiled back. "You are a rat-bastard," she said. "And you," I countered, "are the bravest, most wonderful woman in the world." Then I hugged her and held her for a long time as the darkened boat sped westward at eight knots across the Pacific Ocean.

As it turned out, her nose wasn't broken. However, the flesh was badly torn and she had two black eyes to boot. "If there is a domestic-violence unit on Fatu Hiva in the Marquesas, well, then you are gonna be in big trouble, Fatty!" she mused. Luckily for me, after 22 days and 3,200 ocean miles, the island's welcome wagon consisted of a laughing group of pareu-clad children offering us baskets of fresh fruit in exchange for *bonbons*.

As I tacked into the harbor, I couldn't stop thinking about the circuitous route that led me here: the schooner *Elisabeth*, the double-ender *Corina*, the ketch *Carlotta* and the modern sloop *Wild Card*. And most importantly, all the things my father had taught me, which made this voyage possible.

"Being a captain is all about responsibility," he once told me. "The safety of your vessel and its crew rests solely on your shoulders. This can be a heavy weight. If you can't heft it, don't pick it up. The sea is a harsh mistress, son. She doesn't suffer fools gladly. But if you're careful and study her moods closely, she'll willingly carry you safely on her back around the world."

As our anchor chain rattled out, we were hailed by the crew of *Subeki*, a German yacht we'd met in the Galápagos.

"How long did it take you," they asked.

"Forty-seven years," I replied. "Forty-seven years!"

Booze, Boats and a Modest Proposal

Each sailor charts a unique course through the typical rum squalls of the cruising life

I am, at my very core, a lover of life. I know it sounds simplistic but I believe in the motto "Live while you're alive!" I'm an unabashed, unrepentant hedonist. This isn't entirely my fault. I was raised to enjoy myself, to accept responsibility for my own happiness, to kiss life full on the lips.

Once, when I was young and looking at a picture of the Puritans aboard the *Mayflower*, I asked my father why they were all frowning. "Puritanism is the sneaking suspicion that someone, somewhere is having a good time!" he told me. I've never forgotten that lesson: it made clear to me that we all have a choice of whether to go through life smiling or frowning.

What has this got to do with boating? Bear with me, dear reader. I seldom whisper in your ear. Indulge me for another paragraph or two.

In addition to hedonism, I crave freedom. Freedom is my drug of choice. And independence. I'm fiercely independent.

I believe many cruising sailors share similar views. They expect a lot out of life, and, since they're generally highly effective people, they get it.

Hooray for us.

However, perhaps all this lusting after freedom and independence makes us thirsty. Booze and boats seem to go hand in glove. I literally grew up in yacht club bars, beach bars, marina bars, waterfront bars, port bars, and various other 'sailors haunts,' as my wife Carolyn, refers to them.

I liked to drink. It enhanced my life—for awhile.

When I'd race, I'd wear a shirt with my vessel's name on the front and our crew motto on the back: "A Drinking Team with a Sailing Problem!"

I found this quite funny—then.

My talk would be gin-soaked, too. "Well, we encountered a stationary drunk front aboard last night... damn, those rum squalls were severe!" or "So I told her, 'Honey, we only have room for five cases—one of food and four of rum!'"

Oh, I reveled in it. "Last night, while innocently staggering down the beach of Jost Van Dyke, I was attached by a group of *very* aggressive palm trees!" When I was discovered late one evening swimming alongside my overturned dinghy, I made a public vow, "Never again, in an eight-foot rowing pram, will I wrestle with Jack Daniels!"

Writers are another group known to tipple. Wearing the hat of a marine columnist I'd tell people, "Once a month I sober up for an hour. Then I write down anything I remember, which, alas, often isn't much!"

When I was in my early 30's, I can remember wondering if everybody was putting me on about hangovers. I could drink from morning to night without cessation and feel re-energized the following day.

"Rum is food," I'd rant. "Rehab is for quitters!"

It was fun. I'm not saying that facetiously now in hindsight. It really was *really* fun. For a while.

In 1995, while racing Lasers at the St. Thomas Yacht Club, I had a little "event" which sent me scurrying to the cardiologist in Puerto Rico.

He told me I could only drink two glasses of wine a night.

"Can I borrow your telephone," I asked the doc.

"Sure," he said, and I called Carolyn at the sail loft where she was working and told her to buy the two largest glasses in the Caribbean.

He frowned.

But I watched my diet, exercised and gobbled the contents of my pill tray—all the way around the world. The only problem was that as I got closer and closer to my goal of circumnavigation, I also got laxer and laxer about my health.

Who could resist finding out, firsthand, whether New Zealand or Australian vineyards make the best Shiraz? And the Chateauneuf-du-Pape was cheap in Tahiti. Oh, Madagascar was a trip—a five-gallon fuel jug of 151-proof rum was $20, if you brought your own container. Cape Town was another wine orgy. And then back to my beloved, rum-kissed Caribbean, dotted with as many grog shops as grains of sand.

Alas, I hadn't been to a doctor in five years since I'd left St. Thomas, and I discovered why immediately upon returning home to St. John, U.S.V.I.

"It is like this, Fatty," said Dr. James Clayton, a multihull sailor and good friend. "You can drink for a short time or you can live for a long time."

Well! That shocked me, and didn't seem to leave much wiggle room.

"But—," I said, and he cut me off. "No 'buts,' Fatty. It's your choice. I can't decide for you. Nor can Carolyn. Just you. Good luck."

That was on June 11, 2004, and I haven't had a drink since.

To stop drinking after 35 happy years of unlimited indulgence wasn't easy. Twice I had to pay a visit to Bill's house (to attend an AA meeting) to strengthen my resolve. But I did it.

I'm proud of myself.

But I'm also a different person from the one I was.

At first, I found it impossible to be around people who were drinking. This put a severe crimp in my "sea gypsy" social life, especially in the Caribbean, where a spot of rum is practically included in the baby formula.

After about a year I was able to relax around people while they were drinking, but I still can't abide drunks. (Fact: only drunks can tolerate drunks.)

The hardest part—the saddest part—was disappointing people. Some people just couldn't handle my decision. One dear friend flew in, rushed down to *Wild Card* and blurted out, "This isn't right, Fatty! OK, maybe your liver or heart can't handle the hard stuff, but wine? Or grass? Have you tried LSD or mescaline or peyote, or even a judicious line or two? I mean, all over the world people get high on *something*!"

It was very difficult to calmly inform him, "I'm sorry, Vin, I'm just not—not doing it anymore."

This happens to me often. "Just *one* drink, Fatty, for old time's sake!"

Yeah, right.

A year ago we were anchored in a quiet bay, and a lovely, old wooden cruising boat anchored close on our starboard side. As soon as the hook was set, its grinning skipper sang out to us, "Come on over! I'm about to realize a life's dream—to get drunk with Cap'n Fatty!"

It made me so sad to quietly but firmly respond with, "Oh no, you're not."

Please don't get me wrong. I am not advising anyone not to drink. Carolyn drinks. Hell, I delight in buying her good wine. I have a bar aboard my own boat. What you do is your business.

All I'm asking is to be allowed the same courtesy. Some people don't like to drink. Other people, like myself, can't. I don't demand that you tell me, in excruciating detail, why you drink, forcing you to morally or immorally justify your lifestyle choices to me—so why should I have to?

In essence, I allow you to drink around me without comment or moral censure and I respectfully request that you to allow me to *not* drink around you without comment or moral censure.

That's simple, isn't it?

Yes, sailors *do* traditionally gather for sundowners all around the world. Since that's where all my cruising friends are, I'm there too. We gather in cockpits, on beaches and in various watering holes along the waterfront.

Fine. No problem. Just don't expect a song and dance when you ask, "What's your poison?" and I respond with, "None, thanks!"

A Winch for the Wench

In which the Cap'n asks: Is a promise made at 16 still binding 35 years later in the court of marital law?

It was 1968 and we were gearing up for the Summer of Love. Carolyn and I were both 16 years old. And we were at anchor in Lake Michigan, near Chicago. I'd just replaced seven planks and sistered a dozen frames over the winter, and this was our spring shakedown aboard *Corina*, the 22-foot Atkin-designed double-ender I'd purchased the year before. It was all good news. *Corina* was barely leaking now. The world lay at our feet.

I was happy in the uncomplicated, straight-ahead way that only the young can feel. But now it was late Sunday afternoon and there were storm clouds on the western horizon. Tomorrow Carolyn would have to be back at school, and I back at work. "I'll crank the engine and power forward," I told Carolyn, "You haul in the anchor rode. Tell me when we're directly above the anchor and I'll stop. You cleat it off, then I'll reverse and break the anchor out. Then I'll stop again, and you'll haul it aboard. OK?"

"Sure," she said.

It was a small anchor with very little chain and she'd done it before. But this time there must have been a mountain of Midwestern mud on its flukes. It was heavy. I could tell that by the way she flexed as she hoisted it. OK, I'm a cad. I admit I enjoyed watching her. She paused in mid-hoist to catch her breath. "Isn't there something to make this easier," she asked me. "I mean, like an electric anchor reel or something?"

"Yeah," I said from the cockpit. "It's called an anchor windlass, and I'll buy you one when you're 50. It was just a throwaway line. I didn't even think about it, really. I just opened my mouth and it fell out. Who knew the gold digger would hang around for the next 35 years in patient expectation?

Back in those days, I was far more of a traditionalist than I am today. I had kerosene running lights outside and kerosene cabin lamps inside. Every spring, with an open *Dutton's Navigation* in front of me, I'd swing my compass, and adjust my father's trusty World War II sextant. My only two concessions to modernity were a large-looped radio direction finder and an electronic Accutron wristwatch.

Most of the time, Carolyn had no problem with *Corina's* small anchor, short chain and half-inch rode—not in the Great Lakes, down the Mississippi River, or in the tropics.

"I don't need an anchor windlass," I'd tell my friends. "I've got a Sicilian on the bow!"

It became a joke, I guess, but it was also a strange and backward way that I showed her respect. She was strong, on all levels. She didn't need coddling. So what if other people couldn't—or wouldn't—do it. She could. And did. With a smile. An alluring smile.

Carolyn's strength became legendary. "Watch out," I'd threaten my rum-soaked drinking buddies. "One word from me and my wife will knock out what's left of your teeth!"

When local sailors wanted to move an engine, launch a dinghy or shift some cargo, they'd stop by our boat and ask me if Carolyn was available.

There was a dinghy race in St. Augustine, Florida, and Carolyn was such a strong rower it was a foregone conclusion she'd win. As a joke, a friend (still a friend, though, admittedly a dumb one) tied a cinderblock to the trailing edge of our dinghy's skeg, thinking Carolyn would get a good laugh when she discovered it after a couple of strokes. But he used too much line. It wasn't visible to Carolyn, who thought she was just nervous about the competition and thus slow. But the town folk watching from the Bridge of Lions could clearly see the cinderblock rotating underwater astern. They screamed and pointed. This just confused Carolyn. But she never gave up and finishing third out of 20 despite her... er, handicap. As she stroked like an Amazon throughout her long, hot ordeal, I remember thinking, "I'm the luckiest man in the world to share my life with that woman."

So it became a tradition. Whenever we'd travel in the company of other boats, I'd famously "relax" in the cockpit as Carolyn ran the foredeck. Occasionally, I'd help out with a little moral support. "Come on, Carolyn, asses and elbows, please! Yank it up, honey. That's right, yo-yo it back on the deck

Carolyn would be up there, covered in mud, dripping blood and swing anchors around as if they were cocktail purses. But time marches on. As our wallets grew, so did our boats—and their related anchor gear.

In 2002, our daughter, Roma Orion came from college to visit us in Australia as we cruised the Great Barrier Reef. One day, we attempted to anchor off Thursday Island, in the notoriously windy Torres Strait. We couldn't get our anchor to hold. There was a swift current, and it'd evidently, hard-scoured the bottom. Again and again we tried: hoisting, lowering, backing, and rehoisting. Luckily, Roma was with us. She works out, plays rugby, and mountain bikes. But in the middle of the third hoist, even Roma fell backwards, sat down, and rested. Only Carolyn continued to hoist, with agonizingly painful slowness. And Roma gave me a peculiar look: not accusingly, really, just puzzled. As if something was happening here that she couldn't quite figure—but didn't like.

Three years ago, Carolyn turned 50. We were in Chagos, about as far into the Indian Ocean from a West Marine as you can travel. "Well?" Carolyn asked.

"Well, what," I said.

Carolyn reminded me of my promise, as she had numerous times over the course of the last three and a half decades.

"You're serious?" I ask. "Think about the extra weight of the chain and the added expense of the windlass."

"Are you reneging on your promise," she said curtly.

"Of course not," I said. "But I promised 'when you are 50,' not necessarily 'for your 50th birthday.'"

"Ah," she said. "I'd have never married you if I'd known you'd become a sea lawyer!"

That stung. With a sigh, I went anchorage begging. I didn't find a lot of sympathy, but I did find an about-to-be-discarded windlass in the bilge of *Canadian Sunset*. "It's a SL 555 manual," Jim Gracie said, "It's frozen up solid. But, hey, maybe with a big enough sledge hammer..."

It took a *huge* sledge hammer. Internal parts were squashed, bent and twisted. I beat shafts straight, drilled holes truer and rasped bearings larger.

Finally, it was reassembled and bolted to the foredeck. And it worked. Sort of. Well, nearly.

"But I thought," Carolyn said glumly, "you know—an electric one!"

"I'll buy you one of those electric ones when you're 70," I said brightly.

This did not get a laugh. Not even a smile. Worse, not even a glare.

I realized that what is funny at 16 years, can be sad at 50.

About six months ago, anchored within the fringing reef of Tahiti, we were hit by a small but powerful squall. We dragged. (I've only dragged six times in my life. But that's six times too many, and this was one of them.) This wouldn't have been so bad in sand, but we'd rested up against a large coral head and I was scared to put the engine in gear to power away, for fear of damaging my prop or bending my shaft. So I zoomed out our emergency lunch hook in the dinghy, and returned to *Wild Card* to kedge her off with brute force.

Carolyn was already straining at the rode when I joined her. I gave it my all. Nothing. A slight sea was building. We were pounding a bit.

I wanted *off*, like, *now*!

"Pull, damn it," I cried. "...don't *just look at it*, Carolyn, *pull* on the gawd-dang thing!" Nothing.

"Let's pump it," I shouted. "Get a rhythm going. Now and *now* and—."

Carolyn fell backward. I heard a sob. She sat down with a thud, buried her face in her hands, and said, "I can't."

I froze. I couldn't believe it. Atlas had shrugged, and for a moment, my world blurred. Then, with brutal clarity, I refocused. I was asking her to do the impossible, and fully expecting her to accomplish it. What a fool I'd been, to miss the pivotal moment when the joke had soured. "That's OK, honey" I told her gently as I trotted the dripping rode aft to the sheet winches. "I understand, and I'm sorry I—."

"No, I'm the one who is sorry," she said as she helped me tail, "It is just that—"

"I know," I said. "It's my fault. Truly. I apologize for being deaf, dumb and blind."

After that incident, our first port-of-call in a developed nation was New Zealand. I dashed ashore and purchased a Maxwell VWC1500 windlass with all the trimmings. As I installed it on the foredeck, Carolyn, at my insistence, worked on her tan, fussed with her nails and drank pina coladas.

"It'll pick up 1,700 pounds," I told her. "And it's fast: 56 feet per minute. We'll be able to raise and lower the anchor automatically from either the foredeck or the cockpit. And there's an electronic chain counter with docking alarm."

"It seems like a dream," Carolyn said yawning, "A hi-tech dream."

"No," I said. "Just fair payment on a long-overdue bill."

A few days later, just before we began field-testing the windlass, I presented her with a small, carefully wrapped, belated 50th birthday present. There was a card, and it said things too private to repeat. Inside the box, artfully set amid black velvet, was a small knitted pouch.

"What is it," Carolyn asked, holding it up for bemused inspection. "A gear shift cover?"

"A toe sock," I explained. "To prevent your big toe from getting calluses on the foot switch!"

She laughed. "Seems like you thought of everything, Fatty" she said.

Better late than never.

The Treble Clef Ensign

When the jam fest flag goes up, the question is not how well you play but how enthusiastically.

"Ahoy," I shouted at the Peterson 44, *Sojourner,* from New Zealand, "what's the flag mean?"

Carolyn, my wife, and I were in Bantam, Indonesia, within sniffing distance of Singapore's air pollution.

Alan Hogan, a vineyard owner turned sea gypsy, popped his cheery head out of the hatch.

"The Treble Clef ensign?" he asked, indicating the flag flying just below his courtesy flag, "It means 'music-starved musician' aboard! Do you play?"

"Guitar," I said. "Horribly."

"He isn't being modest," Carolyn chimed in, perhaps a tad too vehemently. "This is one of the few times that my husband isn't exaggerating!"

Alan laughed, and held up a tiny flute case. "Come on aboard," he said. "Having an informal jam session isn't about excellence, it's about having fun. I try to find musicians to play with everywhere that we cruise. Hence, the flag. You would be amazed at all the wonderful music I've enjoyed because of that silly flag. I've played with some of the best professional musicians in the world and, well, some of the most enthusiastic, too! For me, music is about joy and the flag is about sharing that joy!"

Needless to say, we immediately fell in love with Alan (and his lovely-but tone-deaf wife Joyce.) My guitar and I were back within the hour. That evening, we played ashore at a little happy-hour gathering of cruisers on the beach. Later in the week, we played poolside at a nearby resort. Soon we were getting together whenever our wakes crossed in Southeast Asia, playing not only with each other, but others as well.

The magical musical moment with him that I remember best, took place late at night anchored off Ao Chalong, Thailand. It was just one of those times when I could do no wrong on guitar. "I would have never thought," Alan said happily, toasting me with a precious glass of his very own wine, "that 'Sympathy for the Devil' could sound so good as a folk song accompanied by flute and accordion."

A couple of months later, I was anchored off Langkawi experiencing the other side of the coin.

"What country the flag is flying?" asked a passing Malaysian fisherman.

I explained the purpose of the Treble Clef ensign that we'd made: to alert fellow musicians that I liked to jam. "Do you play," I asked him.

"No play me," he grinned back, "but in Kuah coffee shop is both the rock and the roll!"

It took some time to find the coffee shop. When we did, there was a language problem. I wanted to play, but I didn't want to be pushy. Besides, it was such a strange scene: did I really want to play American rock & rock in a strict Muslim country?

More and more people wandered in, and joined our halting conversation. Finally, one guy clapped his hands happily and said. "You from Chicago Blues Home, yes?"

"Yes," I said.

"B.B. King!!"

"Yes," I agreed. "B. B. King is indeed a famous Chicago blues guitarist."

"OK, OK, Mister B. B. Blues Guy. Come back tonight, we jam it hard!"

"You don't think," Carolyn mused on the way home, "that they think you're B.B King, do you?"

"I hope not," I quipped, "for Mister King's sake!"

That evening was perhaps the strangest musical experience I've ever had. There were a lot of people there, standing room only. All the women wore scarves, and many of the men wore their little square-topped hats. And, of course, the coffee house served no alcohol.

I played and played and played. They listened in silence. Nobody clapped. I gave it my all: I screamed, I emoted, I bled. They watched. You could hear a pin drop.

Finally, I could play no more. I wanted to cry. I'd completely failed to move them.

But, before I could leave the stage, one of their leaders stood up and conferred excitedly with the audience.

"Excuse me Mister Blues Guy Sailor," he said. "Would you play us again one song?"

I said I would.

"Fine," he said, careful with his English. "Then play us again the wildest one you call 'Big-Butted Momma!'"

I could barely contain my laughter, but I played it. Finally, at the leader's signal, they clapped long and loud, as if they'd just been serenaded by Eric Clapton, Jimi Hendricks and Mark Knopfler—all together on the same bill.

Then the local band took to the stage and backed me up, and we all played together. I couldn't believe how much rock 'n roll they knew. These guys could play more standards than I could!

"Same world," one told me proudly. "We love Elvis too!"

Later, as we walked back to the boat on a lovely cloud of international brotherhood, Carolyn leaned into me and said, "That was amazing, Fatty. We all grew up with the same music!"

"Yeah," I said, "and thanks for sewing up the Treble Clef ensign!"

A year or so later we were clearing into Richards Bay, in South Africa. The customs guy was with me in the cockpit, officiously filling out a dozen forms. It was tedious. I was irritable. But, as usual, Carolyn wasn't the least bit uptight. She was down below, straightening up from our Agulhas Current crossing and planning our evening's activities.

She popped a CD into the player, and started wiggling her butt to the music. The customs man's jaw dropped. "You like Ray Charles, too?" he shouted down to Carolyn.

Carolyn said she did, indeed, like Brother Ray. Carolyn pointed out our Treble Clef ensign, while I sprinted for my bulkhead mounted guitar.

I was only a couple of notes into "Georgia On My Mind," when the customs guy said, "Wait, wait, wait," and tossed his numerous forms into the air. It only took him a couple of minutes to retrieve his instrument from the back of his car.

"Muzi is my name," he said with a wide grin as we tuned up together. "I play gospel music—American gospel music—in my church. But I love Ray Charles and country and western, too!"

We became good friends. He was a member of the Zulu tribe. He stopped by *Wild Card* a couple of times to play. Once I asked him, since our clearing in process had been rather truncated due to more important matters, how long our South African visas were good for.

"For as long as you keep teaching me Chicago blues riffs," he replied.

Confession: I didn't start out to be a writer. In fact I didn't think I could be a writer, because I thought writers had to know something. It was only later that I learned that writers can be just as stupid as everyone else. Because I thought writing was for intellectuals, and I knew I was a standard-issue-dummy, I started out to be a songwriter.

No to Shakespeare, yeah on Bob Dylan!

Anyway, I took up guitar. Soon, I started writing songs. To learn which songs "worked" and which didn't, I started playing in public—first at parties, then at coffee houses, and, ultimately in bars.

The entire time I cruised on *Corina* (in the 1960s), *Carlotta* (in the 1970 and 1980s) and *Wild Card* (in the 1990s till now and beyond), I played. Come to think of it, I actually started earlier than that aboard the *Elizabeth* {1950s} by singing duets of "When I was a Student at Casey" with my guitar-plucking father.

No, I was not going to earn my living by playing music, but, yes, it did occasionally supplement the cruising kitty.

Mostly what it did was give me pleasure and allow me to share that pleasure with others. Music truly is the universal language. Yes, it *does* soothe the savage beast. And, whether I was playing for the children of Borneo, the fishermen of Madagascar or the beggars of India, it's always fun.

But nowhere is the marine music scene quite as much of a hoot as the Virgin Islands.

Just recently, Jimmy Buffett played on the beach of Great Cruz Bay, St. John, where I've moored on and off for almost three decades. Foxy Callwood is always crooning on Jost Van Dyke. Eileen Quinn regularly passes through. Hell, even the Mamas and Papas used to play for tips in the seedier dives of Charlotte Amalie. Just ask Bill Grogan, who is sort of the official music groupie of St. Thomas. "The first thing that Sir Paul McCarthy said to me," says Bill fondly, "was, 'Do you have any papers?'"

But it's the local guys and gals, many of them sailors, who keep the music scene so vibrant on both St. Thomas and St. John, where, on any given night, you can hear numerous good musicians playing everything from contemporary jazz to classic folk.

And some of the strangest people come to see some of the worst acts!

There was one night recently when the crowd was rocking at Latitude 18, a seedy sailor's dive in Red Hook on the east end of St. Thomas. I'd just finished my set, and now ocean racer and Caribbean 1500 organizer Davis Murray was on stage belting out "Junk in the Trunk" in Calypso counterpoint to my signature-tune, "Big Butted Momma." Mighty Whitey, a familiar patron of the rum shops of the Caribbean, was going to play later. He was the only "white boy" to ever place in the final top three competition for Calypso King of the St. Thomas carnival. His wife, Janet, who heads up The Pop Tarts, a glitzy girl-band, had, just returned from sailing to the Galápagos aboard a steel sloop named *Buster*. Neil Lewis, the folk singing skipper of the famed charter vessel *Alexander Hamilton*, was in the audience, too. He'd just returned from a summer aboard his canal barge *Berendina* in the French canals. Andrew Pan, just out from behind the counter of Island Marine Outfitters, was off in a corner playing percussion. John B off *Sloop John B* was backing up Davis on rhythm guitar, and passing out his trademark flyswatters between sets. Why John distributes free flyswatters throughout the Caribbean was a mystery, but one that nobody wants to ask a former lawyer from Alabama with no last name about. There were a lot of multi-hullers in the audience: they always turned out to see designer/builder/racer Joe Colpitt of the 56-foot speedster *Virgin Fire* play his lovely show tunes.

I was belly-up to the bar, attempting to apprise the bartender of my massive thirst, when a nattily dressed bareboater slid up to me purposefully, leaned into my ear and shouted, "That 'Dark Meat' tune was just about the most disgusting thing I've ever heard!"

Luckily, he gave a thumbs-up sign to indicate his naughty approval.

"Do you know Fatty?" he asked, scanning the crowd.

"I do," I said. "All too well."

"You don't like him?" the guy asked.

"I didn't say that," I said. "It's just that, well, he's really gotten me into a lot of trouble lately.

"We hear he's gonna play tonight."

"I heard the same," I say.
"What kind of music does he play? Any sea chanteys?"
"It varies," I said. "Mostly it varies between poor and worthless!"
"You got some issues with the guy?"
"You could say that," I said.

Just then The Fiddler, Dick Solberg, strolled by with his Sun Mountain Band. Circumnavigator David Wegman of the schooner *African Queen* was with him; the last time I'd heard David play was in St. Barts with Buffett. David's new girlfriend, a multilingual runaway bass player from Czechoslovakia named Channing, decorated his shoulder. Greg, of the Bob Perry-designed double-ender *Four Winds*, was taking the stage now to blow some blues harp. Parker Hall, of the Nicholson 32 *Peace Pipe*, was swinging his washtub string base over the heads of crowd as he prepared to join Greg onstage. I scanned the room, hoping to see other fiddlers like Peter Muilenburg of *Breath* and Dave Dostal of *Rob Roy*. Michael Beans, sailing troubadour and professional stage pirate, was going to miss it; he was gigging on Marina Cay this evening. Somebody told me LouLou Magras of the gaffer *Pluto* would play his squeeze-box, but I knew LouLou was too shy for a public venue. Mandolin James, cigarette-dripping as always, had actually left the cockpit of *Lonesome Picker* in Great Cruz long enough to join us.

By this point in the evening, the visiting bareboater appeared to be having difficulty focusing. He was holding two pina coladas in each hand and looking delightfully lost.

As I passed him, he tried to speak, but seemed incapable of it. "Don't worry," I said in continuation of our previous conversation, "You'll meet him. I guarantee it!"

"Great, great," he blubbered back, "I'll be here!"

Then, just as I was pulling away, he added, "Are all boaters in the Virgin Islands musicians?"

"Some does, but you don't must!" I replied in my best West Indian dialect

Carolyn slid up beside me, and quipped, "That guy ought to drink slower—or faster!"

I surveyed the milling crowd of sea gypsies on both sides of the stage and bar and thought about our upcoming Round Two circumnavigation.

"How's our Treble Clef ensign," I asked her. "Still serviceable?"

"Tattered but game," she said as she leaned into me.

"Just like us," I whispered into her hair.

The Guru and His Gospel

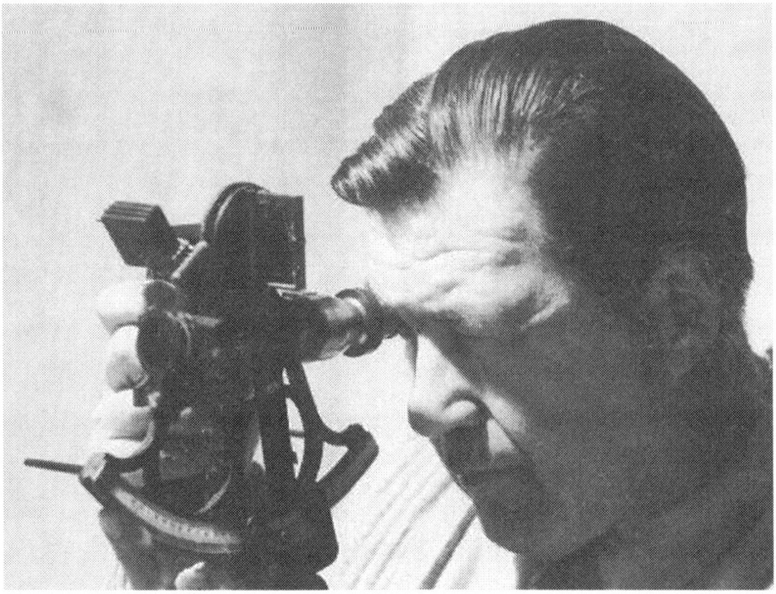

It wasn't what my father knew that earned him his moniker; it was how he imparted his wisdom to those willing to watch him ease joyfully through the day.

On a bitterly cold, late-November day in the mid-1970s, we were finishing up our sea trials of *Carlotta*, the 36-foot Peter Ibold-designed ketch I'd just built, making sure that she was ready for the trip to the Caribbean. I could still see the Boston skyline shimmering to the west in the gloom. We were going to windward in a building sea and taking green water over the bow. Damn, it was chilly.

"Tell The Guru it's his watch," I told George Zamiar, my school chum and first mate. George and I had sailed many an ocean mile, first as teenagers aboard my Atkin double-ender *Corina*, and now aboard the just-launched *Carlotta*.

"Are you crazy?" George whispered back. "Don't even *think* about it, Fatty! He can barely stand up."

I looked at George, who was more brother than friend, and smiled. He loved me, and I knew he loved my father just as much. Still, I ignored his heartfelt advice. I stared up at The Guru, who was clinging to the mainmast on the starboard side. His Parkinson's disease was particularly bad that day: His head jiggled, his boney arm spasmed, and occasionally his brittle hips rotated obscenely.

"Your watch, Dad," I said as nonchalantly as could, just like I'd done a thousand times before on the schooner *Elizabeth*, the family vessel he'd raised me aboard. There was a familiar sparkle in his eye, and I could see The Guru was up to something. He stood tall, let go of the safety of the swaying mast for a brief moment, and did a happy little jig on the foredeck. "God, this is fun!" he hollered with a boyish grin.

To say that boats were central to my father's life is a vast understatement. Boats were, after his love of family, his main focus. They were his ticket both away from the mean streets of Chicago and, eventually, to traveling the oceans of the world. But for a while, he thought he'd blown his sailing career before it began.

He'd been invited to crew aboard a well-known racing vessel in the Great Lakes and had quickly risen through the ranks. It was the first time he'd ever had the respect of men of power, prestige and wealth, and he was bursting with pride. So he'd invited his best South Side pal, a Chicago street kid, aboard for a daysail as his guest. The sail had had gone well until, on the bus ride home, his companion brought out a pair of expensive kid-leather gloves. "Just laying there," his friend said, "so I nicked 'em!"

My father was horrified, grabbed the gloves and rushed off the bus, too angry to speak. Heavy with shame, he walked back to the harbor. "I'm—I'm sorry," he stuttered to the boat's owner as he returned the gloves, so distressed he thought he'd vomit on the cabin sole. "You'll never be able to trust my judgment again, so I think it's best if...."

The owner was smiling, not angry. "Trust?" he said. "Before, I had no reason to trust you, son. Now I do. It's nice to find a young, eager sailor, and even better, to find one who's honest. You're welcome on this vessel anytime. In fact, if I'm not here and you want to let yourself belowdecks, we keep the companionway-hatch key hidden in the steering-quadrant box."

That was the pivotal moment in my father's life. A future of possibilities opened before him, one with sailing vessels, palm trees, and his laughing, loving children scurrying up ratlines while anchored in tropical lagoons.

He'd finally found his tribe, his extended family, his salt-stained social clan—the one place in the universe where he truly fit in. "We're sailors," I often heard him say. "The sea is our home, and regardless of where we sail, there's family."

Yes, James Edward Goodlander's head was in the clouds, but his feet were firmly planted in reality. He'd always been intrigued with the stars, and he was good at mathematics, so celestial navigation came to him easily. Soon he was in demand as a racing navigator, especially during the annual Chicago Yacht Club Race to Mackinac. But it didn't take him long to realize he needed his own boat."She cost $10," he always said proudly, "$5 for the boat and $5 for the team of horses to haul her over to my back yard."

He also purchased an ax and a hammer, and he eventually figured out which to use when. Everyone in his Chicago neighborhood thought he was nuts, but soon his beloved 22-foot sloop, *Dorothea*, rode proudly on her mooring at the Jackson Park Yacht Club.

Oh, yes, the far horizon was already beckoning. At the Chicago Library, he checked out most every book on boating, especially the tales written of Joshua Slocum and the other early circumnavigators. He practically memorized these volumes, and in the process, he not only found his tribe but also discovered his goal in life: to take his family to sea to see the world. The thought of ocean sailing intoxicated him, with its freedom—*true* freedom—adventure and challenge. Yes, the cruising life would provide him and his family with the sweetest existence imaginable.

Years later, on rainy days aboard *Elizabeth*, when my two older sisters, Carole and Gale, my younger brother, Morgan, and I begged her for the family stories, my mother, Marie, would tell us, "He took me down to the harbor and pointed out into the water. I couldn't see a thing, really, as I was too vain to wear my eyeglasses while we were courting. But he kept pointing out into the harbor and saying 'Isn't she beautiful?' I could hear the love in his voice. He was so confident; your father was, so sure of himself. Later that evening, we talked about children—how we both wanted them—and I asked him about a boat. Could he really live on one, raise his children aboard, and sail hither and yon?"

Having heard this one before, we'd giggle and squirm, knowing the good part was coming soon. "Then he reached over and...uh…patted one of my...breasts," she said, shock still evident in her prim, little-girl voice. "Well, I wasn't having any of *that*, so I slapped his hand away, hard! If he had his dream boat, I said to him, then what else would he need. He replied, 'A whore in my bed and a slave in my galley.' I couldn't believe what I'd just heard," my mother would tell us laughing children. "It was the most disgusting thing any man had ever said to me, and, well, I couldn't wait to be his bride!"

The wedding bells sounded just as World War II loomed. Luckily, a skillful celestial navigator could write his own ticket then, and my father was soon living the high life as a commissioned officer in New Orleans, teaching cadets to navigate under the pressures of war, just as he'd trained himself to do under the lesser pressures of yacht racing. Since his skill as a teacher was in such high demand, his military masters wouldn't allow him to go to sea, but his friends were fighting and dying in the South Pacific, and he wanted to go, too.

One day, he learned that his base commander had a big problem: Three small supply ships lying in Mexico had to be in New Orleans "yesterday," or his commander would swing for it. The Guru immediately galvanized his drunken "ragin' Cajun" sailing buddies into action, sweet-talked their way aboard an Air Force plane headed toward the Yucatán and had the three ships in New Orleans before anyone could ask, "On whose authority?" Thus, he earned his orders to the South Pacific.

Luckily for us, the war ended before he saw any action, and he was soon back in Chicago with his young family, looking at boats and the future. A beautiful Maine-built Friendship sloop was for sale; in rough shape, but easily repairable. Alas, he had no money. But, hey...

He talked a doctor into putting up the cash. The Guru did all the shipwright work, the doctor paid all the bills, and the two partners had one of the nicest gold-platers on the Great Lakes. When it finally came time to sell the *Friendship,* the doctor surprised my father by only taking back the money he'd originally invested, and giving the sale's considerable profit to my father for shipwright services rendered. "Usually the best end to a friendship is a partnership, but not always," my father would say.

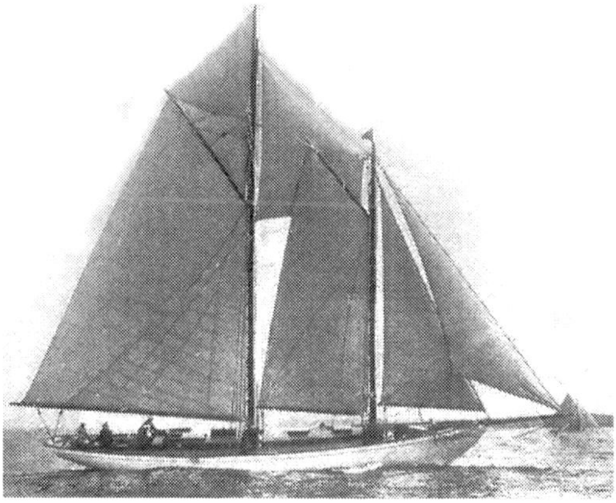

In 1953, when I was a year and a half old, he purchased the John G. Alden-designed 52-foot schooner *Elizabeth.* She was totaled by the insurance company after an onboard fire, and then she'd sunk. "A typical Goodlander vessel," my wife Carolyn says wryly whenever she hears the story.

The Guru paid $100 for *Elizabeth*, and for the next 10 years we lived aboard and cruised her down the Mississippi River and in the Gulf of Mexico. My earliest memories are of being hauled out in Chicago, helping to tend the fire for the steam-box for plank bending, roasting marshmallows as we melted the bilge tar, and getting hit in the head with the ship's axe wielded by my sister Gale. "Nobody has been able to knock any sense into Fatty since," Gale recently quipped during my mother's 87th-birthday bash.)

The winters aboard *Elizabeth* were the worst. We'd huddle under blankets as the snow swirled inside her plank-gutted hull. To stay warm, we dreamed of the South Pacific. "It will be toasty hot in the tropics," my mother would whisper through the frost, "with flower-scented air as sweet as cotton candy."

As a child, it was beyond me how it could be cold in one place and hot in another—until we started down the Mississippi river, bound for Tahiti, and went through our first lock. Then everything began to make sense. We powered *Elizabeth* in, the lock door closed, they pumped out the water, and in my mind's eye, I fancied we'd suddenly arrive in the tropics. The tall lock door seemed to stretch upward into the heavens—the cold air would be pumped out and replaced by the warm air—and I was certain *Elizabeth* would emerge among sandy islands, waving palm trees and cartoon whales breaching and blowing softly on the horizon.

But life isn't fair. Nor just. Nor logical. Life just is, which is a difficult lesson to learn.

Shortly after we set sail, The Guru got sick with Parkinson's and watched his dignity disappear with his muscular control. *Elizabeth* was sold in St. Petersburg, Florida. And the dream of sailing to Tahiti was put on hold until I purchased *Corina* in the 1960s, build *Carlotta* in the 1970s, salvaged our current boat, *Wild Card*, in the late 1980s, announced I'd circumnavigate in the 1990s, and then sailed into Tahiti in 2000, exactly 47 years after my father gathered us around the galley table of *Elizabeth* and said, "Tahiti or bust!"

During the last years of his life, he was bed-ridden, surrounded by the tattered charts, blurry photographs and coffee stained journals of my offshore passages. Once I called him from St. Thomas. "How do you say the name of the main town?" he asked, his weak voice aquiver. "*Shar-let Ah-mal-lee*," I answered. "Yes," he said, eagerly, almost disbelievingly, "that *is* how you pronounce it!"

I wasn't at his bedside when he died. I was exactly where he wanted me to be: in deep ocean, with a fair breeze, and Carolyn, the woman I loved.

While pouring his ashes into the Gulfstream on his final passage, I thought I'd be incredibly sad, but I wasn't. I was filled with a strange, giddy joy for all he'd given me: my love of the sea, my love of writing (he'd written a couple of navigation articles for *Yachting* in the 1950s), my unquenchable hunger for personal freedom, my zero-tolerance for bureaucracy.

The most astonishing thing he gave me was the right, even as a young child, to make my own mistakes. He led by example only. If I wanted an answer, I had to ask for one. I can hear his replies now: "It has a dull blade because you're not storing your wood plane on its side," or, "Never rest it on its heel," or, "Let the saw do the cutting, son; don't jab at the wood; just allow the saw to gently fall through it."

Yeah, he was aptly named The Guru, and I clearly remember when he got his nickname. We were hauled out in Florida, and right beside *Elizabeth*, some college kids were working on an old wooden ketch they'd just purchased. They often turned to my father for advice and bad jokes. At the end of the project, they decided to bring the ketch down to bare wood so she'd really sparkle with smooth topsides. Alas, they weren't thinking ahead and ground off the boot top stripe without marking it.

"Now what'll we do," one of them lamented.

"Well, you could relaunch her and rescribe it with a pencil on the end of a stick, but that would be expensive," said my father. "And she'd soak up water like a sponge, you'd have to let her dry out again. Why don't you give me the brush and I'll take a shot at it?" he said nonchalantly waving a clear cedar batten at the primed hull.

"Have faith," my father added when he saw the anxiety in the young men's faces. Down one side of the hull he went, around the transom and back again.

"But it has to be absolutely level, and straight as an arrow or it will look awful," one of them warned.

When my father—who was also a commercial artist/sign painter by trade, finally returned to the stem, the two lines joined perfectly. "The Guru!" one of the college kids cried as he fell to his knees in respect. And the fact that I'd secretly helped my father mark the waterline *before* they'd ground it off, didn't make him less of a guru in my estimation but more of one.

About the only thing The Guru loved more than boats was his family, and he enjoyed helping my sister Carole and her husband, Joe Borges, build the 36-foot Friendship sloop *Mao* (the Tahitian word for "shark") in Chicago and, later, their 42-foot ketch *Ruby B* in Boston. The Guru was there for my sister Gale and her husband Momo Jensen, when they constructed their 42-foot ketch *Ark*, which they built upside down and gently rolled over with two giant "wagon wheels." And he mentored my younger brother, Morgan, (who now owns *Maxi*, a 36-foot Swedish sloop that he sails in San Francisco Bay,) when he purchased a Roberts 42 bare hull to finish off.

But they don't call you a guru because of what you know; you earn that honor for how you teach. I still think of my father more as a teacher than a sailor. He taught both my sisters to be excellent portrait artists, and he taught me navigation and to play guitar. And best of all, he taught us to love unabashedly—never by telling, but only by showing. He wasn't a preacher, he was a guide.

Once, during one of our annual budget-busting wooden-boat haul outs, we were extremely low on money. My father had promised me that, during the haulout, he'd buy me some gasoline so I could use the dinghy to take my friends water-skiing. Evidently, he'd forgotten all about it when he'd realized our port garboard plank needed replacing. I confronted him one day on a scaffolding plank, and said, "You promised, Dad."

He bent down, stared me straight in the eye, and removed a single $10 bill from his wallet. "This is the only money we have, son. Do you think we should spend it on water-skiing or food?"

I was only 10 or 11, and I wasn't really listening. I just snatched the money, yelled thanks and dashed to the fuel dock.

For the next few days, our family ate only rice and plain water. He never said a word, but the rice tasted like ashes in my mouth, and now, some 40-years later, my eyes still water at my blatant selfishness. No, The Guru didn't tell; he taught.

I replanked *Corina* by myself when I was sixteen, but looking back, I realize now that he was always lurking around the shipyard when I needed him. "How do you taper the new planks?" I'd ask him. "And what about the bevel? How do you pound the cotton caulking by sound? Is it difficult to build a steam box?" Not only was he always there, leading me to my own answers, but he also often just "sort of happened" to have a trunk full of the various caulking mallets I needed as well.

He trusted me, and he cast off my docklines when I first sailed over the horizon at sixteen years of age. In hindsight, that must have been hard to do, because he knew that such freedom, once tasted, would be forever desired.

Perhaps the best thing he gave me was my confidence. Mother Ocean isn't the enemy. The wind is my friend. Even the worst gale isn't evil. Most small boat projects can be fixed with a pocketknife, duct tape and some kite string. Sailing isn't rocket science; it's an art, requiring passion, love, and tons of hard work.

"The world is our oyster, son," he'd tell me, and only now, at the jibe mark of my own salt-stained life, can I fully appreciate the joyful wisdom of his loving words.

Doin' The Tassie Tango

On a dark night in the western Pacific, 40 seconds can seem like forever.

The passage from Whangarei, New Zealand to Brisbane, Australia is only about 1,300 miles—but it skirts the northern boundary of the Tasman Sea, an unsettled stretch of chilly water notorious for its prolonged gales, adverse currents and rogue waves.

"Don't do it, Fatty," advised Captain Timothy McAuliffe of the Beneteau 37 *Forever Young*. "Too many boats have dismasted, rolled and sunk out there. The risk of hitting truly severe weather just isn't worth it. Do what everybody else does, go up to New Caledonia and Vanuatu first, and then come back down to Australia the next season."

It was tempting to keep following the sun-worshiping South Pacific cruisers we'd joined up with a year ago in the Panama Canal area. But it was also appealing to branch out from the Coconut Milk Run for some slightly more adventurous sailing in the higher latitudes.

We weren't crossing the Tasman, just scooting by its northern edge. How bad could it be?

"How bad?" said Aussie Bob Mackie of the Bruce Farr-designed cruiser/racer named *Ninth Wave*. "Well, it can be bloody awful, the Tassie can. But if you watch your weather and time it just right, it doesn't *have* to be awful. It can be just miserable instead!"

For a third opinion, I went to Kiwi John Bramley, on the S&S 47 *Nakoni* who'd done the passage before. "The Tassie? Well, it'll blow the cobwebs out of yer rig, that's for sure! Why, one time our barometer dropped so low we had to retrieve it from the bilge! That was some storm, I'll tell ya! The seas were so big we needed oxygen on the crests and were worried about running aground in the troughs."

I couldn't help but laugh. "Seriously!" I said.

"You've got a good boat and a good woman," Kiwi John said quietly. "You'll make it."

Of course, I had a reason for wanting to go directly to Brisbane from New Zealand. Our daughter Roma Orion had requested to meet us there. She's putting herself through college by working two jobs while her mother, Carolyn, and I circumnavigate—and thus I think she deserves to be indulged occasionally.

"Spin a globe and throw a dart at it any time," I'd told her years ago, "and we'll meet you there."

Just because she'd never hold me to it didn't mean I shouldn't keep the promise.

But first, I had to discuss it with my long-suffering crew. Carolyn and I have sailed together now for over 30 years, and she knows exactly how my mind works.

"Everybody says it is a stupid idea," I told her.

"I was afraid of that," she said glumly. "Then we'll need charts of the both Howe and Norfolk islands, and you'll have to get me drunk the night before we leave. I'll be damned if I'll head out across the Tassie without a hangover!"

Yes, Carolyn is a stickler for nautical tradition.

Is the Tasman Sea's horrible reputation well deserved? In a word, yes. First, gales regularly sweep up from Antarctica. These intense storms occasionally collide with larger weather systems sliding eastward off Australia, and the isobars in the area between the two systems get rapidly compressed. Barometric pressure can drop a point an hour, and wind speeds can quickly approach hurricane force within these notorious "squash zones."

Other factors contribute as well: Huge ocean swells from distant storms often roll right across the Tasman. When opposed by strong winds, these swells can result in some abnormally large, pyramid-shaped seas. Although we would pass north of the worst part of the Tasman Sea, our route wouldn't steer clear of other thorny obstacles. In areas where the cold water from the south hits the warm water from the equator, local conditions can become unstable in the blink of an eye. The Brisbane area is notorious for its severe thundershowers and devastating coastal tornadoes. Given the right combination of factors, strong opposing ocean currents within 400 miles of the Australian coast can result in a sort of "mini-Gulfstream" that must be crossed along the way. Finally, to avoid the early autumn gales, we planned to depart at the tail end of the November-April cyclone season, when tropical storms were still a threat. In short, the passage wasn't one to take lightly. Like the old salt at the New Zealand Yacht Squadron told us when he heard we were heading across, "You'd best put a reef in your ensign!"

After forty years of living aboard and cruising on small sailing vessels, I'd like to think I've seen it all, that Mother Ocean holds no surprises. But of course that isn't true. She always holds a little back with which to slap you down when you get too cocky, too confident, too blasé.

Obviously, the best way to deal with heavy weather is to avoid it entirely. We've been remarkably successful at this over the years, and with today's improved long range weather forecasting and abundant sources of weather information, it's easier now than ever. My problem isn't getting the accurate meteorological data—it's making sense of it. I'm not an expert when it comes to global weather patterns, so I occasionally rely on skilled assistance before shoving off on a potentially difficult passage. In this case I e-mailed my (aptly named) friend and forecaster David Jones in the British Virgin Islands a month before my target date in mid-April so he'd have time to get accustomed to the general weather patterns effecting the Tasman Sea.

While David peered into his crystal ball, Carolyn and I again went over *Wild Card's* rig with a fine-toothed comb. Since it is not unusual for me to reef and unreef *Wild Card* six or eight times in a single day, I paid particular attention to my slab reefing system. Just before shoving off, I replaced all my reef lines, refastened two of my oversized cheek blocks, and added a line stopper on the lower reef line, so I could keep tension on it while using the winch for the second reef as well. I also hanked on my storm-staysail, which is something I do only if I'm expecting extreme conditions. We'd just heard about a 50-foot steel ketch that was hit so hard by a wave off Sydney that two of its crew members had to be airlifted off via helicopter with broken bones.

All this preparation was in addition to my normal offshore checklist, which traditionally ends in making sure all four of my bilge pump systems are operating, and personally checking each and every item in our ditch bag and liferaft group.

On April 10th, David Jones told us to sit tight as Tropical Storm Sose swept by to our north. Three days later, he told us to stand ready for April 15, when he gave us the green light. The last thing I did ashore in New Zealand was print out his five-day wind, sea and swell forecast. Predicting that wind and seas would diminish, it proved astoundingly accurate. (A huge stationary high-pressure system dominated in the wake of Sose, with two smaller highs following after.)

Basically, it was a light-air trip—all but about a minute of it. Instead of storm sailing through huge seas as initially expected, we ghosted along amid cat's paws with everything up. While I seldom crank up our Perkins while on ocean passage, this time I ran our diesel whenever boat speed fell below three knots for one hour, which was fairly often. "Don't dilly-dally out there," I'd been advised repeated. "You never know what the next system might bring!" Instead of averaging almost 6 knots for the trip, we barely averaged 4, taking 12 days to cover the 1,300 miles to Brisbane.

The Thing

The only remarkable event took place about three-quarters of the way across as a relatively small and benign front between two high-pressure systems moved through. I wasn't worried because I knew that on the other side of the front were light-to-moderate conditions.

It was on the night of the April 23, just before midnight, when it happened. The sea was calm. The sky was pitch-black. The wind was blowing about 10 knots from the northeast—but much higher under the squall lines embedded in the passing front. We'd already passed through two large squalls with brief gusts of 40 knots, and I was ready for the third.

Or so I thought.

It started normally enough. The wind quickly built to 35 knots, and then the hardest gusts hit us just as the rain really started to come down in buckets. As soon as the rain eased up, so did the wind—back to 30 knots or so. Just as I was thinking we'd seen the worst of it, things got very strange indeed. I couldn't see anything on our starboard side. The squall moving overhead looked like a menacing blob of darkness.

But then I began to hear something. Something I'd never heard before. It was high up in the sky off to windward, a sort of turbo whine or jet noise. Like static electricity, it raised the hair on the back of my neck.

I managed to say something clever, like, "Whatdafhellisdat..?" just as it struck.

There was a physical presence to it. I mean, it was a *thing* rather than just a strong wind. It wasn't normal. I can't explain it—but somehow I knew it wasn't *right*. And it was very scary. I gulped, and attempted to figure out what was happening. My mind was alternating between being completely blank and total overload. Then the air temperature plummeted, and I shivered. I blinked again and attempted to see to windward. I couldn't. Whatever it was, it was vibrating the air, the seas, and the boat. We rumbled like a freight train on an ear-popping plunge into a cold and dark tunnel.

Wild Card heeled sharply to port. Then she heeled some more. God, even more, and her port rail slowly submerged up to the cabin side. We were being pushed underwater by a giant invisible hand.

I began to shake. Disoriented, I simply couldn't process what I was seeing. Our mast was almost parallel to the water. I could see its port spreader sort of ice-picking towards the surface. In ten years and many of thousands of ocean miles *Wild Card* had never done anything like this.

OK, it was a lot of wind— exactly how much wind I have no idea. The masthead anemometer cups were almost directly in the lee of our sideways hull, and getting hit on the *bottom* of the cups. They actually *slowed down* during the highest gusts, right before my astounded eyes!

"Oh, God," I said aloud, and gulped. "Damn!"

I knew I had to drop the tiny, double-reefed mainsail we were carrying, or we'd founder. At the same time, I knew that moments such as this, when a sailor is slightly panicked and acting in extreme haste and fear, is when tragedies often occur.

I didn't want to be a tragedy.

And, frankly, I didn't relish crawling along the weather rail and hugging the base of the mast long enough to blow off the main halyard either. But I knew that I *had* to do it, so I grabbed my harness—and fell backwards into the tilted cockpit attempting to don it. With shaking limbs, trembling hands, I gasped and tried to put on the harness.

Suddenly, water was all around me in the air. I knew I wasn't actually in the water, but the air was replaced with spume. I turned on the small flashlight in my left hand. What I saw made no sense. White frothing water surrounded me, but it wasn't blowing with the wind in a normal manner. It was just *there*, writhing and pulsing around the boat. We were falling and turning through—a waterfall?

It was so unreal, as if I were watching a B movie, and the hokey model boat they were using for the movie was heeling too far to port, wallowing too low—obviously a fake. At this point it dawned on me that we were taking water belowdecks. Small amounts of water were already squirting into the boat through the ventilators and hatches—wherever there wasn't a watertight seal.

I had to blow off the main halyard now. *Now!*

With my harness completely tangled around my neck and both its useless clips trailing behind, I crawled out onto the howling, wave-hammered starboard-side deck. "Do it, you coward!" screamed a part of me.

I was pressed as thin as a coat of paint against the tilting cabin top.

"Don't listen to that macho bastard," another voice warned. "You're not clipped on. Carolyn's below. It's suicide!"

Then it was over. The fan shut off. The masthead lifted away from the sea. *Wild Card* stood upright. I couldn't believe it. It was, truly, over. I felt giddy. We were perfectly safe. The wind was back to 35 knots. Hell, I could pop the chute in this breeze!

The whole ordeal lasted only about 40 seconds.

Suddenly, the main companionway hatch flew open. Carolyn's upper body appeared. She looked insane. She was pointing aft. Her eyes were huge. Her mouth was twisted open in a snarl. And she was shouting something.

"Waterspout, Fatty!" she was yelling. "It's a waterspout! See the funnel?"

I saw nothing. I said nothing. Instead, I just kept smiling to myself and thinking, "Ain't life grand? Isn't being alive swell?"

God's Own Ax

A yuletide light show is something more than a kitchy holiday spectacle when you're truly at sea.

At first I wasn't sure it was lightening. We were heading west, just south of the Bay of Bengal. It was late December two years ago. At first I thought that it was the setting sun sort of flickering in the atmosphere. But, as the sun got dimmer, the flashes got brighter.

"Wow," I said to Carolyn, my wife, my lover, and my navigator for the last 35 years. "If that's lightening it's the worst electric storm I've ever seen!"

"I really don't need another lightening strike," she said as she chewed a lip. "We haven't replaced all the electronics that got zapped in Malaysia."

The Indian Ocean is a strange place. It is full of drama and mystery and (far too much) excitement, especially in the unsettled weather between monsoons. Conventional wisdom is to wait in Southeast Asia until just after the New Year. But we'd jumped the gun and left a couple of weeks early, as soon as I felt the winter easterlies were well established. I wanted to get to India. For the first three days, it seemed I was right. Then the wind veered north by northwest and became puffy and erratic.

Now I was beginning to feel I'd made a mistake. Normally I'm not homesick, but tonight I was. I could just picture all our family and friends visiting each other this evening—all their love, their laughter, their joy.

Life is full of choices, eh? For every door you open, another closes.

Generally speaking, we were happy being sea gypsies—usually *very* happy. But there were times when I thought to myself, "Why aren't you by your mother's side in California this tonight. Or with your daughter in Boston? Or your sister in Tennessee?"

Carolyn was sitting at the nav station, within easy speaking distance of the cockpit. "Get the binocs and come up here," I told her. "You won't believe this lightening storm. The strikes are, like, continuous!"

She poked her head up through the hatch and peered ahead. "Lovely," she muttered, which is something she says mostly with dread. "I bet you wouldn't mind having *Astounding Garcia's* radar now!"

We don't have radar. Nor refrigeration. Nor a watermaker. Nor, well, a lot of stuff. What we do have is a modest 38-foot production fiberglass sloop that sails, on average, about 10,000 ocean miles a year and has for a long time. But just because I don't have many of the more expensive toys doesn't mean I don't appreciate them. I'd once delivered to Cozumel a 65-foot motor yacht named *Astounding Garcia.* I came away duly astounded by the clarity of its 48-mile Furuno radar and by how easy it was to outmaneuver squalls with it, as if I'd been playing a video game.

"Yeah, it would be interesting to see what this mess looks like on the scope," I replied. "But I don't think we could steer around it. We're too slow and it's too big. Look, babe, it stretches almost 180 degrees in front of us."

"I don't like this, Fatty" Carolyn said, and her statement just hung in the air.

Carolyn seldom complains. Almost never, in fact. So I knew the approaching lightening storm was truly making her nervous. "I'm kinda gun-shy after Langkawi," she muttered.

To be honest, I was concerned too. Lightening is a real problem in Southeast Asia. In the three months we'd anchored off Ao Chalong in Thailand, eight boats in the anchorage had been struck.

But not us. I was beginning to think we were immune. Then we were motoring by the island of Langkawi on the Thai-Malay border, and there was a single brilliant flash of lightening off to port. Our anemometer and single-sideband radio blinked off.

The following day I climbed the mast and could find no damage—no burn or weld marks, no melted insulation. The VHF radio had been switched on at the time of the incident—its antenna is the highest thing on our mast—and yet it still worked fine. Ditto the tricolor masthead nav light.

Only the SSB and anemometer had been affected. We were puzzled but happy. We have friends who've had every single piece of electrical gear on their boats knocked out by lightening, including spare parts (alternator, GPS, handheld VHF) that were neither installed nor even removed from their original Styrofoam packaging! Worse, lightening occasionally blows holes in boats—not a happy midocean thought.

What, exactly, had happened during our lightning strike? We weren't sure, and we still aren't. But, we came up with a working theory: Lightning hadn't hit us. It had struck the water close to us, and the resulting electromotive force had pulsed through our boat via our lead keel and ground plane, randomly blowing diodes as it went.

But that was only theory. Right now, we had more pressing things to worry about—like how much wind and sea this electrical storm might have in it.

"Should I take down the tree," Carolyn asked. She tried to say it as nonchalantly as possible, but I could tell it cost her.

"Oh, no!" I said too brightly, "I mean, I think I'll heave to and just park her here for the night. Would you like that?"

"Fine," Carolyn said. "There's no rush, is there?"

"Absolutely not," I replied.

Aboard *Wild Card*, heaving to is easy as pie. I just tuck in a double reef, roll up the jib, centerline the main boom, and tie the tiller to leeward. It only takes a few moments, and she's good to 50 knots if nothing breaks. By the time I got *Wild Card* squared away and dead in the water, Carolyn was stirring a pan of powdered milk on the stove and grimacing as she taste-tested it. Finally she poured some in a cup, added a dollop of Virgin Island's rum and passed it to me.

"What do you think," she said.

"Not bad," I lied.

"Well, it ain't nog," she admitted.

"But, it is *grog* and it tastes mighty good all the same."

By now the lightening storm was beginning to tower over us. Its flashes never stopped, but just strobed in different places and at different intensity levels. Occasionally a vivid blue bolt would crack and rip and tear its jagged way downward to the sea, the arcs momentarily stitching heaven and earth together in a cataclysmic explosion. It takes 25,000 volts to make lightning jump one inch. We were seeing miles of the stuff.

"What a light show," I said.

Standing in the companionway, looking out, sipping our drinks, I could feel Carolyn fluttering against my chest.

"Dinner?" Carolyn asked.

"Let's skip it and fast for the big feast tomorrow," I said.

"OK, then I'm going to hit the sack."

"I'll tuck you in," I told her, and followed. She awkwardly climbed over the tattered leecloth of her port main-cabin berth, fluffed her pillows and lay down. I bent over her, kissed her forehead and said, "Sleep tight. Don't let the bedbugs bite!"

Carolyn replied, "And if they do, grab a shoe and beat 'em till they're black and blue!"

The boat swayed. I swayed. Pools of blue-white light swept crazily across our cabin sole. It was a very strange, very disorienting feeling. We were both needing the comfort of family to deal with it. Our daughter was in Boston, a grown-up professional lady now. But whenever we'd recite the baby rhymes of her shipboard youth, we'd feel close to her. And we always missed her most during the holidays.

I went back on deck and sat in the cockpit for a while, watching as the storm unfolded towards us. It was utterly awesome, as if God had scheduled an extremely long grand finale.

The sea was relatively flat. The breeze was under 15 knots. I expected at any moment to be hit by a wall of wind. But it never came our way. Whatever was causing those massive updrafts, all this gazillion-volt friction, somehow missed us entirely.

But the thunder and lightning passed directly overhead. At the height of it, I too, took to my bunk. I didn't say anything to Carolyn but I knew she was wide awake. No one could sleep through this noise. The flashbulb bursts of blue-white light were nearly continuous now. Each peel of lightning was a cosmic coconut being split open by God's own axe—craaaaCCCCKKKK!

Just when it seemed the strikes couldn't get any closer or louder, they did. We'd both jump, hold our breath, and wonder if we'd been hit. My ears popped. With each concussion, everything shook and quivered, even the water around us. Our dishes rattled. Something fell off a bulkhead. A metal grate vibrated in our gimbaled oven. It was a scene from one of those old World War II submarine movies, the crew waiting breathlessly for the depth charges to explode.

I could smell burning ozone in the air around us. It was a rich smell... a burning, wet smell that made no sense then and still doesn't now. I couldn't take it anymore. My fingernails were cutting into my palms. My veins bulged in my neck.

Finally I opened my mouth and shakily sang, "Silent night, holy night..."

"...All is calm, all is bright," Carolyn joined in.

It felt good. Safe. Familiar.

Then it was on to "Jiggle Bells" and "Rudolph the Red-Nosed Reindeer" and "Frosty the Snowman."

I'm not sure when I fell asleep, but I was awakened half an hour later by one of the two digital kitchen timers I clip to my T-shirt collar for just that purpose.

The electrical storm had passed to the east of us now and was moving away. We were fine. It was over. I could have easily gotten back underway, but that would wake Carolyn. Besides, I hadn't really wanted to get to India so much as I'd wanted to get back to sea. I was at sea, all right.

At dawn, Carolyn joined me in the cockpit wearing only a silly, contented grin. "Little boy, what do you want from Santa on this fine, fine Christmas Day?"

Panama Canal Dash

Well, it took three times longer than we expected, we had two major repairs, we partied with friends, and we might've seen an international drug deal, so perhaps it was more of a casual slog.

As *Wild Card* dipped swayed, and curtsied to the first of the ocean swells, I felt like I was being transformed. I looked behind me: Land was fading to dull grey. I looked ahead: The blue of the ocean was rich with promise. Adventure loomed. I felt lighter, freer, happier. I could feel my shore-induced cares and woes slipping away into our gurgling wake.

I excitedly paced the storm-battered decks of *Wild Card* while marveling at my good fortune. I was heading out to sea again. With the woman I loved. In God's own cathedral. *Yes!* The Panama Canal and the Pacific Ocean beckoned, a mere thousand miles to the west-southwestward.

"Ready on the jib," Carolyn said, then. "Lazy sheet is clear!"

I pulled out the jib, flicked three wraps onto our Barlow 28, and put out my hand. Carolyn slapped the winch handle into it and took the bitter end of the sheet in one seamless motion. I cranked the jib home in an instant—actually, a tad too far.

"Ease a touch," I said, then, "Good!"

Wild Card heeled, and bounded off like an eager dog with a bone in its teeth. A halyard tattooed an ancient rhythm on the mast. Our ensign slapped smartly. I grinned. Carolyn grinned back. "Happy now?" she asked as we did our housekeeping chores of coiling the sheets, arranging the tagline, and connecting up our self-steering gear.

"Very," I said, with understatement.

We were leaving St. Thomas late, endlessly delayed by the vexations of shore. Hurricane season was almost upon us. Tropical wave after tropical wave had marched by. We had to go *now*, or wait another season. We went. I expected heavy air off the northern coast of Columbia. There, I'd once made 150 miles in 24 hours under bare poles; the seas had been huge. So I was ready, peering over my shoulder at the low-pressure systems rolling off Africa.

As usual, I was wrong. A large tropical wave veered northward as it approached the Lesser Antilles and sucked all the wind out of the trades. Instead of bare poles, for the first six days, I was hoisting large jibs, big drifters and gigantic spinnakers. So much for vast experience, eh? "Well, we have the technology," Carolyn joked as she hit the starter button and our faithful Perkins M30 sprung to life. While she busied herself attaching our tiny electric auto-tiller pilot to our Monitor windvane, I dashed below for my Bose2 noise-canceling headphones. Unfortunately, I "'melled a 'mel," as I used to say as a child. "Shut it down," I told Carolyn, "I think we still have an exhaust leak."

This was unfortunate. I'd just replaced the entire (galvy pipe, alas) system from manifold to transom, but I must have not sealed one of the pipe joints properly because I could distinctly smell exhaust fumes below.

"We can't run the engine, I'm afraid," I told Carolyn. "Carbon-monoxide can cause brain damage."

"You're handsome, kind, and a good wage-earner," she said to me dreamily.

"Drat!" I replied. "Too late!"

The one place in the Caribbean I'd rather not spend too much time is off the coast of Columbia. I don't believe I'm overly paranoid, just prudent. Weird things happen in this area. People go missing. Speedboats brandish weapons. Fine yachts sail by with their sails poorly trimmed and extremely bad, hand-brushed enamel paint jobs. It makes you wonder, and I'd prefer to wonder from afar.

But that's life—filled with irony and surprise. I'd told Carolyn we'd avoid that crime-ridden coast. I'd promised myself we'd stay a minimum of 50 miles off. So, there we were, on a moonless, windless night with neither steerage nor engine just 28 miles from a very dangerous place.

Shady Dealings

At precisely 2000, at exactly 11 degrees 20 north and 76 degrees 30 west, a large rusty freighter steamed briskly up to us and stopped dead in the water. It was disconcerting. There it was, lights blazing. Just a mile away. Hours went by. It just stood there, only engaging its engine occasionally to stay in exact position.

"I don't like this," Carolyn said. "Let's crank up. We can sleep on deck."

"The entire interior will be ruined," I said. "Remember back in the late 1960's when *Corina's* exhaust fractured? How we couldn't scrub the thick grime off and, even after repainting, it showed through?"

"Well..." she said, not convinced.

I tried desperately to sail away, but we had no wind, no steerage—no luck. If anything, we'd drifted closer. Damn. They must know we're here. I tensed, hearing outboards cranking up. At midnight, they lit a bright strobe on the aft deck. Within 15 minutes, the low-throated roar of a large lumbering aircraft could be heard. It was going slow, very slow. No lights. It passed directly over the freighter. Outboards revved, then silence. Twenty-five minutes later, the same thing: airplane, outboards, silence. Twenty-five minutes later, same thing again; only this time the freighter shut off the strobe, doused all its deck lights and steamed away rapidly within five minutes of the final pass. Carolyn and I heaved a tense sigh of relief.

"Fatty," she said, "this is *not* a fun place to loiter."

"OK," I agreed. "Tomorrow, if it's calm, we'll repair the exhaust system at sea."

I did not want to do this for several reasons. It would take a long time. The boat would be an utter mess during the repair. I hate having the floorboards out at sea with the possibility that we or things could fall into the bilge/engine room. I'm basically a lazy guy who equates sailing with leisure, and wrestling with large heavy pipes in a seaway is *not* my idea of a good time. And the entire galvy pipe system would have to be disassembled from aft to forward so that all the joints could be tightened sequentially along the way. This isn't an easy task.

The hardest part was shifting all the stored stuff under the cockpit, quarter-berth and in the bilges forward and then put it all back. The whole process took from dawn until late afternoon. We were both covered with sweat, bruises and cuts, but the boat was once again orderly and the engine ran like a top without the slightest fumes inside the vessel.

"Success!" I cried out as we sped westward under power at six knots. "We had big fun with pipes. Why, we even got to monkey with our monkey wrenches."

Busted for Joy

Carolyn wasn't quite as pleased with the day as I was. "I'm beat," she said, as she headed below for a nap. "And stop bubbling with joy or I'll call the U.S. Coast Guard and have you arrested for Excessive Happiness."

"Guilty as charged," I mumbled, and tried to keep a straight face.

The following morning (or was it a couple of days later?) Carolyn was back to her usual self and suggested, "Let's bang a left and pull into the San Blas Islands."

I wasn't too keen. We were running late and I wanted to get though the Canal. But Carolyn had a strong argument: "I hear it is very romantic in the San Blas," she said.

"Helm's alee!" I cried.

Nobody in the world knew where we were or where we were going. We'd just sort of tossed a dart at the chart to pick a hole in the reef to slither through. So I was quite surprised to catch the tail end of an excited female voice saying, over the VHF, "Is that *Wild Card*? Fatty and Carolyn?"

I dashed below to the nav station, snatched up my VHF microphone and said, "Who calls *Wild Card*?"

"*Ithaka*," said the voice, "*Ithaka* calls *Wild Card*."

"Bernadette?" I said in disbelief.

The Cruising World Turns

Yes, the *Cruising World* family might be a small one, but we're well traveled. I'd just partied with Herb McCormick in Culebra, Puerto Rico a few months ago. Elaine Lembo regularly visits St. John, U.S.V.I., where we've headquartered for many years. Tim Murphy regularly plays music in New England with many of the same degenerate guitar pickers I play with in the Caribbean. Once, in French Polynesia, I waved at Steve Callahan as he sped past in a delightfully strange multihull. And now Doug and Bernadette Bernon, two of my favorite marine writers, were guiding us through the reef, inviting us to dinner and giving us the literary lowdown on the whole wide world of salt-stained inkslingers.

Did we enjoy the ensuing party aboard the lovely *Ithaka?* I assume we did. "Their reds were better than their whites, Carolyn groaned the next day. "Though it sure was a judgment call!"

That's the best part of cruising: constantly doing unexpected things with lovely/crazy people in places you've never been.

Later that same afternoon, Carolyn discovered one of our engine-mount flanges was loose. Yes, I know, I know: Most women don't root around in the engine room, but Carolyn isn't 'most women' in almost any regard, and she knows a loose flange when she sees one. "This thing is looser than your morals," she said to me as she pointed at it.

I raised an eyebrow in surprise.

"Well," she reconsidered, "maybe not *that* loose."

It took us 10 seconds to tighten the bolt and all day to realign the engine. I have a vibration plate/isolator between my prop flanges. In order to align my engine, I have to remove the plate, remove my underwater shaft zinc (actually, Carolyn removed it this time), slide the shaft aft, carefully align the engine, then reassemble it all, above and below water.

The Bag of Broken Parts

On the final run to Panama, our engine started to run hot. Since I hadn't replaced the impeller in two years, I figured, correctly, that it was the problem. Knowing I'd just purchased three new impellers, I shut it off the engine, whipped out the old impeller (only two out of six blades intact) and tried to slap in a new one. No luck. None of them would fit. Too tight. Damn! Luckily, I carry a bag of old "ruined" engine parts that still sort of work despite being replaced, and we were soon back in business.

Finally, cargo ships became thick as flies around us. It was still dark when we called Cristobal Port Control on VHF Channel 16 for permission to enter, and it was just dawn when we shot through the breakwaters off Colón, Panama, at the entrance to the Canal. "Anchor down," I shouted forward at Carolyn and heard the chain rattling out almost with my words. I reversed and she daintily placed a toe on the rode to feel if it was hopping or dragging. "More power," she called aft.

I gunned it. "Fine," she shouted, and began her foredeck housecleaning as I shut down the diesel.

"Coffee, tea or me," she said as she ducked back into the cockpit.

"Hold the tea, thanks," I replied. "Nice passage."

"Really?" she smiled as she started the kettle boiling. "I mean, we didn't have our engine for most of it, it took us three times as long as we expected, and we had to do a couple of major jobs at sea. Just the engine alignment alone took us an entire day. We might have been right next to a major international drug deal. And we're dead broke."

"Yeah?" I said. "So what?"

"So," she said, "so maybe not everyone would think it was such a nice trip, is all."

"That's because they wouldn't have shared it with you," I said and grinned.

"You're the sweetest liar I've ever married," she said as she put her coffee cup down and moved slowly toward me.

Don't Get Lax in the Locks

It took 52 million gallons of water, $600, and two days to spit *Wild Card* into the Pacific Ocean. The passage was quick, we could have transited within three days of our arrival in Colón since it was off-season. It was easy. Everything you need—fenders, approved transit lines, and, if need be, professional line handlers—is available at the Panama Canal Yacht Club (PCYC), for a price.

On top of the $600 it cost us to transit; we had to make an additional $800 deposit. (Use VISA, as they merely put a short hold on your money.) We also rented four lines for $60 and bought 15 plastic-wrapped tire/fenders for $45. The same people who sell the tires for $3 each charge $1 each to "dispose" of them by selling them to the next guy. We paid our taxi driver/agent $30 and the Panama government about $120 in various fees. Thus, we spent around $875. Most vessels spend around $1,000, slightly more if they hire professional line handlers from the PCYC.

We flew in Momo the Astrophysist (boy, is *his* head in the clouds) as our primary line handler and kidnapped Bud and Judy Kennedy off the Out Island 41, *Gonzo,* for the two day party through the canal. Carolyn baked a cake for the occasion. Most crews "do reciprocals," meaning that they eventually crew as line handlers for those yachties who crewed for them. Since Bud and Judy had, in part, cruised to Panama in hopes of "getting a free ride" on the canal, not to transit it, this was a win-win. Six people—a captain, an advisor, and four line handlers, are required to transit, even on the smallest boats.

Besides the normal stuff you know you'll need: lines, air horn, etc, you must provide shade for your pilot, plus toilet and cooking facilities. We were asked if we had a holding tank, we said yes, and we used it during the transit. However, no one checked the tank, if it worked, or if it was in use. Make sure your cleats are strong and your lines can be led to winches. There will be extraordinary, *nearly vertical* loads on them. Your line handlers don't have to be body builders, but they should be physically fit and focused every second of the time you're in the locks. Both pilots we had, a different one each day, were OK; we even got the notoriously solemn Jimmy Wong to loosen up and laugh at some Fat Jokes. Edgar was our favorite, truly cared about our vessel, its crew, and our transit. He was extremely safety oriented and explained things simply and thoroughly long before they happened.

We were supposed to lock through with a large, slab-sided steel vessel whose wild-acting, hard-drinking crew gave me bad vibes. I mentioned this to Edgar, concerned that my rig might hit the vessel's 18-foot high sides. He immediately concurred, and he had us raft up for the transit with a lovely little Lyle Hess-designed sloop named *Whisper*. The large steel vessel in question damaged its port side within minutes of the lock doors closing.

For *Wild Card*, transiting the Panama Canal, some 40 miles of it, was easy and fascinating. The locks are engineering marvels and the large lake in the middle, Lake Gatun, is spooky with its sunken trees strange birds and slotted hill range. Recently, we've heard negative reports of the transit, including 10-19 day waits to pass through, launch fees to ferry advisors back and

forth, and mooring in Lake Gatun, but our transit in 2005 was a delight. Every skipper planning to transit the Canal should do his or her own homework well beforehand, and two good places to start are *Noonsite (www.noonsite.com), Jimmy Cornell's* "Global Site for Cruising Sailors," and the website of the Panama Canal Authority (www.pancanal.com.) They even have a webcam at one of the locks.

Your trip from ocean to ocean could prove to be pure fun, too; if you plan ahead, use common sense, and don't get lax in the locks.

Wild Card's San Blas Time Warp

We were in the San Blas islands, off the deserted north coast of Panama, this archipelago is perhaps the most intriguing group of islands in the Caribbean. A Kuna Indian woman with four children rowed a long, heavy canoe and stopped about 100 feet off *Wild Card*'s starboard side. She was dressed in typical style; brightly colored blouse, a lovely scarf, gaudy beaded leggings, a gold ring in her nose.

She was shy. I waited. She was working up her courage. I helped. "*Hola*," I shouted over to her.

She was solemn, as she expertly maneuvered her cumbersome canoe alongside *Wild Card*. The youngest of the children shrank away, visibly frightened by the pale white ghost of bristly grey hair which was I. Carolyn joined me at the rail and we both smiled encouragingly.

The Kuna woman placed her handcrafted appliquéd fabric pieces called *molas,* on our rail. "Ten, five, one dalla," she said, using up all her English in four words of plea.

Carolyn carefully inspected them, making murmurs of approval. I gave the older child, a girl, four cookies and pointed to the other children. She passed them out. But I'd made a mistake, and the momma corrected me by tapping her chest. I gave her a cookie too. All the cookies were gone in the blink of an eye. Silence.

"*El Gato*," Carolyn pointed at a small, crude mola. "One dalla?"

"*Si*," the woman said, and visibly wiggled with pride.

"*Muy bueno*," said Carolyn, taking the mola and, with a slow, respectful flourish, giving the woman a single American dollar bill.

"*Gracia*," the women beamed and beamed and beamed. I could almost hear her thinking, "Yes, the three-hour row was worth it. Now I have money, and my fisherman husband will be proud."

I watched her for an hour or so as she began her row back home. To me, it was as if she was fading back into her time. I could picture her life and I could picture my life. But as we'd spoken, I'd noticed a jet contrail behind her, and it didn't seem possible that we could all be sharing this same moment. It seemed that if one of us existed, then the others must not.

The Kuna are extremely pro-American, as the United States protected them from slaughter during the construction of the Panama Canal. They are, perhaps, among the most independent and culturally rich Amerindian groups surviving. They govern themselves completely, and we had to first visit the *sahila*, the village chief, to pay our respects (and $10) for the privilege of touring his island of Artitupu.

Later in the day, in a different deserted anchorage, we were visited by another cultural Kuna icon: a transvestite. This person was locally revered for the brilliance of his molas, the making of which is usually woman's work. He majestically displayed his lovely, carefully crafted wares. Then, the master mola maker rowed back to his nearby island, an island without electricity, fuel, or plastic. A little while later, I fired off this story via my laptop computer, Pactor digital modem, SSB radio, shore side server, and, thus, the Internet. While doing so, I wondered if he was wondering the same thing I was wondering: which one of us is smarter?

South Pacific Love Affair

From the Galápagos Islands through 30 days at sea to a difficult Tuamotus landfall, their second circumnavigation already has them thinking about a third.

"We're calling it "Round Two" because it is twice as hard," joked Carolyn to the clearance official on Isla San Christobal in the Galápagos.

"Yeah," I jumped in, "the only thing we've learn during our second circumnavigation thus far is that, well, we really didn't learn anything during our first"

"*Si*," the smiling man said as he stamped our mound of ship's papers, "July and August are our windiest months. The seas are rough. It is a good time for kite flying, not sailing!"

Boy, was he right! Sailing from Panama to the Galápagos, we'd expected the same gentle, open-hatched, light-air, weeklong passage we'd experienced in 2000. Instead we'd endured southwest winds of between 22 and 28 knots for 15 solid days of pound, pound, pounding dead to weather.

Carolyn summed it up best. "Yeeck!" she said. I could only agree. It wasn't just the high winds and their relentless direction—it was the seas. They were large, lumpy and, often, breaking. Why? Ocean currents. This is an area where they collide, causing extreme changes in air temperature, sea temperature and sea state. It's the reason the Galápagos were called the 'Enchanted Isles' by early explorers: Their shifting currents and sudden fogs made them appear and disappear as if by magic.

Nothing has changed. It is a strange place. At one point, we were in VHF contact with *Rontu*, a Taswell 44 from California, and they were basically sailing in summer (warm air, warm water and clear skies) while

we were trapped in the Humboldt Current with 30-degree-colder water, fog, and overcast skies!

But the Galápagos are worth it: You're literally sailing through the world's most isolated, most exotic zoo and surrounded by wild animals that aren't the least bit frightened by your presence.

The experience was wonderful and utterly unique. Craziest of all are the sea lions. They're everywhere—in the water and on the beaches, sure, but also in the dinghies, on the docks, and in the roads. Hell, they'll waddle right into your cockpit if you have a transom scoop. And, truth be told, they're nasty, grumpy, complaining beasts! I mean, I never knew what happened to irritable, bitter old men when they died, but now I do. They get reincarnated as sea lions. The old curmudgeons love using your dinghy as a combination swim platform and outhouse. Which is fine—unless *you* want to use it. Then their attitude is, "Hey, pal, find yourself a *different* dinghy. I was here first."

Of course, you're supposed to respect the fauna, as all the tourist brochures advise. And we did; the problem was, they didn't return the favor. If we wanted to use the dinghy, they'd just sort of lazily wave us away with casual flip of the fin, as if to say, "Maybe later, right now I'm napping, OK?"

If you got into the dinghy—and, frankly, I never had the courage—some of them would leave; others would sullenly "move to their half" with a baleful stare; still other ones would bite you repeatedly until you left.

"Just because they aren't scared of you doesn't mean you shouldn't be scared of them," said a shaken Carolyn immediately after waltzing with an aggressive sea lion on the dinghy dock.

They're, like, everywhere! I was cleaning the prop, with my head stuck in the tiny aperture of *Wild Card's* skeg-hung rudder, when a passing sea lion decided to minutely inspect my work. To say that finding his whiskered, disapproving face within inches of my mask startled me would be an understatement. I must have come three feet out of the water when I surfaced, because Carolyn, who was clothes pining up her delicates, asked me if I was OK.

"Yeah," I gasped, "but a sea lion just shot me the bird down there!"

"They don't have fingers, hon," she lisped through the pins in her mouth. "He couldn't have!"

"Well," I said, glancing nervously around me in the water to see if he was still lurking about. "He made some sort of an up-yours gesture!"

Yes, it's a zoo! Bluc-footed boobies decorate your bow rail. Penguins waddle about. Large red iguanas slither down the paths. Jellylike crabs slide by sideways. Giant tortoises sleep like rocks. Hammerhead sharks cruise for prey.

"We'll be back," Carolyn whispered to them all as the Galápagos shrunk into tiny grey dots and vanished over our transom. "See you again on Round Three!"

A Month of Sundays

The 30-day passage that followed was really the first "major leg" of our current Big Fat Circle. If I'd harbored any doubts about the wisdom of my recent life choices, they vanished almost instantly. This was the right thing to do. It was OK to go back to the well and drink further. Yes, the long ocean passages are always the best for me. Time stopped. The rest of the world shut off. It was just me and God and the most wonderful, sensuous woman in the world. And we had all the time in the universe. Utter peace. Zero stress. The warm embrace of Mother Ocean. Nature at its finest, starkest, and most beautiful.

We fell into our routine: reading, writing, singing, creating, and loving. Carolyn and I never seem to have quite enough time for each other while ashore—only in deep ocean can we really focus on each other's needs. I'm kind of awed by the fact that she gets more and more beautiful to me every day. I'm married to a goddess who is equally at home on the foredeck and in the cockpit as she is in the galley. Lucky, lucky me.

Flying fish were a problem. They bedeviled me. One once gave me a black eye 25 years ago in the Bahamas, and since then, I wince every time one buzzes through the cockpit, even if it doesn't stop. In their death throes, they seem perverse: wedging themselves under jugs, inside coils of line, underneath the solar panels. I had to be careful every second. I was searching the starboard cockpit locker for gasket material, glanced away for a couple of moments—and it took us weeks to track down the putrid smell! "How did the sumbitch git in *there*?" was our constant refrain.

Carolyn, of course, loves flying fish. She enjoyed going on daily fish patrol each dawn, asking me, scientific-like, "Which ones are the freshest, do you think?" She'd pinch, poke, and prod them all until she'd selected a couple of the most tender, then happily fry them up in bread crumbs.

"Delicious," she'd tease me. "And well within our miserly cruising budget!"

In some ways, I think of ocean sailing as a food orgy. Carolyn kept a steady stream of gastronomical delights flying out of the galley: crêpes Florentine, strawberry short cake, cinnamon buns.

Twice we were visited by large schools of pilot whales. One group of dolphins was jumping straight up out of the water to an incredible height. I don't mean a mere 10 feet; I mean 20 or 30 feet in the air, straight up!

Large whales also moved by, like stately cruise ships on leisurely schedules. Three mahi-mahi stayed with us for four days; it was marvelous watching them on our quarter wave nonchalantly snatching a particularly tasty flying fish whenever their appetite called.

The actual sailing of *Wild Card* offshore in the trade winds is laughably simple. I drop the main and cover it. I roll up the jib, deploy my oversized whisker pole, and roll back out the jib. That's it. I call it my chicken-jib rig. People laugh that I'm only flying about half the sail area I should be, and sure, if I'm racing a storm into port, I do occasionally fly an additional drifter on the other side. But the vast majority of miles *Wild Card* has sailed have been under chicken-jib alone. And if the yacht racers of the world don't like it, they can lump it!

Without the mainsail, the center of effort is so far forward that my Monitor self-steering device hardly has any work to do. The mainsail doesn't keep popping nor the boom slamming. Quite simply, it is heaven! Quiet, safe heaven! If a squall looms up astern, I just roll up as much jib as I think prudent and continue on. For weeks on end, my only sailing task is to adjust the sheet to minimize chafe. Yes, I could make my sail systems more complicated and my job as skipper more difficult. But what's the rush? We average 128 miles a day.

On Day 16, just after we were recovering from our halfway celebration, a large high-pressure system slid by far to the south of us. It was nothing dangerous, but gave us 35 knots, a large following sea, and massive southwest cross swells. It was exhilarating to see Mother Ocean in such a grand mood.

The waves morphed into liquid mountains, relentlessly flinging themselves forward. *Wild Card* seemed always to be sailing downhill. A particularly large wave would approach, creep forward, rear up—hesitate, hesitate, hesitate—tower threateningly, loom large—and then lunge! There was no way we were going to escape this one. She'd get us. Swamp us. Fill the cockpit. Oh, yes. Damn! I'd brace, check my safety harness, grit my teeth, and hold my breath as *Wild Card* presented her transom like a brazen hussy. She'd lift her skirts and, at the very last possible second, lift them slightly higher till the massive sea hissed and bubbled and gurgled harmlessly beneath her. What a show! I never tired of it. A thousand waves seemed sure to engulf her this time, and a thousand waves slid by.

It's moments like those when I clearly saw the benefit of keeping my boat light. The temptations of weighing her down, adding windage with a massive "tower of power" aft, or collecting too many heavy electro-toys below is hard to resist, yet these are the times that make me glad I did. In any event, it was a wonderful show. Thank you, Olin Stephens, designer of *Wild Card!*

Of course, some waves did slop aboard—mostly when *Wild Card*, a large following sea, and a massive cross swell attempted to share the same space at the same time.

Perhaps the funniest moment came during an attempt I made to take a leak while in the cockpit. I have a special plastic container that lives in a PVC bracket dedicated to this purpose. I don't want to become one of those sailor-found-drowned-with-his-zipper-down statistics.

In any event, just as I was completing my task, a green sea rolled into the cockpit from the port quarter, completely drenching me and taking said container (and contents) to Davy Jones' Locker. Sputtering, I leaned below to ask for a towel as Carolyn said, "Forgot to pee to lee, did we?"

I laughed. How could I not?

The air was crystal clear around me, as if God had just cleaned my sunglasses. The sun sparkled upon each majestic wave. The clouds were perfect: towering, pure, whiter than white, billowing, puffing, growing before my marveling eyes. Everywhere I looked made me happy to be alive.

We did, alas, have one serious problem. We'd taken on 50 gallons of dock water in the Galápagos—and purchased 20 gallons of bottled water as well. We'd heard that the dock water "wasn't good." But it was far worse than that: It was completely unusable for anything but washing. Again and again we'd boil it for 10 minutes; both slowly drink a glass, and then frantically elbow each other out of the way as we dashed for the head. This meant that we'd each have three-quarters of a gallon of water per day, not a luxurious amount.

This wouldn't be a problem, say, cruising in Maine. But in the tropics, well, water is life. Carolyn went into full conservation mode—dishwashing only with salt water, rinsing only with the "bad" fresh water, using small amounts of seawater for cooking instead of adding salt, and saving the individually bottled and now precious "good" fresh water for drinking and cooking only.

On passage, I eat at least one large can of fruit every day; thus we had over 50 cans aboard. Each day at noon we'd carefully divide and ritually share the juice from these cans.

Full disclosure: Yes, I *did* wonder if Carolyn remembered the quart of distilled battery water stowed next to the engine!

When we were down to our last five gallons of water, I said to Carolyn, "Well, Ms. Navigator, where's the closest watering hole?"

Landfall at Makemo

Until now we'd just been heading westward, vaguely in the direction of French Polynesia. We didn't want to visit the same islands we did during our last circumnavigation, so we'd discussed making landfall in the Îles Gambier. But the more I watched the weather down there and the closer we got, the more I noticed how rough it was that far south. We began to consider a gentler destination.

"Let's see," she said, "we could slide into the Tuamotus. Say, Makemo?"

"What do we know about Makemo?" I asked.

"Nothing," she said.

"Have I ever told you how much I admire your honesty," I said.

Makemo, as it turned out, seemed the perfect atoll. It has a large lagoon, a deep-if-narrow pass, and small village with a store. It also had another attraction: The famous pearl carver, a giant of a Polynesian warrior, named Becko, lived there. I suspect Carolyn the Pearl Addict knew this. But being a happily married man who wants to stay that way, I never asked.

The rest of the voyage was either absolutely wonderful or complete boring, depending on one's attitude. I loved every second. Each day I'd sketch in the log, play guitar in the cockpit, and read and read and read. There is so much a person can do if unshackled from shore drudgery: I write songs, take notes for my novel, snap photos for my articles, study piano theory. One morning I grabbed my harness, dashed to the foredeck, clipped on, and sang the entire score of Sigmund Romberg's *The Desert Song* at the top of my lungs.

"We're 300 miles from shore," said Carolyn pointedly, "so your singing isn't bothering anyone *yet*!"

Finally, after 30 glorious days, a lone, comic-book palm tree popped over the horizon. The End. It always makes me sad. I wish I was a dolphin and able to play forever. But, alas, humans are my species. I must drop in occasionally to check the e-mail, cash the checks, and, in this case, water up.

"It's dead low at 0800," said navigator Carolyn, "and they say the cut can be really nasty."

"What's the tidal range," I asked.

"Not much," she said, "Only a couple of feet, or less."

"How bad can it be?" I said, stupidly. I've been through a number of so-called "dangerous atoll passes" in French Polynesia without a problem. In fact, I was wondering what all the fuss was about.

Makemo taught me.

We went in one hour before slack low because I thought (incorrectly, it would be demonstrated) that it would be best to have a slight negative current. There was a navigation range, clearly visible from sea. But the current was far stronger than I'd bargained for. Well, hell, I just increased my rpm a tad, with a judicious glance at the temperature gauge. Visibility was good, but our chart was slightly off; it put us over dry land as we headed in. Always a bit disconcerting!

The closer I got, the more I realized I should have waited. The current was screaming. Our speed went from six knots to four to two to less than two! (My ancient GPS doesn't read accurately below two knots.)

"Toilet bowl!" shouted Carolyn from the foredeck.

"What!?!" I yelled, and then saw it: a huge whirlpool of water, sucking down greedily, as if someone had just pulled the plug of the cut. I considered turning around, but didn't. It would take a lot of room to turn *Wild Card* in this maelstrom, and I was perfectly lined up with the range. The deepest water was also the roughest. It was hard to head directly at it.

"Toilet bowls galore," shouted Carolyn, "and watch out for—!"

The cross current almost knocked us off our feet. I glanced up at the range markers ahead—*damn it! I was way, way off!*—and crabbed 30 degrees to starboard to get back into the center. Just then, another eddy shot me forward, directly at the edge of the breaking coral.

"Geezus!" moaned Carolyn.

We were creeping ahead, just barely moving forward, and all the while being constantly jostled, heeled, and spun by the capricious current. Sweat clouded my eyes. It was unbearably tense. If the Perkins M30 were to stutter for one instant, we'd be driven ashore. Damn it! I'd misjudged the current. Despite of lifetime of training, I'd been overconfident. But now wasn't exactly the best time to berate myself.

"Major flush," Carolyn was singing out, "have you ever seen anything like this, Fatty?"

I was too busy to answer. I lunged back and forth in the cockpit, yanking at the tiller with all my strength, while attempting to get a better view of the range, current and now frothing reefs close on either hand.

"Shudda waited," said Carolyn, an easy expert after the fact.

Inch by inch. Foot by foot. Yard by yard. I could see smoother water ahead. Would we make it? Now the GPS was reading 2.2 knots, 2.4. Definitely rising! *Yes!* We were in the lagoon. If only we didn't get sucked back out or onto the reef. Faster, faster, *yes!*

Finally we were in the deep blue of the vast lagoon, in 65 feet of water—perfectly safe according to the little sketch chart I was using.

Carolyn came laughing back into the cockpit, "Oh, my God," she said, "that was just *too* exciting, Fatty. I don't ever wanna do that again. How much is one of those large, double-bladed choppers to lift us out?"

"I don't care what it costs—" I started joking, but stopped in mid-sentence.

There was a tiny cloud on the water ahead. The sun was in my eyes. I squinted, and shaded my face from the glare with an upraised hand.

"Those whirlpools were a couple of feet deep!" Carolyn was staying as I knocked her over with the tiller.

Wild Card almost hit it: a small, unmarked coral head jutting straight up from 60 feet. I turned sharply, but we were so close I had to spin the boat back for an instant to prevent the rudder skeg from being clipped.

Afterward, I took the engine out of gear and just drifted a bit. Panting. "Don't tell my cardiologist about this, OK?" I said to Carolyn.

We put the hook down in 45 feet of water just off the settlement of Makemo. It was calm. The palm fronds waved welcome. I could smell the flowers.

"I'll open you a bottle of wine," I told a now-relaxing Carolyn.

"I'll make you a cappuccino," Carolyn said as she air-kissed me back.

"Here's to us," Carolyn toasted in the cockpit, "and *Wild Card!*"

"And Mother Ocean," I added.

I looked around me. It sure *seemed* like paradise. I breathed in; I breathed out.

I was happy—completely and utterly relieved and happy.

Neither of us knew that the next 72 hours would be among the most difficult of our lives. But that's a story for another day.

The Hell and Heaven of Makemo

Who knew what forces of nature would confront us in the heart of this tropical lagoon?

From the Galápagos, we arrived at the Tuamotu Archipelago, in French Polynesia. All we had to do was get the hook down, and go ashore for ice cream. "A hard-frozen Magnum Double with almonds," Carolyn chanted dreamily up on the foredeck. I made a couple of lazy circles off the Polynesian village, like a dog attempting to get comfortable. The lagoon of the atoll of Makemo, with depth of 60 to 100 feet, is deep for anchoring and is studded with thousands of unmarked coral heads. We'd almost clipped one coming in. There was only one narrow patch of shallow water anywhere, just off the village beach.

The problem with the town anchorage, besides the eight-mile fetch, was that the sandy, 35-foot deep patch was too small and narrow. I decided to drop the hook just upwind of the sandy shelf.

"Anchor aweigh," I told Carolyn.

"OK," she said, and rattled out our 44-pound Bruce, fifty feet of five-sixteenths-inch chain and 200 feet of brand new five-eighths-inch braided black nylon rode. I reversed the engine and the anchor set. *Wild Card* was in 45 feet of water, over pure-white sand. The only slight problem: we were about 200 feet off the frothing heads, with not much reaction time if we dragged. "Weight?" asked Carolyn.

"Absolutely," I said ambling forward and she dashed below. A few moments later, the forward hatch opened, and with a grunt, Carolyn offered up our 40-pound anchor weight. I immediately clipped on a snatch block and its snap-shackled 50-foot retrieval line, and then lowered it down the rode.

Why not use an all-chain rode? *Wild Card* is narrow forward and only weighs 13,000 pounds, which is why she goes to windward so well, and is easily driven. But, when I placed the 250 feet of chain from my previous boat in *Wild Card's* bow, it threw her off her lines and the prop was nearly out of the water. As a result, for 15 years and 50,000-plus miles, I've used mostly rope anchor rodes, replacing them every couple of years.

We splashed the dinghy, slung on the outboard, and powered directly to the tiny village store, where we immediately squatted in front of its cooler and began to inhale frozen milk of all descriptions. We cleared customs, raided the bakery for French pastries, then attracted a crowd of local kids to marvel at my stupid magic tricks. ("I betcha I can make your money disappear," is one my favorite, most sophomoric lines.)

Everything was going great. We were having a swell time. Land was under our feet for the first time in a month. We were surrounded by smiling faces, laughter, good vibes.

"Let's go," I said.

"What?!?" said Carolyn.

I spent my entire childhood dreaming of Pacific atolls—how wonderful they were, how full of fish, and how they offered 360-degree protection. Well, that last part is bull. They offer 360-degree lee shores!

In any prolonged blow with a veering or clocking breeze, you're in trouble here if you don't move. And often, you can't move because it is too windy, it's night, or the visibility is bad. Nor can you go back to sea: The passes between lagoon and deep ocean can only be transited at high or low tides. This can be dicey enough in a flat calm, but shooting through one in high winds and non-slack water could be suicide for most small sailing vessels.

"Did we get a GRIB weather file today," I asked as we rushed back to *Wild Card.*

"Yeah," she said. "Eight to 12 knots out of the southeast, like it's been for weeks."

"Good," I said. "Then it's probably a squall. We'll be fine where we are. I'll put out the 20H to be sure."

I love my 20H Danforth anchor. Ounce for ounce, it's the most dependable workhorse in my quiver of anchors. In fact, I'd use it for my primary anchor except that I've found that Danforths regularly foul themselves in reversing wind/current situations.

With Carolyn's help on the foredeck, I deployed my 20H on 200 feet of half inch twist, fanned out about 30 degrees to the south.

"Barometer's up four points in only a couple of hours," said Carolyn.

That wasn't good. "I should've dived the main anchor," I said, hunting up some chafe gear for the bow roller.

"Should we try to move to a safer spot?" asked Carolyn.

"No," I said. "This might be short-lived. And move where? What if we were underway amid the coral heads with a strong wind and zero visibility?

The rain came first, often a bad sign.

Then the wind came out of the southeast at 25 knots, which gave us an oblique lee shore. The chop quickly built, slap-slap-slapping our hull. The upper-atmosphere clouds were moving fast. The barometer continued to rapidly rise, sinking my earlier optimism.

"Damn it," I said. "Fire off some e-mails and find out what's happening?"

We live in a strange new electro-cyber world. Soon, Carolyn was showing me various "weather products" revealing a humongous high-pressure system to the south of us—far stronger than forecast.

I cursed myself for not paying closer attention to the weather. As I'd gotten closer to our destination, it had seemed less and less important. So I'd gradually stopped lurking on the weather nets, chatting with my weather router, or downloading the weather faxes because, hey, no matter what the weather gods threw at me, I was going to go to the same place via basically the same route.

But I hadn't considered the weather *after* my arrival, on what turned out to be a dead lee shore without a speck of protection for eight long miles.

The wind built to 35 knots, and *Wild Card* was taking a beating. It was getting dark. I had to decide, and fast.

I reached into the bilge and dug out the parts for the *Big Gun*, my big, but light, Fortress aluminum storm anchor, and Carolyn immediately began assembling it while I lugged on deck our 300 feet of three-quarter-inch Sampson braid storm rode, which we'd carried for 30,000 miles but never used.

Setting it from our small inflatable dinghy wasn't easy. I was in danger of being swarmed or capsized, and the anchor flukes were sharp. But I managed. Carolyn paid out the entire 300 feet, plus a lighter 30-foot-long extension line to give us maximum scope.

Of course, at this point we were soaked and worried. And we both knew that by putting down our storm anchor, I'd decided to stay put, come hell or high water—a fairly apt description of what followed.

By the time the wind was a constant 40 knots, *Wild Card*'s bow was dipping right into the breaking seas. The foredeck was awash. Occasionally a large sea would hit us when her bow was reared high—and the ensuing shove backward was brutal. You could hear the lines start with the sudden force of tons of water hitting us. I didn't see how my gear could take such continuous shock-loading. In my entire 45 years of boat handling, I'd never been anchored in higher winds in a more exposed anchorage or been so close to a dead lee shore.

I didn't think our gear could take it for more than 10 minutes, but it did. It took it and took it and took it. Every hour I'd crawl forward on my hands and knees to change the chafe point, veering out an additional inch or two of rode while visually inspecting the chafing gear.

Every two hours I'd crank the diesel to keep it warmed up and ready to go; we'd only have seconds of reaction time if our rodes parted. Actually, there was zero chance of successfully powering away from our predicament, but, hey, I will grab at the tiniest of straws.

It was impossible to stand inside *Wild Card*. Mostly we flopped on our main cabin settees. And it was strange to see our dinghy airborne and regularly being yanked through breaking wave crests—well above the level of our stern-rail

Our dinghy is a very light Apex 9, and I was worried it was so light that it would flip in high winds. But it just semi-fills with water and tosses the excess back out.

At this point, I was beginning to turn into "a big fat numbskull," as Carolyn delicately puts it. We'd lacked sleep when we arrived and then we'd had a very exciting day. Now I was too tired to sleep or think.

"I've got the watch," Carolyn said. "Don't worry."

I felt sick to my stomach. I was going to lose *Wild Card.*

I'm 53. I've got about 10 bucks in the bank. I've already swum away from two sinking vessels. I really, really don't want to go for "third time is charmed!"

I must have dozed for a second, and I awoke with a start. It was worse. Far worse. Carolyn was sitting at the nav station, dazed. I stood up, fell, and lurched to the companionway. The sight was like nothing I'd ever seen—as if astern of us was a movie screen of a computer-generated gale, close but not quite accurate, a tad too "Hollywood surreal." There was a strange sensation of speed, as if we were being towed fast to windward. I kept staring aft in disbelief at how the waves were being flattened by the wind and machine-gunned by the pelting rain, their torn and breaking crests ripped off in long strings of foggy spume.

The island of Makemo had completely disappeared in the breakers just astern of us. Sometimes *Wild Card* was underwater; other times she tossed off the waves like a brave swimmer shaking her defiant head; a second later, she'd be airborne and plunging down, down, down into the cement trough of the next vicious sea.

"One sustained gust was 57 knots," she said.

My hopes sank. My arms seemed heavy, my mouth dry. It was still five hours to dawn. We'd never make it.

"The dinghy is losing its sun cover," she noted. "It's half off and in the water. I can't believe the dinghy is still there."

I don't have a spare dinghy. And my dinghy and outboard cost more than the initial purchase price of my yacht.

"I'll cut the cover away," I said, "and clap on an additional safety painter."

"Not a good idea," Carolyn said, and she was right.

It was almost impossible for Carolyn to haul the dinghy far enough forward along the starboard side for me to get in. I only had an instant to make my leap. I landed well, and laid flat, knowing we'd get a horrible spin when the painter took up 40 feet astern. We did. It was like being on a berserk circus ride. There was so much spray in the air, I was having difficulty breathing. Within moments I was getting dizzy, and having trouble determining which way was up. Tying on the extra painter required going forward and leaning out over the tubes. I was being pulled through the waves. I was underwater. I was airborne. I didn't know *where* the hell I was.

It was within these disorienting, almost non-thinking moments that I came closest to serious injury. Somehow the dinghy and I became airborne and *Wild Card* savagely yanked at the same instant. The dinghy and my body were glued together and both reacted instantly. My head, however, had been kind of extended at the precise moment of yank. Inertia can be cruel. I heard a crack and felt a sharp pain—and swallowed back vomit. Things were getting dim. Quiet. But I pulled myself aboard *Wild Card.* I didn't realize at the time, but I had just gotten a fairly good case of whiplash.

I didn't sleep another wink that night and Carolyn kept saying, "You OK?" because I was turning my whole body to talk to her.

Incongruously, she kept e-mailing our weather router in New England who informed us, politely, that he thought we were nuts. "It's just some imbedded squalls on the edge of that massive high to the south of you!" This has happened to me before: some sweater-clad guy sitting in front of his fireplace in his slippers telling me not to exaggerate, as I fight for my life at sea.

But weather routers can only go by what their data sources tell them. He was doing me a favor by just being there. So we thanked him for his input, calmly informed him of our instrument readings, and said we'd chat tomorrow—if we survived the night.

By this point, waves were pounding *Wild Card* so hard that their spume was blowing right over the top of her and landing in the dingy, 40 feet astern!

Worse, the wind was clocking south. This meant we were now almost 90 degrees from the reef, and closer to it; and the seas, if possible, were larger.

The next time I crept forward to veer out an inch or two of rode, I was puzzled to find an almost equal strain on all three of my anchor lines. I'd expected the southernmost Fortress to have it all. Could they be dragging and auto-equalizing the strain? I didn't think so—but what?

All night long we took it, and again and again I went on deck—to inhibit halyard slap, to triple lash the roller jib, to tend the suffering rodes.

Ashore, we learned later, villagers were frantically sandbagging their houses as the blow intensified—and, being sailors all, knew *Wild Card* had little chance of survival in such a wind. Each time there was a break in the weather; they'd peer out of their houses and expect to see *Wild Card* splattered all over the beach. Instead, they'd be amazed to see her still intact, at anchor.

When dawn arrived, the wind was down to 32 knots, and the waves were considerable smaller. I just collapsed, both mentally and physically. I thought it was over—like a bad nautical dream. And, frankly, I was just too tired to do anything but pass out. I slept until late afternoon, and expected to awake to sunlight. But I did not. It was rougher again, the barometer was up again, and there were more dark scuddy clouds.

"We'll be fine," I told Carolyn. "We've still got three of the finest anchors in the world, and I reckon they're dug in pretty well."

But there was one thing that continued to puzzle me. The wind had veered back to its original east-southeast direction. This should mean that my northernmost anchor, the Bruce, was now taking the majority of the strain. But that was not the case. They were all taking the strain. They hadn't dragged or I'd be on the reef, and they were still fanned out at approximately the original angles. But we seemed to be riding to less and less scope. Was that normal?

I can only blame fatigue: The evidence was there; I just didn't put it together.

It blew between 30 and 40 knots all night. I would've been totally freaked out if we hadn't just gone through so much worse. In fact I was almost relaxed, until just before dawn in the second night; my Big Gun rode went limp

I hauled it in slowly, hoping it had only dragged. No such luck. It had chafed clean through. Evidently, the deeper water concealed coral heads. Worse, my other big anchor, the Bruce was leading funny too. There was a strain on it, but it didn't feel right when I gave it a tug. I tugged more and realized I was pulling up only its outer black cover. It hadn't chafed through its inner core yet, but was about to. We were hanging solely by our tiny 20H and our oldest, smallest, most sun-damaged half-inch rode!

I didn't panic, exactly. Let's just say I went into hyperdrive.

"Find me the time of the next high or low tide," I shouted to Carolyn. "We're gotta go. At dawn, I'll take a minute or two to dive up the Big Gun, but if I can't do it quickly, we'll just abandon it. Ditto the Bruce if it is caught on a coral head. Maybe we'll just retrieve the 20H and, with our fourth day-hook anchor—well, that will have to do.

It was still blowing 30 knots—and just getting us and our salvage gear into the dinghy was a trick. The moment I dove into the water I could see the problem: while the spot *Wild Card* hovered over was sandy, the sloping shelf beyond was studded with thousands of small mushroom-shaped coral heads sticking only a foot or two above the hard-packed sand. My anchor lines were zigzagged between the numerous heads, chafing in dozens of spots. Evidently, each time the wind veered and slack developed in a rode, it would fall to the bottom, lace itself under a coral shelf—and then take the strain from a closer and closer position.

I easily found my Big Gun 300 feet away in 65 feet of water, but it took a while to snag it with my trusty grapnel hook and then haul it to the surface—all the while nervously glancing back at *Wild Card*, hoping I wouldn't see her bow suddenly pay off.

After I got back aboard, we actually had *Wild Card* under weigh, slowing powering up to her anchors, when two Polynesian fishermen realized we were attempting to leave and came out to help.

One was just about the ugliest, roughest fellow I'd ever seen—huge boils all over his face, broken nose, scars and sores all over his tattooed body. And, man, that fellow was one of the most talented seaman—one of the most beautiful people—I've ever met.

He knew zero English, but he immediately understood the complex series of tasks that needed to be done. First, he dove over the side, swam down 50 to 60 feet, and leisurely unwound our two remaining rodes from the coral heads.

Next, he surfaced next to *Wild Card* and magically pulled himself aboard. Then, he dashed forward to help Carolyn.

Best of all, he instinctively knew when to acquiesce to her experience with the complicated anchor gear and when to just use brute force.

Soon both the Bruce and the Danforth were aboard. I shook his hand gratefully, hugged him hard and pointed, first to the inlet we'd leave through and then to his dinghy. He shook his head, meaning "No," and pointed at the village pier where the only other vessel within a hundred miles, the inter-island supply vessel *Tahiti Nui*, had ridden out the storm in a tiny pot of water.

I didn't think there was any way I could get *Wild Card* to the dock with *Tahiti Nui* there, but our new friend kept confidently motioning with a curved-to-starboard hand. It was obvious he wanted me to slide alongside the freight boat and duck under her bow. Did he realize we needed almost seven feet of depth?

"What do you think, Carolyn?"

"Up to you, Skip," she said, "but I'd hate to leave these lovely people before we've gotten to know them!"

Thus, with our local pilot calmly pointing the way, I slid alongside the lee of *Tahiti Nui* and immediately ducked under her lofty bow, my masthead just inches away from her rusty steel plate. Soon we were spider-webbed to the village pier, directly under the bows of *Tahiti Nui.*

In the confusion of line handling and fender rigging, our Good Samaritan slipped over the side, swam back to his vessel and left without a good bye. ("Thank you, sir. You're a salt-stained prince of sailor!")

A crowd of teenagers gathered around *Wild Card,* many of them carrying their traditional ukes. I grabbed my guitar, and soon had them rolling on the dock with my exaggerated Mick Jagger/Rolling Stones impersonation. They even helped me with the chorus: "Pleased to meet chew. Hope ya guess my name!" they sang along.

The next few days were as much heaven as the previous ones were hell. We were befriended by the famous pearl-carver Becko, a massive Polynesian warrior who was gentle as a proverbial lamb. And soon he and his lovely school-teacher wife, Janice, and half the kids of the village were hanging out aboard *Wild Card.*

I played guitar. I did magic tricks. Carolyn baked and baked and baked pastries, and handed them out to a continuous crowd of outstretched, laughing arms. We meet the village chief, the town drunk, and the local boat builder, in that order.

On Sunday, we went to church. We prayed that everyone should be as lucky as we'd just been. We felt surrounded by love, laughter, and friendship. We sang along with the entire island until the ancient church rafters nearly lifted off with our soaring, happy voices. It was glorious. It was every single Polynesian fantasy rolled into one—and all the sweeter for our paid-in-advance misery.

On the day we finally departed, Becko brought us down our pearls. They were so big, so beautiful and so delicately carved that we were speechless. Janice cried as we started casting off our lines. Carolyn, too.

Becko and I solemnly shook hands—mine disappearing into his giant maw like a ping-pong ball enveloped in a catcher's mitt.

"Where to next?" asked Becko.

"To the nearest island that sells chain," I said.

Friendship, Tongan Style

You can be absent from these islands for years, but a part of you will remain in the hearts of those you left behind.

Five years ago, when we first visited Nuku'alofa, the capitol of the Kingdom of Tonga, we met a young Tongan family headed up by a dynamic woman named Star.

"I grew up on a small island in the Ha'apai group," she told us. "Our only contact with the outside world was the yachties."

"Every time a boat visited, it was an island-wide party," Star continued. "Our village would cook a big feast, and everyone would get to know each other. As a young girl, I turned the—how you say?—I turned the iron rod the sizzling meat was cooked on. Because of this, I got to stay up late into the night and listen to the adults talk, and the yachties talk. So I turned and turned and turned the handle until my hand would blister! Other kids would do it for a few moments and get bored. Not me. I wanted to listen, and to learn."

Her village received its mail, its supplies, and its entertainment mostly from passing yachties, who were held in high esteem.

"I would listen to their stories," Star told us, "and I just couldn't believe some of the crazy things they said. I mean, flying up in the air, and passing through mountains inside of iron boxes" —trains— "and talking across the ocean"—telephones— "had to be impossible, didn't they? I'd listen and turn the crank, and think to myself, 'They are making this up, to trick a poor Tongan girl!'"

So even after Star left Ha'apai, she longed for her yachtie friends. "Back then, all the boaters knew me as the cooking girl, and, combining my name, I was known as the Star Cook of my island. So, even after I moved to the big city—the capital of Nuku'alofa—I wanted to hang out with the yachties!"

Tongans are friendly to a fault. If you walk into a small business to ask directions, be careful! They will close the business, drive you to where you want to go in their car, wait for you, take you home and feed you, introduce you to all their relatives within 20 miles, and be waiting at dawn on the beach to give you some fresh bananas the following day—all for free, without any expectation to profit, only for the pleasure of your company.

But Star was, when it came to yachties, even friendlier than that! We happened to be buying vegetables at the huge open-air market in town and she overheard us saying something about our boat *Wild Card*, and she immediately asked us about it. The next day, she stopped down to the harbor to see *Wild Card*, and hung around until we showed up. One thing led to another, and we soon became fast friends. We invited her, her husband Afu, and their two children for a gourmet meal aboard our boat. They marveled at the "soft" food we ate.

The following night, we went to their house and had a traditional Polynesian Lu, with the breadfruit, yams, pig and lamb cooked in an umu, a hole dug as an oven in their backyard. (Note: Don't ever hop fences or run through people's backyards in Tonga; they are dotted with covered pits of burning coals!) Every day we did something fun together: island tours, observing the fishing pigs, hunting the elusive sea cucumbers, watching the flying foxes, exploring the blowholes, etc. We ate together, worked on the boat together, and laughed together.

Star and her family were intrigued with us, and, we, with them. They'd just come down, sit in the cockpit and announce, "We want to watch!" And they would. Watch. Giggle. Point. Now, with almost anyone else, this would've been an imposition. But not with them. They were just too cool, too natural, too open-hearted to be the slightest bit irritating. One day, they stopped down while I was writing on my laptop. For a long time they just stared and stared and stared, until finally Star blurted, "We keep hearing how computers are so good for work, but yours does absolutely nothing!"

How can you respond to that except to laugh?

Then, one day, we told them we were leaving. Star shed so many tears that our cockpit scuppers barely kept up. She urged us to change our minds. We politely demurred. She then solemnly extracted a promise from us—to someday return to Tonga. We agreed.

Now, Carolyn and I are always searching for ways to repay the kindness of strangers. So, after we left Tonga, we dropped Star and her family a postcard every few months with a brief note telling her where we were and what we were doing and that someday we'd be back to visit.

Although I'm often poverty stricken in a monetary sense, I'm never so broke I can't pay attention to the people who have helped us so generously over the years. So I keep in touch on an irregular basis with The Chinaman of Malaysia, The Orphan of Lumut, Becko the Pearl Carver, Palmerston Bob, Sandeep the Reverer, Professor Mani, Little Abner, and of course, Star.

Anyway, we first wrote Star every couple of months, then twice a year, then yearly. Of course, we received no reply (international postage costs money and Star is penniless) but we didn't expect any. We weren't writing Star in hopes of profiting from our relationship in the future, only to repay her kindness from the past. However, we did hear *of* Star.

Steve and Irene Macek, old friends from the Caribbean island of Nevis, pulled into the Ha'apai group on their Herreshoff-designed, three-masted, Marco Polo schooner—appropriately named *Star*—and a woman rowed out with a canoe full of babies. She said her name was also Star, and she asked if they knew Cap'n Fatty, and his wife Carolyn?

Graham Morfey of *Flight of Time*, a well-known British yachtsmen who's a member of the Royal Cruising Club, pulled into Tonga and e-mailed us shortly afterward that Star had been rowing around the harbor, asking about us—two years after we'd left. That seemed odd, but delightfully so

This trip we didn't plan to go to Tonga, let alone Nuku'alofa. And we had every reason to believe Star was a few hundred miles away in Ha'apai. Thus, when we showed her picture around the capital of Nuku'alofa with no response, we were sure we'd missed her. But Star, like many Tongans, is a patient person. She'd continued to stop down at the harbor every few days to check for *Wild Card*, and if a boater happened to stroll by, she'd ask them about us.

Finally, exactly five years later, almost to the day, Star came down to the harbor and sat in the cockpit of *Wild Card* once again. Needless to say, we treated her like nobility, like the Princess of Friendship that she is. "You sailed away," she told us happily, "but you never left my heart."

Trading New Zealand for a Feast in Fiji

As the austral seasons turn, it's time to ride a gale north and let reality trump preconception.

I'm always eager to go to sea. Like an impatient student on the final day of school, I just can't wait to be off. Everything else fades into insignificance. I long for it. I desire it. Mother Ocean is the one place I feel completely alive, free, and happy. Sailing offshore isn't what I do, it's who I am. It's my definition, my raison d'être. I'm hopelessly hooked.

Carolyn, my wife/lover/navigator and best friend for nearly four decades of offshore sailing, and I loved our summer in New Zealand. The Hauraki Gulf is a marvelous, windswept cruising area. We could've happily spent the entire season discovering "hidden" anchorages on Great Barrier Island alone. The Bay of Islands still enchants. And perhaps the best part of summering in New Zealand? The friendly, fun-loving and notoriously hardy Kiwis themselves.

Needless to say, the place attracts sailors from all over the world—and it's lousy with marine scribes as well. Lin and Larry Pardey fed us many a meal as our wakes repeatedly crossed. I met Alvah Simon, author of *North to the Night* and a man I greatly admire as a writer, sailor and Arctic explorer. It was great to roll around the cockpit with the legendary Webb Chiles while we lamented the SSB "worry nets," the dangers of occasional shore dwelling and the fact that his wife has a money problem. ("She's *got* it, which is *her* problem—not mine!" he giggled.)

I even tossed flowers into the water in the exact spot where Eric Hiscock died. (Instead of telling me bedtime stories my father used to read Hiscock aloud while I fell asleep in the forecastle of our family schooner, *Elizabeth.*)

But the weather in New Zealand, especially in autumn, is notoriously tricky, and it was time to go. Procrastination would only make the passage tougher. The Southern Hemisphere's hurricane season was over. The tropics were safe once again—if we could just get there. New Zealand was getting colder, windier and rainier by the day. Storms were popping off Bass Strait and roaring across the Tassie like spinning popcorn. Inside *Wild Card,* the condensation dripped from the underside of our fiberglass deck, drenching our suddenly mildewy sleeping bags.

Last year, seven boats had been dismasted on this run, with three vessels a total loss as their storm-battered crews elected to be airlifted off by Kiwi SAR helicopters. And if that wasn't enough to intimidate us, there was the memory of the famous Queen's Birthday storm: That June 1994 blow, in exactly these waters, featured a destructive squash zone—a region of tightly packed isobars between high-and low-pressure systems—that forced the crews of 16 well-found ocean-crossing vessels to set off their EPIRBs. Seven boats were lost. Twenty-one sailors were plucked to safety by courageous Kiwi rescuers. Three people lost their lives.

We weren't even out of the harbor before the first gust staggered *Wild Card*, our modest 38-foot S&S-designed sloop. "Are you sure you want to leave?" asked Carolyn. "It's blowing a steady 30, with gusts to 36."

"Sure I'm sure," I said as I eased the deep-reefed mainsail. "Tell me, have I ever called a weather window wrong?"

"Yeah," she said as she nonchalantly allowed the mainsheet traveler car to drop down a couple of inches to further spill the wind. "The last dozen or so."

"Well," I said reasonably. "Perhaps you're right, which means I'm in for a change of luck, eh?"

Another savage gust hit us. *Wild Card* heeled sharply to starboard. Damn. Perhaps she *was* a tad overpowered.

"I'm gonna drop the mainsail," I said as I donned my safety harness and dashed forward. "Tend the sheet and leeward boom preventer, please."

"Don't you think it odd that you're dropping the main *before* we're out of the Bay of Islands?" she shouted forward at me, some of her words snatched away in the gusts. "Isn't Fiji over a thousand miles away, and isn't it reasonable to expect that it will be both rougher *and* windier offshore?"

"Never use the term "reasonable" around me," I admonished her through the sail ties in my clenched teeth. "You had your chance 37 years ago, when you were surrounded by 150 million very reasonable American men, many of them gainfully employed, and then you picked the goofiest, gawkiest teenage boy you ever met. Well, too late for marital regrets now!"

We're like this. Always joking. Always kidding. Always, on some strange and twisted level, telling each other how much we appreciate our mutual sea-borne silliness. If you only maintain one thing on your vessel, let it be your sense of humor.

"Besides," said I, dripping wet as I regained the cockpit, "our weather router says we've got four days of decreasing sou'westerly breezes, perfect for putting some distance between us and these pesky New Zealand gales!"

Only one other boat was visible, an aging IOR racer maybe 45 feet long. I worried about its proximity in the squalls. It had been clearly visible to port as I dropped my main, but then I lost sight of it. Finally it emerged from the gloom close astern.

"Boy, he's lugging it, eh?" said Carolyn. A couple of minutes later, we heard what sounded like a cannon shot from the other boat, and he rounded up into a full luff.

"Maybe just the jib sheet parted," I said.

"Something worse," she said. "Maybe a broken jib car or pulled deck track. Anyway, it looks like he's turning back for Opua."

She was looking through our trusty 30-year old Fujinon binoculars. "Can you read its name?" I asked her.

"Yeah," she said, and something artificial in her voice allowed me to guess what was coming, "The transom says *Smarter than Fatty*," she said.

"Not *Less Prepared*?" I asked.

"Touché," Carolyn said, and then suddenly settled into her normal offshore mode. "Want some coffee to warm you up? Are your feet dry? Can I e-mail our daughter and tell her we're off?"

"Sure," I said. "And my toes are fine. Yes, on the coffee."

The trick to leaving New Zealand in the autumn is to hop on a fading sou'westerly gale and allow it to slingshot you northward above 30 degrees south before the next one strikes. This takes guts, luck, and an accurate forecast. It's easy to get it wrong. Wait too long and you have no wind and huge rollers. Leave too soon, and you have to heave to.

Our timing was fairly good: We had 30-plus knots of sou'westerly breeze over the port quarter when we left. With a small storm jib, we were occasionally touching eight knots on the surfs. The following day, it dropped to the mid-20s for a lovely downwind sail. Gradually the wind got lighter. By the evening of the third day, our boat speed fell to less than three knots, and I reluctantly cranked up our faithful Perkins M30.

It was wonderful to be meandering back to the tropics: heading for more warmth, fewer storms and more ease. That's what the tropics are to me. Ease. Languidness. Slowness. Peace.

When the wind came back, it was light and from astern. That suited. With her deep keel and high ballast-to-weight ratio, *Wild Card* barely rolls. I set the pole. The feeling wasn't so much that we were moving through the water, but that the water was flowing around us.

It's during times like this, when nothing special is happening, that I get my most delicious, most sensual thoughts offshore. I feel like I'm floating high above the brave, jaunty *Wild Card*, watching her plow the oceans. Or that she isn't a sailboat but a magic carpet, ready to go anywhere at whim.

While cruising Southeast Asia, I once met a Zen master. He told me about living in the now, being in the moment, and how all the happiness we'll ever have is already inside us.

When he finished, neither of us spoke for awhile. We both just smiled. Then I said, "I know—I'm a sailor."

The island of Viti Levu drifted closer, from pale grey, to firm smudge, to vivid, verdant green. Adventure loomed.

Fiji, formerly known as the "Cannibal Isles," consists of more than 330 islands located about 1,000 miles north of New Zealand and equidistant between Tahiti and Australia.

Its tumultuous 3,500-year history is an extremely violent one. Only within the last 100 years or so have its citizens stopped munching on their enemies, who were referred to, with an eye to their transition as table fare, as "long pig."

Carolyn and I always attempt to keep an open mind. "Hope for the best and plan for the worst," is wise advice for the waterborne wanderer. Many of our cruising friends had told us that Fiji was their favorite Pacific stop. We were here to find out why.

I blinked as I emerged from the darkness of the chief's hut. The Fijian sun was bright. My mouth felt like I'd come from the dentist, and my knees were wobbly. I'd had too many bowls of kava with the village elders.

"To travel is to be surprised," I was thinking to myself. I'd expected the Fijians to be as fierce as their violent past, yet I found them to be polite and friendly. How could history and reality be so different? Hadn't I just purchased a cannibal fork from a local carver? And hadn't Carolyn and I grimaced at the forlorn pair of leather soles displayed at the National Museum, the only remaining reminder of the early Christian missionary Thomas Baker? (In 1867, cannibals ate him and his boot uppers!)

When I left *Wild Card* to go meet the chief, Carolyn had quipped, "Watch your prepositions—only accept invitations *to* dinner, not *for* dinner!"

But everything about Fiji struck me as refined and civilized. Example: the kava ceremony. They were so serious about it. Every time the chief's son handed me the coconut-shell bowl, he clapped formally and bowed low.

I'd drink. Clap three times. Smile. Hand it back. Bow in return.

"How long will you stay," asked the chief's wife.

I was attempting to maneuver my thick tongue into coherency, when the whole village unexpectedly jammed into fast-forward.

There was a shriek. Running. A crash. Shouting. A scream. Then the chief's wife, an individual size of a small vehicle, scampered away with surprising swiftness. I could see eager young men running towards the commotion; terrified women were running away.

There were about 100 residences in the village, varying from western-style single-room dwellings to tiny thatched galvy huts. All were close together. It was difficult to maneuver between them, let alone get a clear field of vision.

A sweating man, breathing heavily, ran to the house next to me, leaned in, grabbed a machete, and dashed away. I followed.

In between two houses was a group of men, some wrestling on the ground, others standing over them with raised knives and maneuvering for a swing.

Grunting, a horrible grunting.

More eager young men flooded in, knocking me out of the way from behind.

By the time I regained my equilibrium, only dust remained. They were gone. I dashed shoreward in awkward pursuit. By the time I arrived, some of them were already in the water—a wedge-shaped stream of young men swimming frantically seaward. Out in the middle of the harbor, off *Wild Card's* port quarter, they formed a circle. Tightened. Closed.

Suddenly all the tension went out of the air. Fast-forward stopped, and life returned to normal speed. The Fijians on the beach were laughing, shouting encouragement to the returning swimmers.

An old toothless woman, skinny and warped in a faded blue bed sheet, cackled to me, "No worries. Kilt!"

"Killed?" I said. "Killed?"

"Dead," she said, and made a motion of holding something underwater.

"Oh, dear," I said, and sounded effeminate even to myself.

"From the mountains," she explained. "Wandered down. Happen not often, only sometimes. Now, we eat. Good!"

I guess I still looked stricken.

"Pig," she said. "Wild pig!"

I have a horrible habit. In times of stress I crack jokes. At various times in my past, this has gotten me fired from jobs, expelled from schools, stomped into unconsciousness, arrested, slapped, and hated/loved forever. I haven't yet learned how to resist the impulse, but I have learned to tone it down.

"Thank God," I whispered to myself, "a short one!"

We'd cleared into Suva, the capital, 10 days before. We spent a delightful week at the Royal Suva Yacht Club, which has gone to seed in a most delightful manner. Picture a colonial yacht club where a young Queen Mother might have frolicked on the lawn as child—then zoom ahead 70 years or so without dusting, and there you have it.

The host and/or commodore was a helpful fellow who advised us with a hiccup he could always be found "at or under the bar!" One of the blue-haired elderly members summed it up best. "Our standards have, well, dropped," she wisecracked when I inquired after the "royal" in the yacht club's name.

In any event, we had a wonderful time in Suva, especially buying kava in the local market, and soon we were cruising the south coast of Viti Levu. Every mile or so is a break in the barrier reef, which offers good protection from the easterly trades. Good light is important to see the coral heads, and we used that as an excuse to leisurely leave at 1000 and then anchor again by noon. "Not a long day, but a good day," as Carolyn would say.

Each reef break and anchorage is spelled differently on every chart. We had no idea where we were exactly. Sure, our three GPS units continually spit out lat/longs, but our charts varied enough to prevent accurate pinpricking. "We're in Paradise," mused Carolyn. "Isn't that close enough?"

The villagers get around by sea. The local fishermen travel to and fro along the coast. One morning, two young men named Esai and Bai, in a canoe full of fishing nets dropped by *Wild Card's* toe rail to chat. It only took me a few seconds to get them both laughing when I told them how in Thailand, Carolyn got mad at me for looking at the beautiful Thai ladies. "But I told her," I said. "'Don't get mad at me, honey, I'm only looking for my unmarried male friends!'"

Carolyn comes up into the cockpit and playfully boxes my ears. Everyone is smiling, most of all us.

In one tiny bay, we visited a small resort during happy hour. The owner, an Aussie from the Darwin area, was drunk. He "shouted" us a round of drinks, then muttered a list of ex-pat complaints. I told him I used to write for Fodor's Travel Guides. "Oh, the stories I could tell," he said and foolishly didn't stop, "about the time we poisoned all the rats, and they crawled into the kitchen cistern to die."

He paused, glared at his wife, and asked dully, "Why are you kicking me?" Then he continued with his sad tales. This made me strangely glum. However, on the hike back to the dinghy, we accidently flushed out a *caca,*

or red-breasted musk parrot from a palm tree. Its iridescent green body, bright red chest and black top-hat head are as remarkable as his giant wing span. Suddenly I was refilled with peace and serenity. Life is good, if we just let it be.

The place that stole our hearts was the island of Beqa, only a few miles off Viti Levu's southern coast, where fire-walking is practiced. Our two-hour passage wasn't long but it *was* lovely. The trades were warm, strong, and consistent. *Wild Card* had a bone in her teeth, as she screamed through the narrow pass in the reef. Yes, there were plenty of coral heads—thousands of them—but we joyfully carved the deep water between.

The huge harbor of Vaga Bay, off the village of Naiseuseu, was completely empty as we anchored. The Fijian chief's long name had a couple of syllables in the middle that sounded like JAH-KNEY, so for us he became "Chief Johnny!"

"*Vinaka!*" he said as we placed the kava before him. "Thank you for the grog! It is the Fijian way. You give grog, we give village. Welcome!"

We were in luck. The entire village was currently involved in raising money for their annual school fees. They'd carefully made costumes in which to perform their traditional welcoming ceremony at a nearby tourist resort. Would we care to see a rehearsal?

The following day, in Chief Johnny's sweltering cinderblock hut, we had the experience of a lifetime. Fifty of the villagers put on for us a traditional, centuries-old welcoming song-and-dance *meke*. Carolyn and I were within three feet of the performers, and by the finale, we'd had so much kava, that we were dancing with them.

The following day I returned with my guitar, and Carolyn and I warbled "If I had a Hammer" and "Blowin' in the Wind" to their hear-a-pin-drop amazement.

The next day was my kava fest with the village elders, which ended in

the unfortunate pig's demise.

On the morning of our departure, we made a modest cash contribution to their school fund and donated six sets of guitar strings (used, but much appreciated) to the village band and a selection of school supplies for the youngsters.

A few days later found us a few miles downwind, anchored off the Robinson Crusoe Resort at Likuri Island. Once Carolyn discovered they had all-you-can-eat Chicken Parmesan on the menu, I knew it was hopeless. Our hosts, Ron and Ann originally from Sydney, Australia, were doing a fine job of entertaining their 38 backpacker guests with a staff of 50 wonderfully friendly Fijians.

The only jolt was finding a sea snake—a banded sea krait, three times more poisonous than a cobra—attempting to slither into our anchored dinghy. "Just grab 'em right behind the head," Ron advised. "If you don't let go, no worries!"

Time faded. The rest of the world dimmed. Two days later, another five miles down the coast, in another perfect harbor, Carolyn and I got into a slight argument about what day of the week it was. There was even some doubt in my mind as to the month.

"I think one of the pages on the GPS will tell us," I said. "Or call someone on the SSB and ask."

"I'd be embarrassed to admit we spaced out," she said.

"Not me," I said. "I'd be proud."

Perhaps that's it is a nutshell: If losing track of the day of the week appeals to you, go cruising. If not, keep the day job

Then we discovered the tranquil island of Malololailai and its unbelievable Musket Cove Yacht Club/Marina/Resort. Why unbelievable? Because it just doesn't make sense how nice they treat us yachties.

Its founder is a long-term Pacific cruising sailor named, er, Smith (aren't they all?) who chartered to Brando in the late 1950s. Anyway, Mister Smith decided to "not build a resort, but create an island lifestyle," and the result is the utopian Musket Cove Yacht Club

I'm a lifetime member—hell, it only costs a Fijian buck (that's 60 U.S. cents) and they even give you a waterproof membership card.

Yes, *Wild Card* is currently anchored in one of the most protected and magnificent harbors in Fiji. We have complete resort privileges: toilets, showers, pool, daily entertainment, access to filtered water, use of the dinghy dock. Why, they even light a nightly barbecue and put out place settings so all the visiting cruisers can eat a communal dinner ashore each evening.

Of course, this isn't free. There is a cost. So far, I've calculated that it's slightly less than 40 U.S. cents per day, but it'll go down if we stay longer. "Finally," said Carolyn as she paid. "A place Fatty can't label 'outrageously expensive.'"

We're deep into our decades-old routine now. I write all morning, while Carolyn beachcombs and flirts with the pool boys. We have lunch together, take a quick nap, then swim, snorkel, hike or do boat work until time for a sundowner. ("One excitement per day," cautions Carolyn.)

Yesterday, as the misshaped tropic sun hissed into the sea astern of us, Carolyn got up to fetch herself another drink. She said, "Want anything?" I thought about it, then thought about it some more. "Nothing, save you and this moment," I whispered.

The Grisly Facts of Cannibalism

For thousands of years, Fijians ritualistically ate their enemies. It was considered the ultimate insult. In some tribes, young men could not receive their adult name until they'd killed in battle. If a victim was captured alive, all the worse. The warriors would then do a *cibi* (death dance) to visually demonstrate what was in store, the women would top it off with an obscene dance of sexual humiliation, and, worst case, the victim would then be fed pieces of themselves.

Needless to say, this discouraged early attempts by the bareboat companies.

Everything was done according to ancient ritual: The priests were given the brains, the warriors the muscle, and the woman the rest. Kids were tossed fingers and toes to gnaw on.

Mementos were kept to celebrate the event: leg bones around the village parameter, teeth to be inset into war clubs, the skull of a particularly courageous opponent for a kava cup.

The number of stones outside a chief's hut revealed how many people he'd eaten.

Since priests were not allowed to touch any food (they were fed by young girls), they ate human flesh only with special sacred forks, which were then kept in the village spirit house and never touched by anyone else.

The Sacrament of Kava

Polynesians take their culture seriously. Never forget that on many levels, it still exemplifies a "warrior" mentality. Example: In New Zealand, a young Maori male was recently hired to greet visiting tourists in a traditional nose-rubbing Polynesian ceremony. One of his first clients was a loud-mouthed drunk who continuously belittled what was happening, right up to the moment he was head-butted into the intensive-care unit of the local hospital. While no one approved of the young Maori's impulsive response, even the *pakeha* (white New Zealander) judge presiding over his trial let him off with a stern warning.

While Carolyn and I were never frightened by a Fijian, it's always best to respect local sensibilities. Kava is serious here. It remains a daily ritual of village life. It's definitely not just an intoxicating drink or a cheap recreational drug; kava is subtly interwoven into all aspects of the Fijian culture.

By tradition—and to this day—all visitors (including sailors) must present the *turaga* (chief) of the *koro* (village) with *sevusevu* (an offering or tribute.) Some cruisers resent this. "Why do we have to bring drugs to bribe an old man so he and his buddies can get zonked all afternoon?" is a common complaint. That's one way to think of it. Another is to recognize that the kava ceremony is ancient Fijian tradition. By honoring the chief, you honor the village.

Here's how it works in current practice. A cruising vessel carries about a pound of kava (unground is preferred but powdered will do; the cost is US$10) for each village to be visited. The first person you come across ashore will immediately say *"Bula"* (hello) to you and guide you to the chief. Present the chief with your letter of cruising permission. He will either read it or pretend to read it.

Now, the important part: Do not hand the kava directly to the chief. Place it before him. He has the right to refuse, and if he does, leave immediately. However, he usually accepts your gift, and he'll pick it up and make a long and formal speech/chant in Fijian, wishing you and your distant relatives well, and assuring you of your safety and well-being while in his village.

I was strangely moved by this. It didn't seem at all cheap or foolish to me. I was honored to be experiencing an ancient ritual exactly as Captain Cook, and Robert Louis Stevenson did.

Remember: Your offered kava isn't a bribe; it's part of a social contract. You promise to be nice, he promises his protection for as long as you are in his domain.

The *sevusevu* doesn't have to be kava; it is just the accepted coin of the realm. We met a New Zealander who recently made a multimillion-dollar real-estate deal with a local chief; he sealed the transaction with a whale's tooth, knowing the tooth would bind the chief far stronger than the money.

If you're invited for grog (another word the Fijians use for kava), attend to the ritual solemnly. Remove your shoes before entering the *bure* (hut or house.) Dress demurely. Clap three times after each *bilo* (cup.) Don't put your knees up or show the soles of your feet to the chief—nor allow your feet to point to the *tanoa* (kava bowl.) While walking in the village, follow directions, even if issued by children: Walking on one side of a hut can be fine, while walking on the other is *taboo.* If your path crosses with another villager, pass behind them, not in front. When in doubt, say "*Tilou*" (excuse me) or "*Vinaka"* (thank you.)

Don't worry: Most Fijian will make allowances for your uncouth behavior because they understand you are uncivilized and lack the good, sensible, refined upbringing they have been blessed with for 35 centuries.

Alaska Jim

When tales of sea gypsies penetrated his cold log cabin, this man made a decision that soon transformed him into a sailor.

It was cold outside, 48 degrees below zero to be precise. In northern Alaska, Jim Sublett huddled under his mound of quilts inside his crude log cabin. He gave his balky flashlight a few whacks with the palm of his calloused hand. It flicked back on. Dim and getting dimmer.

"Darn," he whispered into the dark, drafty room, hoping the light would last until the end of the article he was reading under the covers.

Jim was like that— he didn't swear even when he was alone. There was a stillness about him, a politeness. He was a gentleman's gentlemen. But there was something more, too. A wildness. An unpredictability. He was a banked fire, a coiled spring, an enigma wrapped in a question mark. People walk softly around Jim. And he was bone-tired from dressing out that moose

But Jim laughed and chuckled and sighed as he read. The words seemed to dance in his head: "sea gypsies" and "wonderful waterfront wackos" and—his favorite—"lush tropical vegetables."

His flashlight was dying now. He could no longer see the print, so he had to stop reading, and just flip through the pictures: the black shabby hull of the boat, those colorful pareus, that crazy bulkhead.

The light sputtered out. Jim stuck his head out from under the breath-frosted covers and said aloud, "Why not?"

The answer was plain, even to him. He didn't know how to sail. He'd never been on a boat. Hell, he'd never *seen* the ocean. And, something which really gave him pause, he didn't know how to swim.

"So what?" Jim said and was surprised by the fierce defiance in his voice. He was 50 years old. It was now or never.

Suddenly, he felt warm all over. As if he was already cruising the tropics.

The Alaskan town of Chatanika where Jim lived, wasn't much of one. "Only 13 people, 12 now that the village idiot has left," Jim would later say. It was fairly spread out: his nearest neighbor was a 90-minute drive away. By noon the following day, Jim was sitting in a cybercafe and hunt-pecking "how to buy a boat" into Google and penning a brief e-mail to the only sailor for whom he had an e-mail address, a guy named Nim Marsh.

Nim, a former *CW* associate editor, wrote him back a nice letter and didn't call him crazy—at least, not flat-out.

"Hot damn!" Jim laughed, and took it as encouragement.

Jim only had one firm idea: he'd hit stuff. Like rocks and docks and reefs and overhanging trees. He had to learn, and he'd figure he'd hit stuff while learning, so he decided on a steel boat. Not big. Not fancy. Around 30-feet or so....

Jim's not real cyber-savvy. Plus, he's dyslexic. So it took him a while to navigate the information highway, and he was surprised that New Zealand kept popping up. Heck, he'd always been intrigued by New Zealand and he'd been reading a lot about it lately.

Jim was nervous standing on the dock at Westhaven, in Auckland. He really didn't know what he was looking at. He stepped aboard. She didn't tilt too much. (Only later did he learn boats don't tilt, they heel.) She wasn't a complete rust bucket. The mast was up, the keel down. "I'll take her," said Jim, and was flabbergasted by how flabbergasted the Kiwi yacht broker was.

"Weren't you expect'n to sell 'er?" Jim asked with an arched eyebrow.

Just down the block was a crowded, boisterous sailor's bar named The Boatshed at Swashbucklers. So Jim started hang'n there—talking about such diverse subjects as boats, bears, and gold-mining at the Arctic Circle—and soon met "Janet the girlfriend" who just happened to have two large touring motorcycles in her garage. My, my, things were looking up for Alaska Jim!

Even better, the Boatshed was owned by a locally beloved biker/sailor with a heart of gold by the name of Ginger Gibbs. He'd once toured Alaska on his Harley and immediately took Jim under his wing. The first thing Ginger did was to convince Jim to take a Kiwi Safe Boating course.

Jim and Ginger soon became good friends—and with some "riding mates" they road-tripped New Zealand to raise $14,000 for the NZ Coast Guard, almost all of it in two dollar coins. Yes, only modern NZ would think of the "Bikers for Boaters" concept.

By now, mostly everyone along Auckland's waterfront had heard of Alaska Jim—and Kiwi sailors aren't exactly shy about expressing themselves. But Jim didn't blink. He knew he didn't know what he was doing. But he figured he had to start somewhere—and this was as good a place as any. If he didn't kill himself first, he'd learn by doing.

"I'll git it," he'd say. "It'll take me a while, sure. I'm slow, but I'm sure!"

Jim finally worked up his courage to take his boat for a sail. "I was much amazed, yes sir, by how a thing that only goes about as fast as a man can trot could so scare the heck out of a fella!"

It seemed to Jim that a boat is a lot like a loco horse. You have to tell it what to do just so, or it will continuously attempt to throw you.

"I was heading out of the harbor into the Hauraki Gulf," he said, "and one minute everything was fine and the next it weren't. Suddenly the boat tilted—tilted *bad*! And then it turned, like the devil himself was at the helm. And the sails started flapping —loud, like a cannon. Soon I was tangled in strings, just tangled and dazed. The worst part was the other boats around me. They was sailing along nice as you please!"

Every day Jim would go out "and mess up less" as he'd say.

Suddenly autumn was around the corner. It was now or never. Jim sailed up to Opua in the Bay of Islands and anchored smack dab into the middle of the cruising fleet to await a weather window to the tropical South Pacific.

His plan was simple. Although he had no idea what a "weather window" was, he'd be ready to go, and when the other boats went, he'd go too.

Carolyn and I were dining in the clubhouse of the Opua Cruising Club with Kurt and Katie Braun who sail *Interlude*, a 74-foot Deerfoot and rapping about music as much as boats. (Their guitar rendition of "A Hard Day's Night" always gets the island kids rocking.) I just happened to glance up—and stopped in mid-sentence. There was an American Cowboy waiting to speak to me. I mean, I could have *sworn* he was wearing chaps! (Carolyn says no.) It was as if he'd just fallen from a Marlboro ad or escaped from "The Good, The Bad and the Ugly."

"Yer the fella, ain't ya?" he said to me, grinning wide. "You're him. The guy who wrote the article about you and them Sea Gypsies

circumnavigating! My, my! Right in front of me. Diggity-damn! Nice to meet you, Fatty, and this must be Miss Carolyn!"

Now, dear reader, let's get something straight. If you are a reader of Cruising World and a cruising sailor there is a good chance our wakes will someday cross. Every time I meet one of our readers I make a special effort to be nice and take a few moments to be as polite and charming as I can be, given the chance circumstance. After all, it is ultimately you who signs my paycheck. But—and I don't mean this harshly—that's *all* I owe you. Civility. Momentary charm. Politeness.

I'm a private person, leading an extremely private lifestyle, and I never, ever, allow anyone to intrude on it—unless I want them to.

But there was something about Jim—something quiet and brave and special.

He's a small, compact man, but there's a hint of danger to him. He likes it on the edge. He's a misfit. A free thinker. A rebel. And his hard stare (even when he smiles) tells you he don't take much from nobody.

Jim's a romantic. Oh, he wouldn't think of himself this way: too GQ, too cologne-kissed, too metro-sexual—but that's what Jim is: a romantic. He's a Big Game hunter on many diverse levels, not only in the frozen woods of Alaska and the hot jungles of Africa, but the mean streets of America as well.

Jim was bounty hunter for many years. He's the type of man who, while sitting quietly with his hands folded, sends off the signal to the big fella next to him who is heading off to jail, "Don't try it."

Anyway, a man like Jim is a man worth knowing. I figure he can teach me more than I can teach him, except when it comes to boats.

Jim didn't even have the names of his sails right—and his lovely 30-foot, Denis Ganley-designed *Bell Bird,* has only a single mast!

The next night, we inviteded him aboard *Wild Card* for dinner. "Just like the pictures of her in the magazine," he marveled. The following night, Carolyn and I dined aboard his boat. For the next week I helped him as much as I could to get his new vessel prepared for sea. Many other cruisers did too.

But when I thought it was time to go, I went. I didn't say good bye—I seldom do. Nor did I tell him (or anyone) that it was good time to go. But a lot of us—the majority of the gathered 40-boat fleet—left at the same time.

The first four days or so were perfect—which is all you can ask from the New Zealand Met Service. Then we were hove to aboard *Wild Card* and hanging on a sea anchor for 72 hours. I tried not to, but I must admit I thought about Jim more than once when our decks were swept by large seas.

Jim didn't have an easy trip. He kept breaking windvane blades, losing stuff overboard, having things stop working. He tried to heave to, to lay ahull, to run off before the wind towing warps, but he was on one wild, crazy steed.

Fourteen days later, however, he pulled into Nuku'alofa, Tonga, and dropped the hook next to *Wild Card.* His hull was rust-streaked, his engine didn't run, and he was grinning from ear to ear. "Howdy, Fatty and Miss Carolyn!" he said. "Mighty rough out there, but I'm starting to get the hang of this sailin' thang. Whoopee, those waves is sum'thin', eh?"

Jim's doing it. He's really here. Now. Doing it. Within days, we had his vessel sorted out. And soon he was hosting our Tongan friend Star and her family in his cockpit. He was "In like Flynn" in his own words. I especially enjoyed it when other boats arrived in the harbor; Jim helped them tie up, gave them advice on how to clear in, provided directions to the local market, and warned them to avoid the dockside diesel fuel— it was, he confided, 50% beach sand.

As always, he was super-polite. When asked for local knowledge of cruising the waters of nearby Ha'apai, he said, "Can't say. I don't reckon I've ever been there, sir."

Jim, of course, is crazy. If he would have asked me if he should do what he did, I would have told him no. But, lucky for both of us, he didn't ask. Jim's a doer, not an asker. And I'm proud to call him a friend. And I'm perfectly willing to admit he's enriched our lives.

Most of all I'm happy for him—that's he's finally found the one last place on this planet where they can't fence you in.

Slow Juice and the Buddha Tree

A reverse somersault helps things fall into place during another day in paradise.

My consciousness rises with the sun, as it does nearly every morning of my cruising life. I looked over at Carolyn sleeping diagonally away from me in the forecastle. Each wrinkle, each year, and each ocean mile makes her more beautiful to me. She is my other half. I'm a lucky man.

Getting into our V-berth is relatively easy, but getting out is far more difficult. I sort of roll out in a noiseless reverse somersault—careful not to wake Sleeping Beauty.

I check the barometer. It's dropping. In the cockpit I look up at the low sky. Dark clouds, moving fast. Despite the benign GRIB weather files of yesterday, I know we are in for a "bit of breeze," as the Kiwis say.

I light the stove and put on the kettle. First I check that the speaker to our SSB is shut off, then turn on our ICOM 710. Ditto, the computer. After checking the propagation tables, I don my headphones and connect with my Winlink e-mail server in New Zealand for my personal messages and with Sailmail in Australia for my commercial business-related mail.

The good news: Everywhere I go, I can earn my living without getting off my vessel. The bad news: Everywhere I go I have to earn my living!

In essence, I'm as much waterborne entrepreneur as sea gypsy. I average a story every 10 days and a book every two years. And I have my photography work, 18-year-old radio show, writing, seminars and more. I have to hustle.

We're still in Musket Cove, Fiji, about 1,000 miles north of New Zealand and a bit farther from Australia. Propagation is good, and my Pactor modem zips me four personal letters and a couple of business ones.

I'm about to read the business ones first—one is labeled "Assignment," which pleases me—when Carolyn emerges sleepily.

She's a night person who wakes up cranky and gets progressively more joyous. I'm a morning person, wildly awake from the moment I arise but losing steam the entire time. We're ying and yang: Between the two of us, we make a normal person.

"Roma?" she asks.

"Yes," I say, and Carolyn's face lights up. Our daughter Roma, with her freshly minted M.B.A. from Brandeis, has just gotten her dream job with the Boston Community Health Worker Initiative. We're excited for her, and, frankly, it is nice to know at least one Goodlander has worked at a normal shore job this century.

"Out of the way, Skipper," Carolyn jokingly says as she pulls me out of the nav station by my ear and plunks herself down to read Roma's missive.

I turn on our portable SSB radio while she reads, scanning the BBC, ABC (Australia Broadcasting Corporation), and Radio New Zealand for the international news. The Middle East is a mess. Oil prices are rising and our dollar is falling. "Oh, dear!" I mutter, sigh, and switch it off.

At 0730, as Carolyn finishes up the breakfast dishes and moves to the foredeck to begin her yoga, I begin my shipboard exercises: 15 minutes of cardio and 15 minutes of light weights. (Actually, I use only one weight, our 40-pound anchor weight, and turn the entire boat into a rope-and-pulley exercise machine. To vary the weight with only one chunk of lead, I use different combinations of Harken roller blocks.)

At 0800 Carolyn zips into the cabin to pick up her mobile jewelry workshop, which could be mistaken for a large tackle box, and begins to head ashore. Before she cranks up the outboard and leaves in the dinghy, Bob Taylor of *Nero* roars up. He's a great guy and a great friend and currently on his fifth circum-navigation, and he excitedly tells us some great news. The guy who just sailed in on the blue catamaran, Canadian surgeon Ken Bradley, has three

recent *New Yorker* magazines aboard.

"Wow," says Carolyn, "should I ask if we can borrow them or just lure him ashore so that one of you guys can sneak aboard and ransack his vessel?"

"Ask first," I advise, "but don't take no for an answer!"

By 0805, they're gone. I sit down at my word processor (one of three aboard) and clear my mind. I put my fingers on the keyboard. I say aloud, softly, "Don't think. Type!" and begin doing so.

Writing isn't difficult. Talent is like a muscle: The more you use it, the stronger it gets. For me writing is like falling down a tunnel. Current reality darkens, and I transcribe the flickering images in my mind. I am just—gone. In the zone. Then, faintly at first, I hear the sound of our outboard approaching and Carolyn returning for lunch.

Carolyn is the social one, and she's full of gossip Southern Joe, host of a perpetual floating party aboard his huge steel Belgium schooner, fell down the companionway ladder *again* last night. Barfie, the scuba instructor on the California multi, is having another one of her migraines. The Fijians who work at the dive concession are on strike—they don't like the new French PADI instructors. Kerry, the fine artist aboard the British vessel *Folly*, has drawn a horse so perfect it appears to be alive. The father and son crew of *Sanuk* have left for Vanuatu. Paul and Ann Marie, whom we first met many years ago, immediately after they rounded Cape Horn, just sailed in on their new racing sloop—with a son!

We take a full two hours for lunch: fresh lobster, fresh salad, and lusciously ripe papaya are on the menu. Carolyn tops it all off with a frothy cappuccino made, amazingly, with powdered milk. (The secret is in the whisk!)

Captain Ilene zooms up in her dinghy. She's an amazing woman who skippered large ships for NOAA (she has a 1600 ton US Coast Guard master's license) before snagging her husband Ken, out of the bar at the Balboa Yacht Club.

"Wanna go dive with the manta rays," she asks. "You might get some fantastic underwater shots."

I tell her we can't—too much to do, too little time.

Before she is out of sight, I dive into the bilge of *Wild Card* and begin tracing down a bad electrical wire that is mildly draining our batteries. It only takes me a few minutes to find it, but to replace and reloom it takes a couple of hours.

The problem with our electrical system is that *Wild Card* was on the bottom for nearly 50 days, before I salvaged her. Over the years, I've replaced most of her electrical system but not all and, it's an unreliable mess. I'm constantly bedeviled by "slow juice," as Carolyn sarcastically calls it. When I turn on a light, it goes on after a few minutes—or hours.

Then I do my daily deck check to make sure my anchor chain is OK, my snubber is chafe protected, and that *Wild Card* is ready more or less to go to sea at a moment's notice.

I've lived aboard, mostly on my own hook, for more than 45 years now. An amazing number of emergencies have happened during that time, requiring immediate, effective and bold action to save my vessel. So I try to keep her shipshape and ready to roll even in safe harbor.

My list of boat jobs is long. I never finish it but I do chip away at it every day.

"How's the deck-tank level," I ask Carolyn, who is swimming alongside now, scrubbing the green slime off our red boot top. We shower with rainwater collected straight off our decks.

"Nearly full," she says, "and we've got new hair conditioner."

I rig the cockpit privacy screens while she stows her snorkeling gear, and then we're both naked and showering on the cockpit floor. It's fun. We slide around like seals on the soap.

Later, I grab my guitar and belt out Bob Dylan's "I Threw It All Away" with gusto, because I know I haven't done so.

Then I'm ashore on Malololailai for my hour-long hike. I've explored almost every square inch of the island over the course of the last month, and I revel in the brisk, bracing exercise.

At the end, I sit on top of the highest hill and look down at the harbor. I watch Carolyn ferrying fresh drinking water back to *Wild Card*. The reefs are lovely: blue-green and yellow-to-white where they dry. It's midtide.

Seagulls float below me.

I hold my breath and think, "How can one man be this blessed?"

Then I'm off to the Buddha tree, under which I meditate for 30 minutes. I surface from this mind-vacation utterly refreshed, rejuvenated, and eager.

As I hike back down the hillside to the harbor I sing spirituals at the top of my happy lungs. I love to sing the songs that I learned growing up in the Deep South aboard the schooner *Elizabeth*.

I stop at the little grocery store on the island and have a Magnum Classic ice cream. It is my one remaining vice—well, that and caffeine.

It is now happy hour. Carolyn joins me and we hoist a few with friends at the beach bar. Carolyn drinks wine, and I have soda water with a twist, so I don't have to explain to all the drinkers why I'm not.

Surfer Kevin, about to set off on his first around-the-world jaunt, wants me to help him install some software and help interface his GPS into his new chart plotter. I agree to help, but not until the weekend, when I'll have more time.

All of us swap cruising tales, and both seek and give advice. Someone notes that three different cruising vessels have gone up on the fairly straightforward reef at Suva on Viti Levu. I point out that each crew was foolishly attempting to enter at night when they could have safely stayed offshore.

Pier, captain of the Swan named *Splash Tango*, invites us back to his boat to play guitar, but it is too close to dinner. While we macho men build fires, our ladies giggle and gossip in whispers, probably confiding, quite rightly, that their spouses are sun-crazed idiots.

About 50 to 100 cruisers from all over the world join together in Musket Cove for a barbeque each evening. Within a week of attending, you can learn pretty much everything you need to know about voyaging from, say, Tahiti to Darwin.

I always leave a small, dim, low-current anchor light alit aboard *Wild Card* so, if we're unexpectedly delayed ashore, she will be properly illuminated. I pick it out easily as we make our way back in the dark with Carolyn playing Statue of Liberty with our flashlight. I believe we're in greater danger at night in our dinghy than in deep ocean aboard *Wild Card* because of unlit fools at the helm of dangerously high-powered dinghies.

Once back aboard, Carolyn makes us herbal tea—Red Zinger for me, Tension Tamer for her—and we read for an hour or two. I finish up Michael Chabon's *The Wonder Boys* and begin on George Pelacanos's *Soul Circus*—two great writers working different vineyards.

At about 2100, Carolyn yawns and says, "To bed or should we get desperate?"

"I'm up for one," I say booting up the DVD player and slapping in a disk of the first season of *Desperate Housewives.* It's weird, watching it in Fiji. I'm sort of losing touch with my culture, but is this what suburbia has become?

Around 2200, I brush my teeth, check that both my (GPS) position and depth alarms are correctly set and somersault into the V-berth next to Carolyn. I'm just about to drift off when I realize, with a weary start, that I failed to read my business e-mail. Damn! I don't want to, but, hey, I must. After all, I'm a professional, or at least I have to keep up the facade.

So I reverse-somersault back out of bed, relight the computer screen at the darkened nav station, and quickly find the e-mail in question.

It's from John Burnham, the new editor at *Cruising World.* I don't know him well, but I'm learning he has a sharp red pen—and that the harder he works, the better I look.

"How about a "Day in the Life" column in which you tell how you while away all those idle cruising hours," it reads.

I smile as I head back to my bunk.

Hooked on Circumnavigating

For this gang, once around the globe wasn't enough.

"Let's see," says 58-year-old American Bob Taylor. "We're currently on our fifth. We completed our fourth circumnavigation in 2002."

Bob's sailor's sailor: a man of great passion, boyish enthusiasm, and a boundless thirst for offshore adventure. A liveaboard child (his family's boat was moored in front of John Wayne's house in California for many years), he can't seem to get enough of sailing. And during those rare moments when he isn't sailing, he's surfing.

He's a larger-than-life, gray-haired surfer dude who loves to joyously shout, "Hang loose! Hold Tight! Live while you're alive!"

It isn't easy keeping up with Bob; I had to fit this interview in between his morning surf run, afternoon siesta and all-evening every-evening mega beach party ashore

"My father was a Transpac racer and we owned *Corsair*, a 12-Meter built in 1912, then a Lapworth 36, even a 65-foot trawler," says Bob. "So I was always around boats, and my parents took me cruising in Mexico when I was 3 or 4. Boats are the one constant in my life. Well, surfing too!"

Bob, and his nice-but-tough-as-nails Canadian wife Glenda, are currently in Fiji and have been for awhile. Why? Because there are five good surf breaks within 15 minutes of their boat. But as nice as it is here in Musket Cove, Malololailai, Bob and Glenda are leaving soon for Indonesia. Why? "Even *better* surf breaks," giggles Glenda.

Bob and Glenda hooked up while Bob was working as a deep-sea diver for a Southeast Asia oil company. "When he asked me to go offshore with him, I figured why not have an exciting week or two sailing?"

The rest, as they say, is history.

"Before I met Glenda I was a tad wild," Bob admits. "I never checked the weather. I'd just leave whenever the boat was ready. Now, I'm mellowing a bit. I watch my weather and I don't push my boat as hard. I'd rather be comfortable for eight days, than fast and miserable for six."

One of Bob's strangest experiences was being hired to deliver a boat from Australia to Greece. The owner never paid him, so Bob sued and ended up with *Neptune's Car*, a 40-foot, center-cockpit steel ketch.

"I sailed it around the world in celebration," he laughs.

His current vessel, the 45-foot fractional-rigged *Nero*, is a 1978 sloop designed by John Lidgard and cold-molded from kauri wood.

"We're real pleased with her after all these miles," reports Bob. "*Nero* is fast, stable and, best off all, well-built. After all she's been through; she's in better shape than ever. We recently added a fixed dodger and better back rests in the cockpit. What a joy she is to cruise aboard!"

What's next on the itinerary?

"Well, we've only been to 93 countries, says Bob with a grin. "I'd like to make that at least 100 before I hang up my Topsiders." That's Bob in a nutshell. He went to sea thinking "isn't this cool" as a child and is still doing it for the same marvelous reason more than 50 years later.

Circumnavigator Michael Grunstein is a completely different story. The New York real-estate investor—he's married to a concert violinist and they have two sons—was 50 years old before he jumped into sailing.

It didn't take him long, however, to become enthralled with the cruising life. "I'm having a tremendous amount of fun," he says. "I'm having new exciting experiences my friends can only dream of. There is always something different happening—new harbors, new friends, new cultures."

His current boat is *Yonita*, a 53-foot ketch-rigged Amel Super Maramu 2000 built in La Rochelle, France. She has all the toys: washer/dryer, dishwasher, watermaker, bow-thruster—even electric reefing and main/jib sheeting!

"We're very pleased with her," smiles Michael. "The company builds a great boat and really stands behind it. We've had almost no problems, and the small issues we did have were remedied immediately. I can't say enough about the boat and company."

Michael first sailed around the world from 1995 to 2000 on board a Choy Lee 42, while his wife, Nily Grunstein, continue with her musical career in New York and Israel.

"I had a wonderful time," admits Michael, "sometimes with pick-up crew and sometimes singlehanding. But now that Nily's with me, it is even better!"

Nily's the first to admit that she finds cruising life a challenge and hasn't adjusted completely yet. But she is also quick to point out how fascinated she is with the whole process.

"I've got a background in psychology as well as music," she says, "And I find the sailing life very strong, very rich. It is a different life than from ashore. I even sleep and dream differently. The whole world strikes me as a playground now. I've undergone a sort of purification of mind. Everything I see, smell, and feel seems more intense. I feel like I'm being healed and cleansed at the same time."

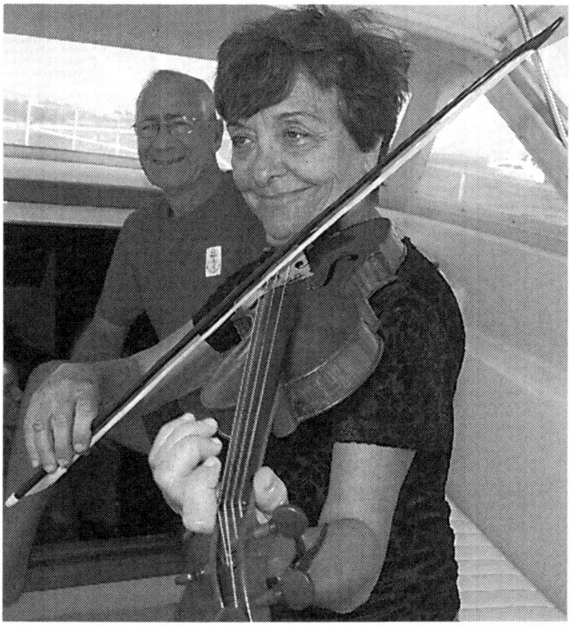

Michael smiles at her carefully chosen words. "She gave a Bach concert to a couple of yachties who just happened to be anchored off a deserted island at Suwarrow Atoll, in the Cook Islands, playing her violin that was handcrafted in the time of Captain Cook."

He pauses. Thinks. Sighs. "It was as lovely as it was unexpected."

Where to now?

"Thailand, then across the Indian ocean to Africa," says Michael. "After that, one of our sons wants to use the boat for a year, so we'll use the time to land travel. Then we hope to rejoin the boat and sail to Brazil, where our other son lives with our new grandchild."

Any plans to sell the boat?

"No," says Nily, "we like her too much. Look at the woodwork. It is lovely, isn't it? Michael wanted to put a picture on the main bulkhead but I stopped him. It is so beautiful just the way it is. Just like living in a violin!"

Kiwis always have a lovely way of understating things and Paul Hickey is no exception. With his wife, Ann-Marie, Paul currently sails the lovely 46-foot masthead sloop *Solar,* a Germain Frers design that was cold-molded in kauri wood in 1982 by Brin Wilson.

"When we finally rejoined the fleet of circumnavigators on the Coconut Milk run in French Polynesia and heard all the horror stories of transiting the Panama Canal—crushed boats, bent stanchions, ripped-up toe rails—I was happy Ann-Marie and I took the easy route!" he says.

Easy Route? That's how Paul casually refers to their Cape Horn rounding in 2000 aboard their previous vessel, the 36-foot *Harlequin*, which was also built by Brin Wilson.

"We hardly ever mention that we sailed around Cape Horn," notes Ann-Marie, bouncing their 2-year-old son Daniel—aka Captain Handful—on her lap. "It is sort of conversation stopper. People think we're weird!"

My wife, Carolyn, and I first met Paul and Ann-Marie just after their Cape Horn rounding in 2000. After some 40 days at sea, they landed on Hiva Oa in French Polynesia, on a Sunday, with no money, no liquor, and very low on food.

As their anchor rode paid out, we immediately delivered to them the equivalent of $100 in French Polynesian francs, a six-pack of cold beer, a bottle of strong rum, a bag of ice, and a sack of gourmet treats.

"But you don't even know us," they said in wonder as we piled the loot in their cockpit.

"No," I admitted, "but if you've been around the Horn, I admire you!"

We became fast friends, and delighted in each other's company on various Pacific islands during the 2000 season. And we were delighted to unexpectedly bumped into them again six years later in Fiji.

"Our 1997 to 2000 circumnavigation was really fun," says Paul. "We sailed from New Zealand across the Indian Ocean to Cape Town, South Africa, up to England, back down to the Horn and home to New Zealand. It wasn't difficult. The funniest part was arriving back in New Zealand and taking part in the local club races. We were used to having a week or two to contemplate a tack!"

"Having Daniel aboard makes cruising a bit different," notes Ann-Marie. "We used to sail six-on/six-off and always be rested. Now, if I come off watch at dawn just as Daniel's waking up—well, forget sleep! He's full-on all day!"

"But he's a good sailor," says Paul. "He's never seasick, and if we're in heavy weather, he just sits in his car seat and amuses himself."

"But I wouldn't want to go around Cape Horn with a child," laughs Ann-Marie. "It isn't hard, but, hey, it is *cold* down there!"

"I just enjoy sailing," says Paul. "Sure, we've been around the world already and we've seen some things, but I just love all aspects of cruising and sailing, even heavy weather. Why, we once crossed the Agulhas Current off South Africa in 45 knots—wow!"

"We'll return to New Zealand for the summer," says Ann-Marie. "Then do more of the western South Pacific the following seasons including Vanuatu and New Caledonia."

"Any major trips planned for the future," I ask.

"Not really," says Ann-Marie, "with the baby we just take it one day at a time." Behind her Paul is grinning, nodding yes in response to my question, and putting a finger to his lips in secrecy.

Then I see it again: that flash in his eye, as if he can stare at things that make other men tremble. The Cape Horn glint, I call it.

"You never know, Fatty," he laughs, "This new boat sails pretty good. It would be a shame to keep her in harbor, eh?"

There is one thing immediately obvious about circumnavigators Alicia Lavigne and Alfredo Vogliardi: They are in love. Every time she looks at him, it's as if she is gazing upon a handsome movie star. Every time he glances at her, he grins as if he can't believe his good fortune to have found such a fun-loving, adventurous life partner.

Alicia Lavigne was about two years old when her father began to teach her to sail. At the age of 10, in Mobile, Alabama, she purchased her own vessel, a beat-up Sunfish. In 1996, she and a former boyfriend took off to sail around the world aboard *On Vera*, a Rifiki 37 designed by Stan Huntingford.

In 2002 they were in Chagos, a mainly deserted archipelago in the middle of the Indian Ocean, where she jumped ship after falling in love with Alfredo, a dashing Italian fellow—and former lingerie salesman.

Alfredo had been singlehanding for more than seven years aboard his 34-foot steel boat—and he didn't take kindly to Alicia's fussiness as a navigator.

"She's good, but worried with the charts," says Alfredo. "I'm more laid-back, more intuitive."

Unfortunately, off the coast of Brazil, with Alicia in her bunk suffering a high fever, Alfredo "got careless for one second" and hit a reef. Within two minutes, his boat—only six days from completing its circumnavigation—was gone. The liferaft failed to open. And, of course, their inflatable wasn't inflated. They were in the water. Swimming. Dazed.

"A can of cocoa floated by," recalled Alfredo, "and I collected it. I passed by some toilet-paper rolls and a jug of diesel fuel. It didn't seem real."

"We didn't panic," Alfredo continued. "But we were sort of in shock. I mean, one moment everything was fine, it was a beautiful sunny day, and then we were swimming."

It was six miles to shore and there was a strong current. Luckily, after a short while, they came across a swimming platform, and had just enough energy to climb up on it.

"I make a mistake," Alfredo says sadly, "One minute I pay no attention. I pay for it big, eh?"

"But," chimes in Alicia, "we immediately had three very positive experiences. We got a sailboat ride to Trinidad within two days of being shipwrecked, and there, we were immediately hired to skipper a brand new Hallberg-Rassy 64. And, even more amazing, when my former boyfriend found out about our situation, he... well, he gave us his boat—the boat I originally set out on to sail around the world."

The world of circumnavigators is a small one. Unusual things happen. People who live this life make decisions and help each other in ways at which landlubbers can only marvel.

"So," said Alfredo, "we decided, hey, we have a new, good boat. So we sail around again, eh?"

"Only this time," notes the chart-watching Alicia wryly, "I do the navigation, and we just take our time."

Where are they headed to next?

"Alicia has talked me into sailing from New Zealand to Chile," laughs Alfredo. "Straight across the Southern Ocean. She is some kind of woman, no? So we lash on the storm trysail, bolt down the floors and see what happens next!"

"I like a challenge," says Alicia. "New places, new people, new horizons. We have no children, no careers. We aren't tied down in any way. Why not live free?"

Yes, there is something strangely addictive about The Big Fat Circle. Life, once tasted at this level of freedom and fulfillment, is forever desired. I know. I, too, can't seem to get enough. But sailing without end isn't all roses. Like anything else, there are downsides. This, too, I know.

"If you can't find the time to tell me exactly where you are," said one testy e-mail from our now-citified daughter Roma Orion, "then at least inform me what continent you're sailing to next!"

But most of the time she understands. She recently asked me pensively, "Do think circumnavigating was the coolest thing you've ever done?"

"No," I said.

"No?" she asked, startled.

"No," I repeated. "Continuing was."

The Ecstasy of Vanuatu

The Fat Man hates to play favorites, but Vanuatu just might be one.

"I'm going back out," I called forward to my wife, Carolyn. "This isn't it. We're almost on the reef, hon."

"No," she said, holding on to the swaying mast. "Don't be silly, Fatty. It's here. We just can't see it. Get in a tad closer."

We were off Tanna, an island in Vanuatu, in the southwest Pacific Ocean, and we were looking for the tiny harbor of Port Resolution.

Wild Card, our modest S&S-designed 38-foot sloop, had just made a lumpy and squally four-day crossing from Fiji. We were ready for a break from windy Mother Ocean.

"I see no harbor or town." I shouted. "I'm going to jibe onto starboard, head back offshore, and then we'll..."

"Wait," Carolyn shouted. "Up there. On the bluff. Is that a nav light?"

"Masthead," I shouted in relief. "And I bet there's a boat underneath it. OK, we've found the harbor. Now all we need is the entrance!"

We'd only traveled a couple of more yards to the west when the shadowed cove suddenly revealed itself like a tropical magic trick. The entrance was plain as day—two breaking white reefs with a narrow gash of deep blue between.

"That's it," I said. "I see it clearly now. I'll crank the Perkins; you drop the mainsail, OK?"

"Yeah," she said. "There are three boats rolling around in there and I could have sailed passed this place a dozen times without seeing them. A perfect hideaway, eh?"

"Then let's hide-a-way!" I said as I put Wild Card into gear and cautiously headed in.

Port Resolution is littered with rocks: small pebbles that are perfect for the slingshots the local kids use, medium-sized stones that are great for throwing, and giant multi-ton boulders the size of large trucks. All these, and millions more, were thrown miles through the air from the active Yasur Volcano, which is at the very core of both the island of Tanna and the psyche of its warm, primitive people.

You can hear the volcano for miles. It sounds scary, and it's still taboo in the minds of many locals. Even on board you can feel its thudding through the bedrock.

You can also see it: in the daytime, sulfurous smoke, and at night, a dull, red flare on the underside of the low scudding clouds. It has been active for a long, long time.

Captain James Cook, aboard the *HMS Resolution,* spotted it in August 1774, and pulled into a small bay, which he named after his ship, to investigate.

From our Western perspective, this was a long time ago. But time in Vanuatu is a Johnny-come-lately thing: the last bad hurricane, World War II, and Cook's arrival, reside in about the same vague time zone: the past. And their rich oral history traditions make it seem like a recent event.

"When our village woke up and saw Cook and his huge boat in the harbor, we immediately decided to kill him," a villager told me, as if he was recounting something that happened last week. "But one of our chiefs, a wise one, said, "First we learn from them, *then* we kill 'em!'"

Luckily, the learning process is still going on.

Vanuatu, which means "land eternal," consists of more than 80 islands running approximately 500 miles north to south. It lies 1600 nautical miles east-southeast of the Torres Strait, which separates Australia from Papua New Guinea. Vanuatu, formerly called New Hebrides, was once home to almost a million Melanesian people. That was before the missionaries arrived to bring "civilization" and quickly reduced the population, courtesy of cholera, smallpox, and measles, to 41,000. Some islands experienced a 95-percent decline in residents. Currently, about 215,000 people live in Vanuatu.

The islands were originally settled by the Lapita explorers from New Guinea in 2000 B.C. Both the Portuguese and the French passed through before Cook. It's still an extremely undeveloped country, with 80-percent of its population surviving off subsistence farming in villages of 50 people or less.

Port Resolution is the only semi-safe harbor on Tanna. It's on the windward side of the island, far away from the main town of Lenakel. But as hidden as the harbor at Port Resolution is, it's still open to the north, and a persistent swell works its way between the narrow reefs. We anchored *Wild Card* bow and stern to face the rhythmic dip, and consequently, we were completely comfortable for the two weeks we stayed.

Around the harbor, it steams in numerous spots. You can find a perfect place to bathe (warmish), while doing your laundry (warmer), heating your food (hot) and boiling your lobsters (very hot.)

Just be careful. Stephanie, who sails the Westsail 32, *Mico Verde,* bathed in one warm pool and waded in another, then foolishly hopped into a third without checking, and boiled the skin off her foot in a horrible instant.

Getting ashore in the dinghy isn't easy either: the water is mucky from the black-sand volcanic run-off. There are no fish, because they don't like the high sulphur content, and coral heads, wrecks, and rocks abound.

Once the tiny village heard that we were Americans, they quickly summoned their chief. Chief Ronnie, 75 years old, seemed like a young, eager man as he hurriedly dashed up to us.

"The river," he cried. "Have you seen the river?"

"What?" I asked, completely taken aback by his intensity and excitement.

"The river in America!" Chief Ronnie cried. "In California! It is *huge*!"

Thank goodness for Carolyn and her valedictorian ways.

"The Colorado," she said.

"Yes!" said the chief, his eyes aglow. "You know it! You've been there. I told them (a sweep of his arm at the surrounding curious villagers) about it. What a river, eh?"

"Yes," I said. "The Colorado is a great, great river."

From that moment on, we were golden in the village.

Ronnie later brought us a tattered *National Geographic* magazine with a much-thumbed story about the Colorado River, which somehow had tickled his fancy.

Clearing in to Tanna should only take a few minutes, but it actually takes an entire day and requires a $100 bill. First, you have to rent the services of a pickup truck and its driver for a day. It's only 13 miles to the governmental offices in Lenakel, but it takes a solid two hours to drive there—and you'll be begging to go slower.

Road building isn't a high priority on Tanna. In fact, *nothing* is a high priority on Tanna.

I was literally black and blue for a week after the ride. Thank goodness I'd had the wisdom to bring a pillow for my seat.

Despite the bruises and expense, we had a great time. The pickup truck is also the informal island bus and farm produce vehicle, so we were constantly stopping to load and unload vegetables, people, and pigs.

The market in Lenakel was lovely, with many of the ladies so shy they had to work up their courage to take our pennies.

For lunch we went to a recently opened local restaurant, and were as pleased with the owner's quaint monologue as we were with the food.

"I am going to have hamburgers soon!" said the owner/cook/busboy. "Maybe next week. And beer, too. I don't have refrigeration, so I'll run to the market and bring it back cold. Oh, yes, carefully watch where you step on the floor because the palm-thatch covers the holes."

Actually, the floor was worse than that! The owner had put down floor braces and planked the floor. Unfortunately, he had no nails, so the planks were loose. Worse, he didn't arrange it so that the ends of the planks rested on the floor braces, instead, they just ended where they ended, often just hanging in space. When you stepped on one of these plank ends, you fell through the floor, while the plank's other end rocketed into the air. Hence the matting, which, (good news) inhibited the velocity of the swinging planks, but (bad news) made stepping on the unsupported ends impossible to avoid.

Our meal consisted of—well, we don't know. Rice and something. But it was good. With fruit juice and dessert, it came to less than US $2 each.

By the time we got back to Port Resolution, we felt we'd met most of the people on the island, and we loved them all.

There's something called the Port Resolution Nipikinamu (literal translation: "fish tail") Yacht Club and Resort. There are a couple of cabins which occasionally host some wide-eyed, jungle-dazed eco-tourists and there's the main "club house" that serves as a bar and restaurant.

"One soda, one beer," I told the girl behind the counter.

She panicked.

Then left.

So much for that.

Of course, we wanted to see Yasur Volcano, but I have a confession to make. I don't like heights. I'm a sea-level guy. Oh, I can handle it, sure. I mean, I go up my mast when need be, visit skyscrapers, even take airplanes flights.

But I like, well, low things.

Let's put it this way: Gravity scares me.

But, I wanted to get an up close-and-personal picture of the volcano and Carolyn wanted to see it, too, so off we went.

We arrived at the base of the volcano just after dark. It was a moonscape peppered with a billion tossed boulders, any one of which might have killed anything it landed on.

We climbed a path, and it brought us to a ledge that actually jutted out over the cauldron below. There was no rail, no wall, nothing. At our backs, trying to push us over the rim to our deaths, was a 20-knot easterly wind which would occasionally lull and then gust sharply to 30 knots.

Every few seconds, there would be a horrendous thundering sound, as if God was removing the lid of a giant, simmering pot, and directly in front of us, molten lava would shoot up hundreds of feet in the air.

Carolyn, of course, was wandering around as nonchalantly as if strolling on a golf course. (She wears glasses and her night vision is awful.)

With my hands shaking, I set up my tripod, thankful for the darkness so that none of the other six or seven onlookers could catch a glimpse my distress.

Frankly, I was too freaked to even think—especially when a fellow photographer with a tripod perched dangerously on the *very* edge, then turned to me and said, "I'm set at f/5 at 20 secs," or some such techno mumbo jumbo.

Carolyn smoothly covered for me, attempting to distract the others. But, alas, her patter had the opposite effect. "You don't say," the photographer cried and rushed to get her husband. "We read you guys all the time. Why, we helped to bankroll Tania Ebi on her circ!"

By this point I was on all fours and foaming at the mouth as Carolyn led them away with, "He really gets into these time exposures."

I won't bore you with more details of my shameful cowardice, just some small observations. One, I never believed in that "fire and brimstone" crap until I saw it first-hand. Two, a week later, a large molten clump of lava was reported to have landed exactly where we had been standing—and a shaken cruiser with a walking stick drew a smiley face on it as it cooled. And three, a year or so ago, two tourists and their guide had been killed by falling molten lava at the exact same spot.

The lofty masthead we'd spotted upon entering Port Resolution belonged to a custom, 74-foot, David Pedrick-designed sloop named *Nomadess*. The crew turned out to be swell folks with a wonderful tradition they'd developed while circumnavigating: Instead of having sundowners aboard to get acquainted with their fellow sea gypsies, they staged a big barbecue party ashore catered by the locals. Thus, everyone—local and visitor alike—got to know each other.

The entire village took part, with the men slaughtering a pig while the women cooked the food and the kids wove the traditional palm-frond plates decorated with hibiscus flowers.

I provided the music with my guitar, and soon we were all singing songs of 'The Bobs' as Carolyn calls them: Bob Dylan's "Blowin' in the Wind" and Bob Marley's "Redemption Song."

Carolyn and I are early risers, and we'd often pass through the village when Chief Ronnie was handing out work assignments. Perhaps we should've varied our hiking routine more. In any event, we were both amazed to hear Ronnie casually telling us to accompany his eldest son Stanley to the Pig's Bay Resort, run by Willie the Pig Man, and there put together a photo/essay to promote it.

At first I bristled. But hey, hadn't we wanted to be a part of village life? What could be a nicer compliment? So off we hiked with Stanley—a two-and-a-half-hour trek each way—along a dense jungle trail.

Now I've had some tough assignments in my day, but nothing to compare with *this* challenge. First off, it is important to realize that Vanuatu is sort of a pig-centric place. Pigs represent both money and prestige. So Willie the Pig Man was a very important guy in Vanuatu—and our village was intent on doing something to honor him.

The trouble was, there wasn't any resort or restaurant; it was all just a vague dream in Willies head. So there I was with my camera, and Carolyn was taking notes, near a pigsty that looked exactly how a pigsty looks. "How the hell are we gonna spin *this* one," I whispered to Carolyn, who at least was able to hide her smile behind her steno pad.

But, hey, I'm a professional, so I clicked away and I even asked a polite question or two for effect.

Afterward, I was playing with a particularly cute pig—the smartest, most affectionate of the group—when Willie asked if I liked that one. When I unthinkingly said yes, the club came down and I was immediately paid in full for my services, Vanuatu-style.

Later that day, I decided, once again, to attempt the impossible. I walked into Port Resolution Nipikinamu Yacht Club and said, "One beer, one soda," to the same girl.

Her eyes got wide. Her nostrils flared. Her hands started to flutter nervously. She jumped up to flee, but I stepped into her path. "Beer and soda!" I demanded.

There was no ice in the cooler, so the beer was warm. The cooler was also locked so the local boys couldn't sample the wares. There was a key but the girl didn't have it. She knew who did, sort of. However, since there wasn't much call for beer or soda because there were never any customers, she hadn't seen the guy in a long, long time. However, if I'd just step out of the way, she'd be happy to attempt to find him, which she was fairly sure she could not do.

Carolyn started laughing as the barmaid dashed off down the path.

By now, an Amel 52 named *Wanderer,* had arrived with an Italian-American named Vito aboard. He was from Brooklyn and had a New York accent, and looked like he just sailed out of an episode of *The Sopranos.*

"Don't worry, Fat Stuff," he told me when he heard my tale of woe. "I'll get the beer!"

It took him days but he stayed focused. With the help of Chief Ronnie and Stanley—and, perhaps, after a little contribution to the tribal slush fund—Vito was soon happily zooming around the harbor while swilling a six-pack of warm beer.

"You the man, Vito," I said, and admitted I'd been bested.

One of the reasons that Port Resolution is seldom visited is because it is to windward of the capitol of Port-Vila, on Éfaté. We'd sailed here first to avoid the windward beat. So when our visit to Tanna drew to a close, we had a delightful, 150-mile, overnight downhill sail to the "big city." We were becalmed in sloppy seas in the lee of the island of Erromango for quite a while. Perhaps sailing to the east of it would make for a slightly smoother passage.

Port-Vila is considerably more modern than Tanna. It felt as if we'd traveled across 150 years as well as the 150 miles in between.

Its entrance presents no problem, but watch for the drooping overhead power cable in the inner harbor: Its height depends upon when it was last tightened. Our 48-foot mast passed under easily, but loftier vessels have hit it at high tide.

Once ashore, we soon bumped into Tony the Taxi, who was overjoyed to hear us sing the praises of Tanna, which was his home island, "where my heart is still!"

"There tomorrow is wedding," he said excitedly. "A Tanna boy will marry a local girl. You invited. There will be dancing and fun. Yes?"

The ni-Vanuatu love visitors and invite them everywhere for everything. It's a prestige thing. (Always bring a small gift, and contribute a little something to cover the food expenses.)

The wedding turned out to be the highlight of our cruising year. The bride-price was steep: a giant pile of gifts, a huge cow, and, of course, some pigs.

The killing of the pig "seals the deal," said Tony. "Once the pig is dead, they're married."

The pig was clubbed to death by a fellow who needed some points in heaven. It was a special honor to be asked, like being best man, Vanuatu-style.

There was dancing and kava and speeches by both fathers and both chiefs, and much merriment all around.

I was particularly touched by the father of the groom urging the father of the bride to accept the dowry: "Please accept these gifts." He said ceremoniously to the other man. "Our relatives have stood with us and helped us through this successful marriage of our children. You and I and them—and our villages and islands—we're all blessed."

Now there are two local styles of dancing: jumping up and down, and jumping up and down while running in a circle. Carolyn and I soon became proficient in both.

Between dances, I pulled her aside and panted, "I finally have the answer to that big question."

"Yeah?" she laughed. "Really?"

"Sure," I said, still huffing and puffing. "As we circumnavigate, everyone is always asking us, 'Which is the best place in the world?' I've always avoided directly answering by dazzling them with a vast list of how many places we've fallen in love with along the way. But, after tonight and last week in Tanna," I continued, "I can truthfully say that it's Vanuatu!"

"You know what I think?" Carolyn asked me.

"No," I said.

"I think you should just shut up and dace, Fatty."

Staying Ahead With the Sea Anchor

Good storm tactics preserve Wild Card and her crew—and remind the captain to buy a new piece of line.

Carolyn looked up as I closed the drippings companionway and began peeling off my foulies, "Oh, she's in a grand mood today," I said. Some of the waves out there are impressive."

"Is that how you think of them?" she mused as she stared out the dim, salt-encrusted porthole at the white horses galloping by. Suddenly another wave hit like a hand grenade on our starboard bow, and the whole boat slowed to a rattle as the tons of water bounded aboard. "I think 'scary' is more accurate," Carolyn sighed.

I went forward and took a look at where the wooden joint of our hanging locker and drawers had cracked with excessive hull flexing. It was a tad disconcerting.

We were heading for Tonga, we were four days north of New Zealand, and we were in a typical autumn gale. The wind was blowing a steady 35 to 38 knots, the seas, in the absence of any cross swell, were breaking uniformly, mostly 12 and 14 feet high. Occasionally a larger, more "exuberant" wave would leap by. The highest wind gust we'd recorded was 47 knots.

We were in no danger. We were hove to. We've come through many gales that were far worse. Still, *Wild Card,* our 38-foot, salvaged, sunk-after-a-hurricane, fiberglass production craft for which we paid $3,000, is a very modest boat. I don't like to push her hard; she was designed and built as a weekender.

Another factor: it was late afternoon. If we wanted to work on deck, now would be the time.

Our last weather report indicated the low that was causing our squash zone might deepen and move southward into our higher pressure. This scenario rang warning bells with me. It was just such a low-pressure zone bomb that caused the infamous Queen's Birthday storm in this very same area, at about this same time of year

The deciding factor was highly personal: I believe in being proactive. I've always felt that many of the Queen's Birthday deaths could have been avoided if decisive, defensive storm tactics had been set into motion early. A lot of things are far, far easier in 35 knots than 55.

Besides, I'd never done what I was about to do and I dearly love what I call "learning by adventure."

"I'm gonna toss over the Para-Tech," I said nonchalantly. "This is an ideal time to see how *Wild Card* will lay to a sea anchor in a breeze."

"Oh, *Fatty*," Carolyn said wearily and didn't continue. She just chewed on her lip.

This is as close as my wife ever gets to insubordination. She knows I'm captain and that I call storm-tactics, but she also knows setting and retrieving a sea anchor in gale-force conditions is potentially dangerous.

"Buck up, babe," I told her. "I'll inspect the sea anchor. You get the rodes together. We can't make any mistakes as it pays out. Once it pays out, it's like a loaded gun until we're laying to it, OK?"

"Aye, aye Captain," she said, and wisely left the unspoken "Bligh" part out.

Despite carrying our 15-foot Para-Tech sea anchor around the world and more, we'd never deployed it. The few times I'd considered it, it was already fairly late in the game to do so. Besides, I've only been truly worried three times in 47 years and 100,000 ocean miles—and each of those times involved an ocean current *and* very severe weather. We had neither this time. So I wasn't deploying it for the conditions we *had,* but rather what we *might get*— as well as for the battlefield experience of it.

The sea anchor was all set to go; even the bow roller bolt—to prevent the rode from being knocked upward out of the roller should *Wild Card* stick her nose into large seas—was still duct-taped in place on the swivel from eight years ago.

The problem was our rodes. In 1998 I'd purchased two "dedicated" 300-foot emergency rodes for exactly this purpose, but had used them as anchor rodes in various gales during which they'd been heavily-chafed. Our sea-anchor rode now consisted of five different types and sizes of nylon line connected with double carrick bends—not ideal.

But there's a lot of stuff that isn't ideal aboard *Wild Card* which is one reason we're able to average 5,000 ocean miles a year on a very limited budget.

Here's how we set the Para-Tech, step-by-step: I took the bitter end of the rode forward, careful to make sure it was outside of all stanchions, shrouds, and the like. I led it through the bow roller, slid the bolt in so it couldn't escape, then tied it off to our main foredeck cleat with 100 feet on deck in reserve.

Once back in the cockpit, I helped Carolyn carefully coil the entire remaining rode onto the cockpit floor, so that it would pay out safely. Since we were hove to, *Wild Card* was barely moving, just slightly fore-reaching. First, I made sure Carolyn's body was completely behind the rode, so an unexpected hockle couldn't snag her, and that my two knives were ready at hand in case the rode snagged around the backstay or self-steering gear. I hesitated. In fact, I stopped for a couple of seconds and carefully went over each step of my plan.

I had time to think now, not once it was in the water.

"Ready?" I asked Carolyn.

She was all business now. "Ready!"

"Here we go," Over our windward side, near our sheet winches, I dropped a small bleach bottle attached to 100 feet of three-eighths poly, a small swivel and another 50 feet or so of nylon webbing. This was the retrieval system. Once I was sure all this had paid out correctly, I unlatched the locking device on the 15-foot Para-Tech anchor, then tossed it and its bag in the water.

Now, it was serious.

I paid out the rode carefully, with Carolyn's help. On the few occasions when problems seemed about to develop, Carolyn was able to warn me in advance, and I was thus able to deploy the entire 400 feet of rode without, literally, a hitch.

Since *Wild Card* was barely moving, coming to the end of the rode wasn't violent. The feeling was more like a hooked fish attempting to swim away.

I dashed forward and dropped the double-reefed main. *Wild Card* fell back. I paid out scope until the boat and the sea anchor were on wave crests at the same time.

It was just like being anchored in a very large sea. I felt perfectly safe. In fact, my only task as a skipper now was to keep *Wild Card* attached to the drogue and keep a sea-anchor watch so we wouldn't be run down. None of the seas hit us too hard or swept us. I wasn't the least bit worried about our rudder snapping off. It was well tied amidships, but it wasn't being shock-loaded nearly as much as I thought it would be.

We spent the first day relaxing, resting, and marveling at the raw power of Mother Ocean. The second day, Carolyn made bread while I wrote in my log and caught up on our shipboard e-mail. On the third day we retrieved the sea anchor.

During the entire three days we felt perfectly safe. In fact I almost wanted the wind to increase another 20 knots just to see how she'd ride. But we were fairly uncomfortable. True, Carolyn made bread and I e-mailed, but we felt like bull riders while doing so. The motion was extreme to the max. Picture the roughest anchorage you've ever been in, multiply it by ten, and you're still short of the berserk-elevator reality.

I attempted to rig a bridle to allow me to rehoist my double-reefed main (at a 45-degree angle to the seas) for stability, but found there were too many technical issues I hadn't thought through. Stanchions, fairleads, and bow-pulpit chafe issues all had to be carefully considered.

Of course, we were safe only as long as the boat stayed connected to the sea-anchor, so I was continuously concerned with chafe. My solution was to use separate half-inch pennants tied with rolling-hitches to my main five-eighths-inch Gold-N-Braid rode. This allowed me to renew the chafing gear as well as keep veering out additional line to change the chafe spot every two hours.

Even so, I broke two pennants. There's a massive amount of force involved when the vessel is struck by a large sea and shoved backward. Massive! So I'd immediately (both times were, of course, at night) go on deck, rig another pennant and veer out the main rode until it would take up.

This is easy and straightforward, but, hey, it's also dangerous. I've been through dozens of hurricanes and have had considerable experience handling lines under high loads. You have to be *very* careful it you want to end up with all your fingers and toes. It was marvelous watching *Wild Card* climb up the backs of the steep waves. Just when I'd think, "This massive 18-foot sea will surely bury her," she'd daintily rise to the occasion. There's a reason for this. Since *Wild Card* is so narrow and light forward, we lash all our anchor chain and anchors to the mainmast base in the head during long passages. And we use the forward-most water tank first for the same reason. Thus, Wild Card climbs large breaking waves as buoyant as a swan.

The only real difficulty was retrieval of the Para-Tech. This should have been easy, with Carolyn judiciously bumping our M30 Perkins into gear while I toed our faithful Maxwell windlass. But it wasn't. My double-carrick knots wouldn't pass easily through our bow roller nor would they rotate smoothly around our gypsy head, which was completely my cheap-skate fault. (I was well aware of this situation and made an incorrect decision not to buy a new sea anchor rode—a decision I now regret and will rectify as soon as reasonably possible.)

Thus I was forced to rig many temporary pennants to inch my way past the knots. But we managed—with only two brief "hissing" moments of the rode almost-but-not-quite getting away from me.

It took two and a half hours of extremely difficult physical work to get the sea anchor back aboard. Our correctly deployed retrieval line was useless—a common problem.

Of course, we weren't the only boat to go through this fairly modest gale. Two other vessels set their sea anchors within 50 miles of us. About half-a-dozen boats hove to under storm trysail. However, another dozen or so just kept going. A few made it through without incident, but two turned back to New Zealand. One had seawater in its diesel engine from excessive heeling. Another broke its boom. One roller furler spit its bearings. Two sails were blown to tatters. Several didn't get to Tonga, and ended up running off to downwind destinations like Fiji and Vanuatu. Numerous boats incurred damages, with repairs costing anywhere from $5,000 to $10,000.

The scariest incident was hearing, "I'm sinking!" on the SSB when the panicky skipper of a very well-found 60-footer discovered his forward cabin was full of seawater from a stove-in hatch. The boat had a watertight crash bulkhead, and its skipper only learned he had a problem when seawater started sloshing into the main cabin from the shared dorade vents!

Wild Card pulled into Tonga a week later with absolutely nothing to fix, buy or repair. And I'm no longer intimidated by my sea anchor. It is a useful tool, but when it is set, the ride is mighty *uncomfortable,* and retrieving it is not easy, either, so neither Carolyn nor I will ever set it lightly or without careful preparation.

Perhaps our last verbal exchange on deck, just before I got the sea anchor back aboard, summed it up best.

"Having fun?" Carolyn shouted forward, knowing I was completely, utterly, absolutely exhausted.

"Perhaps a bit *too* much," I said laughing, but a bit distracted by counting and recounting my fingers and toes.

Shooting the Pass

It's lonely when you're in command, but somebody has to do it.

We were an hour away from North Minerva Reef, south of the Fiji Islands, and we were ready for a rest from the Pacific Ocean. Besides, Carolyn—my wife, lover and first mate for the last 37 years—and I love midocean islandless atolls. We find them utterly peaceful: No land equals no problems in our little water-world view.

Alas, our hopes of finding North Minerva deserted were dashed when our new friends, the inexperienced offshore passage-makers Chris and Des

Trattles aboard *Sky Lark II*, a Shearwater 39, hailed us on the VHF "We're at the pass," Chris said to us. "How far are you out?"

"Oh, don't wait for us," I told him. "We're 6.8 miles away. It will take us over an hour! We'll see you inside,"

"We'll wait," he said curtly. I instantly understood what was going on.

If you're an experienced offshore sailor you are in constant contact with less-experienced cruisers and they often look to you for advice and assistance. Carolyn and I are almost always happy to help, as are most of our fellow sailors.

"I didn't want to make a major mistake out there," Alaska Jim Sublett recently told me after his first ocean crossing on *Bell Bird*, his 30-foot Denis Ganley-designed steel cutter. "I didn't want to screw-up offshore. The price can be too high. The cruising lifestyle is an exciting and wonderful one, but not *always* care-free!"

How true.

I remember how freaked out my friend Jennifer Scheifla was during her first trial-by-error passage from Travelift to marina slip.

"I was so green I was trembling," said Scheifla who sails the Ted Brewer-designed Verity 40 *Vigilant*, "So I used a little too much throttle while backing out, and damn near raked the boats astern of me. I barely got *Vigilant* into the slip without disaster. To check for leaks, I opened the floorboards and heard the shrimp snapping outside the hull. I'd never heard those strangely clicking sounds before. So I immediately rushed back to the shipyard office and demanded my boat be rehauled, it was cracking up or something! The yard told me that the shrimp were making the noises." Scheifla ended up successfully singlehanded her boat around the South Pacific for years. (Singlehanding isn't exactly true. She had a cat and a dog aboard, but, as she put it, "neither could steer worth a damn!".)

Anxiety can visit a big ship as well as a small one. During WWII my father who was second mate and senior navigator, was conning his ship through a submarine net off San Diego. His captain, recalled to service by the war was an old man in his dotage whom my father loved dearly and respected mightily. Suddenly he appeared on the bridge and changed course, saying they were headed for the net not the gate. My father, gently at first and then ever more forcefully, repeatedly attempted to stop the skipper from making a major mistake. But the skipper was the skipper, and the ship hit the cable at speed, severely damaging both the submarine net and the ship's propellers and rudders.

"The moment we struck," my father told me, "the skipper left the bridge and I resumed command. It was a mess, but with the help of tugs I got her to the shipyard area. I turned around and there was the skipper on the bridge in civilian clothes, diminished-looking now, with his two cardboard suitcases, completely disgraced in his own mind. I felt so very sorry for him. His country had called and he'd nobly risen to the occasion, despite his advancing age and physical infirmities. Now he'd failed, miserably. And all I could do was sincerely salute him while praying it would never be me."

These are, perhaps, dramatic examples, but our friend Chris was facing exactly the same challenges. Thus, I understood his hesitation. And the reason I'd politely but firmly urged him to shoot the pass himself wasn't that I didn't want to deal with him, but rather because I wanted him to gain the self-confidence to do it himself. But Chris wasn't quite ready yet—almost, perhaps, but not quite. So I decided to walk him slowly through it on the VHF, step by baby step.

"I've already begun," I told him, "by timing my arrival to have the sun over my shoulder. This will allow us to see the reef clearly—and any coral heads once inside. Also, I'm checking my paper and electronic charts with my actual sounder depths as I approach, trying to get a sense of how accurate my charts are. So far, they seem pretty close. I've also looked up the tide: it's low and just starting to rise. That's good. If we run aground, we'll be lifted off rather than set down. Since there shouldn't be less than 20 feet of depth in the channel, I've set my depth alarm for 15. If it rings, something's wrong. And should a visibility-limiting squall hit, I've plotted a "safe" magnetic-compass course through the pass in the unlikely event my two GPS units go down at the same time."

My talk of running aground evidently concerned Chris, so I quickly explained, "No, I don't expect to run aground. But I'm going to stack *all* the cards I can in my favor, not for what I think *will* happen but for what I think *might* happen. For instance, we keep our main anchor heavily lashed offshore and our anchor windlass disconnected from ship's power. But I just had Carolyn make sure both are ready to go, and that our lightweight aluminum kedge anchor is ready to splash as well." I took *Wild Card,* our S&S-designed 38-foot sloop, out of gear and glided almost to a halt in front of the pass. I checked my engine-temperature gauge and mentally confirmed I had plenty of diesel fuel. Carolyn went forward to read the water. As the bow watch, she knows to only point in the direction she wants me to steer the boat—never at the obstruction she wants me to avoid.

I watched Chris skillfully maneuver *Sky Lark II* just astern of me. "As we head into the pass," I said over the VHF, "we'll have both the wind and current against us. True, the tide is just starting to rise, but there's so much water slopping over the eastern side of the atoll, the current is obviously still flowing out. This has its advantages. It means that until we actually get into the cut and beyond, we're perfectly safe. At any point, for any reason, we can just turn away and have plenty of time to think *before* the cut. However, once we're a couple of inches inside, the reef becomes a dead lee shore and we *have* to gain some distance upwind and upcurrent of it. Oh, and one more thing, Chris, should *Wild Card* come to an abrupt stop, *do not* swing alongside to ask why. Stay behind me. Communicate only by VHF. Here we go!"

As we steamed into the utterly beautiful, completely pristine lagoon of the atoll, I pointed out how I was watching both my speed through the water and my speed over ground to gauge the velocity of the current. I also pointed out that I was checking both my magnetic compass *and* my GPS to see if I was being side-stepped by the current. Many a keel has stuck a reef sideways while the skipper maintained his proper compass course, not realizing the current was sidestepping the boat.

"What appears to be a deep-blue river in midcut is the deep water," I explained to Chris over the VHF. "The eddies are from the current bouncing off the reef. That sort of malignant-looking yellow water on the sides is about five feet deep and the white water is very shallow."

Once we were inside the atoll in smooth water I cautioned him, "Don't break out the champagne yet, Chris. This is where many newbies make the mistake of getting too lax. We're now out of the ocean swell and it feels safe—but it isn't. We don't have any real distance yet on the lee shore behind us. Until we do, we can't relax. And now is when we really have to keep an eye out for coral heads. Don't let our depth of sixty feet lull you—coral heads can rise up vertically from 100 feet, and be hard to spot amid the darkness of a patch of sea grass.

We powered for 2.7 nautical miles to windward until we were close the leeward side of the atoll's windward-breaking reef—but not *too* close if the wind changed. On a white sandy bottom, I put down my main chain rode and 44 pound Bruce, with a medium-sized Danforth as well in case of a sudden squall. I made sure both were well dug in and had a scope of seven to one. This still left me with two more good anchors on deck, should I have to divorce the Bruce and Danforth in the middle of the night.

As soon as *Wild Card* was squared away, I snorkeled around my anchors to make sure they were dug deep and that there were no lurking coral heads.

I was naked in the cockpit and just rinsing the salt off me with our deck-collected shower water when Chris called us again on Channel 16 and said, "I've just uncorked a bottle of red for Carolyn, and Des has put on the coffee pot for you Fatty. Bring your guitar too!"

Then we had the best kind of party aboard *Sky Lark II*; an impromptu one. Chris and Des even roped us into staying for dinner, "for all the knowledgeable help," as Chris put it.

A few days later they left and we had North Minerva Reef to ourselves for almost a week.

But the real end of this story came a few months and 1,000 ocean-miles later. We were approaching Funafuti, Tuvalu, unsure of which pass to transit in the brisk northerly breeze. Suddenly Chris was booming information to us on the VHF, confidently rattling off lats and longs, compass bearings and depths.

Carolyn and I had been at sea for a week. We were tired. It was nice to have accurate, firsthand information laid out so concisely for us. "You shouldn't have a problem," Chris concluded briskly. "And while you're threading your way through the coral heads, we'll be ashore at the Saturday market, can we get you some cucumbers or fresh tomatoes. Or some bakery goods, perhaps?"

"Yes, yes, yes," Carolyn and I both laughed into our radio and then I said, "And thanks, Chris, for your help."

"Don't mention it," he said, "That's what we sailors do, isn't it, help each other?"

"You bet," I said, grinning at the pride in his voice—pride he'd so recently earned and now so richly deserved. "We do indeed!"

Doing the Hemisphere Hop Through Yap

Micronesia's westernmost island group is known for betel nut chewers, coconut-beer drinkers, stone money, and topless women. What's not to like?

I hate being woken up, but it's an important part of a captain's job, so I always attempt to hide my irritation. "What?" I said drowsily, "I don't understand"

Normally, I get plenty of sleep on passage, but not this trip, not in the Intertropical Convergence Zone. It seemed that every time my head touched the pillow, my wife, Carolyn, would summon me back on deck.

"I don't know," she was mumbling. "The last two squalls looked just as bad, but had nothing in them. So I think maybe this one won't be too—"

Suddenly, *Wild Card*, our modest, world-weary 38-foot sloop, heeled sharply to port.

Instead of coming right back up as usual, she hunkered down even farther, as if she were being pressed deeper into the water by an invisible weight. Even worse, I could sense her beginning to round up from the squall's leading edge.

Our new Maximum wind speed indicator started wailing—the alarm was set to trip at 42 knots.

"Shit!" said normally-not-a-gutter-mouth Carolyn as she spun around in the darkness of the main cabin and started to claw her way back into the tilted cockpit. "Fatty, I *need* you!"

I needed no additional urging as I jack-in-the-boxed out of my bunk and joined her outside in the pitch-black, spray-strewn night.

But it took a second or two to get into our respective positions, clear our sheet, and nod our mutual readiness. As a result, we were a tad late in furling the jib. The vicious squall was now fully upon us, hunching and hovering directly overhead like a malevolent genie.

"Easing!" I shouted over the squall's roar as I carefully fed out the jib sheet. "Put your back into it, babe!"

"Need help," Carolyn grunted. I slid next to her straining body and grabbed the iron-barred jib-furling line as well. Within the blink of an eye, the jib was rolled. I clicked the Monitor windvane dead down and *Wild Card* stood as upright as a righteous man in church—and perfectly safe.

"Whew!" Carolyn said with a grin, "Like I was saying, this one looks like it has a ton of wind in it!'"

"Good call," I joked back, as I, too, attempted to catch my breath. "Your hindsight forecasts are 20/20, eh?"

"Pretty much," she admitted sheepishly.

It isn't as if I didn't know better. Twice a year, *Wild Card* runs from hurricane season. Since we like to hang out in the tropics, this means we either change hemispheres or head for the poles. Last year, we spent the Southern Hemisphere's storm season in New Zealand, at 40-degrees south, where the chance of getting hit by a tropical cyclone or typhoon is slim. We could've done the same this year, but instead we decided to switch hemispheres and revisit Southeast Asia. The only problem is that each time you switch hemispheres; you have to cross the Convergence Zone, an area of disturbed weather that lies between the two major weather systems, one in the Northern Hemisphere and one in the Southern Hemisphere, of our planet.

The Convergence Zone isn't fun. It's full of squalls—some quite nasty—and has numerous areas of calms in between them. Thus, the poor sailor within is repeatedly wacked, wacked, and wacked again by high winds only to wallow helplessly in the wave-generated slop amid the calms. The only good news is that the zone is usually only between 150 and 300 miles wide, and if it's traversed at 90 degrees to the equator, well, the sailing misery doesn't last long.

Notice I said "usually?"

On this transit, we crossed the equator back into the Northern Hemisphere in November in hopes of sailing northwestward to the Philippines or Hong Kong in December. Alas, Mother Nature didn't cooperate. Instead of *no* storms tracking west along 10 degrees north, there was a steady stream of them. Thus, because we wanted to spend as much time as possible in the Southeast Asia, we decided to run westward just south of the storms—for 1500 miles of Convergence Zone misery.

"Another great plan gone awry, eh?" Carolyn joked. "What is it with you, Fatty haven't suffered enough lately?"

"Well," I shot back. "I want to practice Zen patience and what better place?"

"Watch what you hope for," she said, waving a finger in warning, "Nothing is more frustrating that squalls 24/7! If you're not on your way to tuck in a reef, you're shaking one out. Remember the time you got so mad, you actually ran forward and punched the jib?"

"That was in 1960s," I said. "A long time ago!"

"And, you're wiser now?" she parried.

"No," I admitted. "I'm a better lover maybe, but not wiser; just more patient, more accepting of life's quirky challenges."

"Then get used to sleeping all-standing (in your foulies) for the next month or so," she said.

The problem with sailing the world for nearly 40 years with a woman like Carolyn is that she's always right. Lots of people talk about "my better half," but that is just the literal, accurate description in my case. And I'm blessed in another way. "I'll follow you to the ends of the earth," she's told me numerous times over the years, while doing so.

Yes, I try to count my blessings but the numbers are huge.

Wild Card, our $3,000 hurricane-salvaged rambling-wreck of a sailboat, is another matter. Since I make only small money, but have big dreams, we're usually running on a micro-budget. This means that if I want to spend our pennies actually cruising, I have to be careful not to spend too many of them on the boat.

Take our whisker poles, for example. Our big four-inch-wide, 17-plus-footer came off a 50-something-foot South African racing yacht, and our tiny 11-footer, only two inches in diameter, was a gift from a 28-foot British twin-keeler.

But, hey, if you get lemons make lemonade, right?

Soon we were running dead downwind in the Convergence Zone with our working jib poled out to port on the big pole and our storm staysail poled out to port with our slender one. That's right; both headsails poled out on the same side.

Goofy, eh?

Well, it worked beautifully. The blanketing staysail didn't hurt our speed too much. I thought it would screw up the airflow to the jib much more, but it didn't. And it made furling the larger, lofty jib much easier; the strain was distributed over both sails.

So we were able to profitably run off under twin same-side headsails and roll the larger one up in the squalls, effectively sailing in 5 to 45 knots safely—without leaving the cockpit.

If a squall were really nasty—as happened twice—we'd just leave the poles up with the foreguy, the afterguy, and the topping lift still attached; then we'd roll away both sails. One wild night, the front of a low-pressure system roared over us, and we hove to comfortably with both poles still deployed.

Thus we proceeded to sail at five knots across the entire length of Micronesia, which covers an ocean area that would span the United States.

About 10 days into this process, Carolyn said wishfully, "I sure could use a cold beer."

Since her wish is my command, I asked her, "What do we know about Yap?"

"Only that they have stone money, are stoned all the time on betel nut, and the women don't wear tops, even in town," she said.

"What's not to like?" I said, as I altered course for Colonia, capital of Yap state.

Yap has been a fairy tale for many sailors. Perhaps you've seen the Hollywood version, a movie called *His Majesty O'Keefe*, which starred a young Bert Lancaster. In a sense, all the hopeful mariners who followed have bobbed in David O'Keefe's fortuitous wake.

O'Keefe was washed ashore in Yap in 1871. He was the lone survivor of the wreck of the sailing vessel *Belvidere* out of Savanna, Georgia. He immediately fell in love with Yap—and within the year had commandeered a Chinese junk named *Catherine* for use as an inter-island trader. Soon he had a whole fleet of ships—carrying copra in one direction and sea cucumbers in another. His most profitable cargo, however, was carrying stone to Yap. For centuries, Yap had used stones mined in distant Palau for money. These stones had to be transported 360 miles via dugout sailing canoe—and were often paid for by the blood of their daring crew. Once back on Yap, the stone was carved into money, many single pieces weighing tons

Anyway, O'Keefe loaded his sailing ship with carvers and stone masons and sailed off to Palau, where he pre-carved the money so it would stow more compactly. When he arrived back in Yap, he was, locally at least, a zillionaire. On one single voyage in 1884 aboard his graceful brig *Swan*, he carried back 1,480 large pieces of money.

So he did what any sensible sailor would do: He bought a private island in the middle of the harbor, started a waterfront bar which still stands to this day, and entertained the ladies—so well, in fact, that nearly every person we met in his bar claimed to be directly descended from him.

Yes, the funny thing about sailing around the world is how many funny things there are. For instance, the outer islands of Yap are usually administered by three chiefs: a land chief, for agriculture; a sea chief, for fishing; and a chief whose job it is to be in charge of regulating the villager's coconut beer intake.

If too many young people are getting too drunk instead of doing the traditional betel nuts, this drug-czar chief cuts back on booze production to encourage them to chew.

Betel nut use is almost universal in Yap. For example, all of the five government officials who showed up to clear in *Wild Card* had a bright-red mouth full of it

People carry an intricately woven purse—sort of a traditional drug kit—for their betel nut stash. About every 10 minutes, they bite off half a nut, sprinkle it with mineral lime, wrap it with a pepper-plant leaf, pinch off a third of a mentholated cigarette (including its paper) and happily chew.

The worst part is the spitting. Betel nut addicts continuous spit, dribble, ooze, leak, and drool. Often, they have so much betel in the jowls that they can't be understood. They just sort of gurgle happily, saying, one assumes, how tasty is their fine, fine betel nut! We had dozens of Yappers—as Carolyn and I began to affectionately refer to them—aboard, and always had to immediately scrub off the red stains they left. There is only one rule in Yap: Don't criticize betel nut. It is part of their culture, and Yappers are proud of it. But the betel nut is just one part of their extraordinarily traditional lives. For instance, many of the men only wear a sort of lavalava thong that hides the fore while nicely displaying the aft.

At first, I thought they were tied all the same way—a typical Western assumption. In fact, the drape and tie of each lavalava reveals much about the wearer: his island of origin, his status, even his age. It's sort of like how wearing Brooks Brothers says one thing and Armani says another.

The women don't wear tops in the home or villages; many don't wear tops into town either. "We have our traditions and you have yours," one proud woman told me while leaning over the frozen-food display of a modern supermarket, her enormous breasts swaying low into its cool fog. A woman wearing shorts and displaying her naked thighs however is considered obscene.

We soon fell into our daily in-harbor routine: I'd toil in my literary vineyards all morning, while Carolyn provisioned and puttered ashore. After a long lunch aboard, we'd often go hiking—always carrying a large leaf in our hands.

"Yappers don't like empty hands," Carolyn told me. "As far as they're concerned, empty hands are the devil's playground. But a stranger coming into a village with a leaf in his hands is saying he or she comes in peace. Thus, they are obliged to welcome him, feed him, host him."

And so, we carried our leaves before us as goodwill amulets, at first feeling self-consciously foolish but later with knowing pride. And we were *always* treated with courtesy and respect by every Yapper we met, even in the most remote villages.

Another thing Yap is justly famous for is its sailing navigators, and I wanted to find out as much as I could about them. At first I was confused when one guy told me, in response to my inquiry, "Go to the video store," as if I wanted to see a Hollywood movie about ocean navigation. But then another guy said, "Go to the DVD place." Then he added, "Martin, the young fellow behind the counter, is a wayfinder"

Perhaps you wouldn't expect a country whose national pride is primarily centered on its maritime traditions to employ said navigational experts as clerks in DVD shops, but that's the reality of modern-day Yap.

Soon Martin was chewing betel nut in *Wild Card's* cockpit, and telling us that such ancient knowledge of navigation isn't to be shared. But he sort of hinted that there are 32 stars in their "sky compass," that they "save their line"—that is, they make dead reckonings—without use of pencil and paper by tacking three hour on each side—the tacks get shallower as they approach their destination—and that they often stop, hove to, and "listen" to the sea.

Like anywhere else, there are time-honored rules governing such things as how to avoid storms, when it's safe to ocean-voyage with family, how many coconuts and fish hooks are to be carried for which destination.

Pacific islanders, some from Yap, regularly sail to Guam and Saipan in the Mariana Islands, and occasionally venture to Hawai'i, Tahiti and Pitcairn Island, completely without compass or charts.

But according to Martin, this isn't exactly true. "You say we don't have a compass, but we do, Fatty. It is just your compass floats in a bowl; ours is better, it's in the sky. Our charts are woven palm fronds with sea shells for the islands, our east is on top where your north is because, we're sailors, and the trades themselves are our best compass. Besides, we don't have to find the island exactly. We just get close and reverse-sail the morning paths of birds back to their nests. And the ocean swells bend around land. The waves are different to leeward. If you look really hard, you will see. It is not complicated, really. *You* make it so, not us."

Carolyn was delighted to learn that women can be navigators, too. "My mother first taught me," said Martin, who grew up on the outer island of Satawal. "And when I was young, she kept pointing at the sailors and saying, 'Go with them and learn.' At first I just followed them about, then helped with the fish and soon I was at sea, free as a bird!"

Boatbuilding is nearly as respected as navigating in Micronesia. There are numerous traditional outrigger craft under construction on Yap. These are basically open dugout canoes that have been planked up using locally woven coconut twine for fastenings, and they have an outrigger lashed on for stability.

There's nowhere to get out of the weather on the boats. "You have to be tough," admitted Martin. "You don't even eat unless the navigator (captain) says to. In the rain, we just huddle. Hoisting the sails isn't hard, but we have to steer, too. The worst is bailing. We have to bail without stop; and in heavy weather, we have to bail even more! So the navigator must have courage and faith. He must know that he'll get his crew ashore in the end, no matter what; and that the gods will smile upon them. A Pacific navigator isn't merely a navigator; he's a true man, a pure-hearted man!"

So there we were in Yap, with Martin the Satawal sailor spewing stories and betel juice around all 32 points of the sky compass he keeps in his head. Occasionally, he'd ask us a complicated question that required Carolyn's hands to dance over her WiFi-ed keyboard. Almost instantly, the internet supplied us with the answer via Google.

"Can all this be happening," I asked. "Right here, right now? Martin? Star charts? Sea birds? Betel nut? Outriggers? The World Wide Web?"

"Sure," Martin said without concern, as he spit and dribbled over *Wild Card's* side and into the harbor. "But it is you guys who make it complicated, not us!"

Macho Mechanics and the Iron Jib

It takes some sailors longer than others to become one with their engine.

I've been bedeviled by marine engines most of my life. The first was a gasoline-gulping, four-cylinder, 1920-ish flathead Scripps aboard my family's schooner, *Elizabeth.* It was huge and produced only a few weak ponypower when it ran, which wasn't often. We called it "The Bomb" in hopes it wouldn't be. It had an old Zenith updraft carburetor with a sticky float. Yes, there was a flame arrester, which considerably shortened the giant blue-yellow flame that shot out of its bronze mesh screen when the engine backfired. Occasionally the beast would decide to drip raw, explosive gasoline into the bilge. My father's solution to this spasmodic problem was to assign a "small crewmember" to crouch beside the running engine and continuously suck up the excess gasoline with a tiny squeeze bulb intended for use inside the human ear.

"Don't stop," he'd say, "or the gas will flood out, gather in the bilge and, well—*kapow*!"

When I later purchased my 22-foot double-ender *Corina*, I assumed the rusted hulk of an engine would never run. I only worked on it so I could throw it away someday in good conscience. But I found that I could start it, sometimes, as follows: First, I'd hand crank it many revolutions to make the oil circulate enough so it would spin freely. Then I'd pull out the spark plugs to clean them of grease and carbon. Next, I'd put a dollop of oil in each cylinder to increase compression and give each cylinder a shot of either, then quickly replace the plugs. Then, using a fully charged battery and while spraying more ether directly into the carb, I'd hit the starter. About a tenth of the time it would start.

At 19, I put a rebuilt 4-107 on layaway at the Westerbeke factory in Boston while building my 36-foot ketch, *Carlotta*. Finally, I owned a diesel, and I'd never have to clean a spark plug again. The 4-107 ran like a top until I submerged it by winterizing it and forgetting to close a tiny, easily overlooked cutlass-bearing water-injection petcock. I got it to run again, sort of, but it made horrible metal-on-metal noises and finally snapped its crankshaft in Georgetown, South Carolina.

So I tossed in a six-cylinder Gray Marine Fireball (alas, back to gasoline and cleaning those annoying sparkplugs) from a local powerboat that had burned, and then I took off for the tropics. The Fireball was raw-water cooled (it had no heat exchanger) and immediately started corroding and leaking seawater out of its expansion plugs (which are there to prevent the block from cracking in the event of a saltwater freeze.)

The first hole was tiny. I stopped it immediately with a toothpick. "Oh, clever idea!" I thought to myself. Within a month I was using wooden pencils, and a year later the entire engine bristled like a porcupine with wooden dowels and various carved-oak plugs. Many of these had to be tapped daily with a hammer to keep us from sinking.

Oh, yes, marine engines have bedeviled me truly!

The first engine that didn't was the Grey's replacement, a new 50-horsepower Westerbeke built on a Lehman block that ran perfectly for a decade or, so, until *Carlotta* was lost in Hurricane Hugo.

Wild Card, the Hughes 38 that Carolyn, my wife, and I salvaged off the bottom after Hugo, had a worthless, barnacle-encrusted Volvo in it. We deep-sixed it and went more than five years without an engine while cruising in the Caribbean and along the South American coast. I didn't particularly like cruising without an engine, but it took us that long (until 1996) to save up enough money to purchase our current Perkins M30. It's never failed to start, and it's never stopped of its own accord. I love it; it's light, powerful and dependable.

Which isn't to say it has been completely free of trouble. I had to replace its rocker arms in Madagascar, with Carolyn snapping low-res photos and e-mailing them off to our B.V.I. mechanic at Parts and Power (thank you, "Diesel Dan" Durban) during the entire rebuild.

But—and now I'm going to sound like an old fart—when I grew up back in the 1950's aboard *Elizabeth*, men fixed things. Continuously. You didn't say you couldn't fix something or that you didn't have the parts, you just gritted your teeth and fixed it, whether you were on a farm or a boat or an island.

My entire childhood was spent in the bilges of various vessels fixing stuff. First my father showed me how to wield a wrench; then a deckhand named Joey Borges; then a southern hot-rodder named The Gyroaster (Jerry

Kennedy); then a "beat-it-to-fit, paint-it-to-match" shade-tree mechanic named George Zamiar. They all took me under their greasy wings and showed me how to fix stuff.

There are a few simple rules: Don't make it worse as you take it apart. Place the parts so you know how they go back together; use string and draw pictures, if needed. Think. Understand how it works, and what each part is there for. Clean stuff. Never notice bleeding knuckles. Swear often, loud, and proud. If you put it back together and it doesn't work, just look sad and take it apart again. Repeat until it *does* work, swearing louder and louder as required.

That's about it.

Engines are simple: Picture a small coffee can sitting upside down on the ground. Put a fire cracker on it. Place another slightly bigger coffee can over both. Ignite firecracker—and that's an internal-combustion engine. All the rest is mere details.

I began this column with lamentations over my various marine auxiliary dramas with older engines. Actually, it's the modern diesel engine that frustrates most boat owners, despite the fact that most of today's engines are incredibly dependable machines if they are properly maintained.

That, of course, is a big "if." The key is basic maintenance. Yes, it's easy—but, as I've learned over the years, it has to be done regularly and right.

This was brought home to me a few years back by Canadian Christopher, a globe-trotting stinkpotter I met in Chagos as he circumnavigated for the third time aboard his lovely wooden motor vessel *Harmony*.

"The reason you sailboaters always have problems with your engine is because you are in ignorant denial," he said as I fell under the spell of this gearhead. "You don't understand them and, thus, you deify them. Instead of maintaining them, you pray they won't break. But engines aren't gods and maintaining them isn't voodoo. It is simple science. Planes don't fall out of the sky often, so why shouldn't marine engines be just as dependable? Well, they actually are. But the skipper must be in tune with his engine. He not only has to maintain it; he has to be one with it. To watch it. Listen to it. Smell it. Touch it. Almost taste it. Engines aren't people. They aren't capricious. They're machines. Everything that happens to them is logical and has a specific reason. All will be revealed *beforehand,* if we but look, listen and learn. Any change is a clue—a change in temperature, sound, smell, you name it. Modern engines almost never suddenly fail without notice; they give plenty of warning to those who listen, look and think. Careful observation is the key. You should regularly study every square inch of your engine. Check for oil or water leaks, discoloration, and corrosion. Belt wear? Hose damage? Read the manual. Better yet, actually *follow* the manual. Engine maintenance isn't rocket science. It's just logic and observation applied. Forget praying and knocking on wood for good luck. Instead, get in harmony with your engine and it will get in *harmony* with you!"

Since Chris practiced what he preached and had been doing so for three "engine-only" circumnavigations—in the process of putting tens of thousands of blissful, trouble-free hours on his lovely museum-quality Gardiner diesel—I took him at his word.

And I devoted an entire week recently to worshiping, observing, and maintaining my diesel engine. I lifted it off its beds to checks its mounts. (Fine, after more than ten years.) Then I aligned it to within .005 inch. I flushed out its cooling system and then "boiled"—cleaned—its heat exchanger in muriatic acid (careful, careful.) I checked its valve clearance, retorqued the head, and tossed in a new impeller for the raw-water pump. I swapped out its transmission, which was beginning to leak. Finally, I added new coolant. (Never use tap water to achieve 50:50 mix; use only distilled water.)

Yes, I changed its 15-40 military-spec diesel-grade lube oil and replaced its one oil and two diesel fuel filters.

Then I ran the hell out of it, and every minute, I carefully watched it. Until I felt the harmony of it all in my sappy, happy, grease-monkey bones.

Lovely, Lonely Atolls

In the middle of nowhere, there's plenty to do, and less is truly more.

After 47 years of living aboard, 37 of them with my wife Carolyn, I'm still enthralled by Mother Ocean. I see God's face in every wave, every cloud, every sunset. My boat is my church. Deep ocean is the only place I've learned to pray. At sea, I'm always in the moment. I taste the tangy salt air. I hear the dove-wing flutter of my jib leech. I feel the life pulse of the waves, chuckle at my wake, watch *Wild Card's* bow throw diamonds at the sky. It is *so* lovely.

Sometime I believe I can hear the earth spinning on its axis and it is difficult not to cry aloud with the perfection of it all.

But the sea is restless, and I, frail mortal that I am, need and desire rest. Thus, whenever possible, we seek out a few special places on this watery planet that span both terra firma and the world of water; these islandless midocean atolls, which are like tiny "lakes" in the deep ocean, include Beveridge Reef (at 20 degrees south, 168 degrees west) and Minerva Reefs (at 23 south and 179 degrees west.)

For us, these places are magic—halfway houses between King Neptune and Johnny Appleseed. I'm not a geologist but I will do my layman's best to explain how these otherworldly atolls came to exist.

Once upon a time, undersea volcanoes erupted and the lava built up to form islands sticking up above the sea. Wind and waves eroded away their tops. Plate tectonics gradually moved the mountain away from the place of its eruption, and it began to sink slowly under its own immense weight. Some tropical islands are surrounded by coral reefs, which grow *up* faster than the mountain sinks *down*. Thus, such landless atolls as Minerva or Beveridge are leisurely formed over the course of eons.

Being anchored within one is a strange, eerie feeling. You're in harbor and you're protected by a fringing coral reef—but there is no land anywhere. Well, it is straight down, actually.

Usually, because they are in the warm, windswept tropics, such atolls are pounded by large waves. The sound of the surf is like continuous but distant thunder; immensely powerful, possibly dangerous, and yet strangely comforting in its remove. The 360-degree reef protects you from the potential fury of the sea. But it's ying and yang within this small watery universe. If you drag anchor, you have a 360-degree lee shore as well.

Often, whales use these usually deserted atolls for calving. During the two weeks we were anchored within Beveridge Reef, at any moment we could just pause to listen intently and hear the family of whales that shared the anchorage with us blowing. The mother would always stay between her babies and us, balefully watching.

Of course, ships occasionally crash into atolls, are holed and sink. You'd think atolls would be littered with large, ugly, half-submerged steel wrecks, but they are not. They are amazingly self-cleaning. Even the thickest plates of the mightiest vessels are soon waving goodbye in the frothing, pounding surf.

The fishing in such atolls, needless to say, is fabulous. In both Minerva and Beveridge, it seldom took more than a minute to catch dinner, and if a different fish than the one you desired attempted to take your hook, you could just slowly tug the bait away in mild discouragement from 40 feet above. Haul in your catch fast, however, before the ever-present and very lazy circling sharks steal it.

Catching lobsters, albeit with a welding-gloved hand, is as easy as gathering Easter eggs.

Shellfish often abound; octopus too, although they're tougher to catch than you might think. Squid are elusive—unless you have a gaudy "squid-hooker" lure, around which they are inclined to want to wrap their amorous arms. Carolyn's the fisherman in our family, not me. I can't bear to watch the horny guy squids being enticed to their death!

True, fresh water is nonexistent. But we have three different levels of water catchment on *Wild Card,* our S&S-designed Hughes 38, and we've gone nearly half a year while cruising rainy climes without having to pick up any fresh water ashore.

Here, our shipboard clocks mean nothing. It's the tide that's the metronome of our lives, whether it's low tide and flat calm or a washing-machine-on-agitate high tide.

Mostly, what a landless atoll offers is nothing. This is exactly why we seek them out, for what they *lack*. But not everyone is so enthralled. Many modern dirt dwellers, long accustomed to being assaulted by urban noise, find the peace of "nothing" difficult to handle. It gnaws at them. It makes them nervous. They can't get to sleep without the sound of car traffic, jack hammers and ambulance sirens wailing in their ever-on-alert ears. They're put off by tranquility.

"There's nothing to do here," they say in hasty excuse, as they yo-yo back up their anchors. What they really mean is that they aren't being externally entertained and are too lazy or incompetent to entertain themselves.

Carolyn and I feel differently. While the sailing journey itself is our destination, we luxuriate within these brief, midocean hesitations. It's at places like these that we realize that we don't have to seek a path to happiness because happiness is already brimming within us. We want for nothing because we have everything. Our daily reality is the reality we desire. Are our lives perfect? No, of course not. We still have our all-too-human problems. But it's in these lovely, lonely atolls that we realize our biggest problems are also our best teachers. We have no fear of the future, the past or the luminous, soft-focused now.

So we quickly settle into the ancient cycles of food, love, and survival. We work on the boat and we work on ourselves. The rest of the world fades. We feel like space travelers—light years from our former cultural context and solar systems away from civilization. There's an entire universe beyond the world of 9 to 5.

It is these precious moments—when we taste eternity upon our eager tongues—for which we work so hard. We are in tune. We are our environment. We resonate.

The reef that protects us is alive.

So are we.

We are the planet.

"Why?" people ask us. "Why, after all these years, do you sail on and on and on?"

I want to tell them. I really do. And it is my job. I take it seriously. I want to convey to them the immensity of it all, but my words are clumsy. They fall short.

"To discover we don't matter," hardly covers it. And "to be one with God" seems blasphemously presumptuous, like sailing egomaniacs run amok.

So we just smile our secret smiles and keep sailing, waving goodbye over our battered, salt-stained transom, while whispering, "Because it's still fun," in pathetic, pale explanation.

Fishing for Honor

Surrounded by pelagic flesh eaters, including his own crew; this sailor's more preoccupied with food for the soul.

Soon after leaving Thailand, we dropped the hook in a remote little island of the Chagos Archipelago, in the middle of the Indian Ocean. Before the anchor of *Wild Card,* our S&S-designed Hughes 38 had even dug in; a fellow yachtie rowed alongside and asked, "Catch anything?"

He was, of course, talking about fish, and it wasn't to be the last time I was asked the question. It turns out the entire island was fish-crazed.

This was bad news for me. I'm fish-sensitive. In 1961, at the age of 9 and living aboard *Elizabeth*, my father's 52-foot schooner, in the sleepy fishing village of Carrabelle, Florida, I reached the apex of my career as a fisherman. My ship's cat had gone missing, and the local fishermen/drunks had told me that it'd been eaten by a giant alligator gar that lurked under docks, waiting to pounce on unsuspecting felines.

I vowed to kill that fish.

"Git 'em yet, son?" the local fishermen asked me everywhere they saw me.

"Not yet," I'd say, "but that thar gar is as good as dead, so help me God!"

I hooked it one Saturday afternoon from the dock behind Lester's Sundry shop, in full view of half the townsfolk. I was using an ancient fishing rig almost as heavy as myself, and I was terrified as the line started hissing off the reel. I flipped on the drag, but after a few jerks, the fish stripped the reel's gears, and I watched with horror as my line started spooling out. I just stood there, scared to my very bones, before I shook myself and clamped both my thumbs down on the line as hard as I could.

Up until now, the fish had been an abstraction. Now it was real. This was war—and only one of us would win.

The line kept smoking out from under my thumbs, so I clamped harder. It hurt, but not too bad, so I clamped harder still. Then the line came to the end where it was knotted on the spool, and I was flying off the dock like a human dart. I belly flopped into the harbor, released my grip on the rod, and surfaced into air.

I'd lost the battle, if not the war.

I held up my two bleeding thumbs high in the air and attempted to kick back toward the shore. Then I heard something I didn't understand at first. It sounded like a distant football game. I glanced up and noticed all the people staring down at me from the docks, cheering me. I was the town hero.

"Right down to the bone," said the local doctor with respect as he bandaged me.

"Dragged 'im halfway out the harbor 'fore the little fool let go," said the clinic nurse in admiration. The sheriff even bought me a turnover at Auntie May's Fried Pies so he could "take a close gander" at the two huge bandages on my thumbs.

The following day, I sewed a shark hook into the belly of a large mullet and shackled it to our vessel's spare anchor chain. I caught the gar, and my father hoisted it into the rig for all to see—all six-plus feet and 200 pounds of it. I'd thought I'd feel pride—but I didn't. The fish looked too noble. My head told me I'd won, but my heart told me both the fish and I had lost. And the victory celebration didn't go as planned, either. Once an admiring crowd had gathered and the local newspaper reporter arrived on the scene, the giant fish came alive again.

The gar shook the whole boat horribly, and then, as in a bad movie, broke the frayed line holding it to the fore halyard and flopped violently to the deck. My entire family started clubbing it frantically with oars, winch handles, and boat hooks. It flopped aft and fell heavily onto the cockpit floor. Then, with a mighty flick of its dying tail, it reduced our engine instruments and steering pedestal to twisted scrap metal before my father and brother-in-law fell upon it with flashing knives and brought the scene to a grim and bloody conclusion.

I'll never forget the horror of that moment. Strangely, I'd been rooting for the fish. It had every right to attempt to escape. Besides, up close, it didn't look like a cat eater. I'd set out to kill a predator and discovered the predator was me.

I decided right then and there never to seek revenge (or fish, for that matter) again. But, I've discovered that being a sailing nonfisherman isn't easy. The concept of "catching you dinner" and "sailing the farm" are very powerful, macho ones. So I've learned to fake it when pressed. "No luck," I say lamely. Or, "they just didn't seem to be biting when I transited the Atlantic, Pacific, and Indian Oceans."

So there we were, my fish phobia, my wife, and I in the Chagos Archipelago, which is an unusual place. A British Indian Ocean Territory, its population is dominated by the U.S. military base on Diego Garcia, though the native islanders (Ilois, in the local vernacular), forced into exile to Mauritius in the 1960s and 1970s, are making gains in their battle to return. The two atolls that cruising yachts often visit, Peros Banhos and the Salomons, have no shoreside populations. There, you'll find only "survivalist"-type yachties who sail in for a year or two to gather coconuts and live off the sea.

Thus, the social hierarchy of Chagos is based upon fishing (commercial fishing and spearfishing in the archipelago are prohibited by law.)Within hours of our arrival, we were instructed on where to catch bait fish, how to jig for squid, and how to prevent the ever-present sharks from eating our catch before we could. Each evening, all the yachties would gather on the beach at Ile Boddam to check the level of their rum bottles and talk about the day's catch.

One more bad thing: My wife and cruising partner of 32 years loves seafood—and started hinting broadly that she would like some fish. Eventually her hints grew less subtle, until they went something like this: "Catch me a fish, OK?"

So I sighed wearily, rummaged through my emergency liferaft supplies to gather together all my fishing gear, and set off in search of dinner.

To catch a fish, the first thing you have to do is catch a fish—for bait. This wasn't as easy as I remembered it was about, oh 42 years ago. The canned chicken I was using quickly fell off the hook. I couldn't seem to snag any mullet with my treble hook, nor could I find any flounder to gig. Finally, using bread, I caught a tiny little fish hiding under a rock just off the nearby beach, a fish so gaily hued it looked as if Peter Max and God had collaborated on its beautiful coloration.

"Damn," I said just as a large, rugged Aussie sailor was passing by. "I didn't bring a pair of needle nose pliers. How am I gonna get the hook out?" Almost without breaking stride, he stepped on the suddenly-eye-bulging fish and yanked the hook out with one brutal, lip-ripping tug.

"Oh, yeah," I said, with a sick smile. "Er, thanks!"

I returned to *Wild Card* and started fishing in earnest. It didn't take long before I hooked a large coral trout. I hauled it aboard and looked at it. It was shaking its gills in fright. Then its mouth moved, and I could swear it spoke to me in a voice remarkably similar to the one Mister Ed, the talking TV horse, used while querying his owner, Wilbur, "Have you considered tossing me back?" asked the fish.

"It's asking to be released," I announced to my wife.

"Don't anthropomorphize it, Fatty," she said. "It's a fish. You eat it, you don't talk with it!" And with that, she laid it on our cockpit cutting board and calmly chopped off its head. I sighed.

An hour later in the same cockpit, she served it to me on a plate. I took a bite. It was delicious. Then I set my fork down. Carolyn loved her portion, and she went back for seconds. She praised its taste, texture, and aroma, all the while pretending not to notice my distress. Finally, I leaned my full plate over the side and tilted it. It was her turn to sigh.

"I'm sorry," I said. "I'm just not much of a fisherman, I guess."

"OK," Carolyn said briskly, and I could tell she was about to make a decision. Then her voice softened, and she said, "That's fine, Fatty. If I want to eat fish, I guess I'll just have to catch and kill it myself. That's OK. I can handle that."

"Do you still love me?" I asked.

"Yes," she said, exasperated, and then laughed. "But I haven't the faintest idea why."

"Me neither," I said.

Nine Cats, Many Lives

A zany flotilla marked by shiny multihulls and sailors' boundless enthusiasm helps to make old territory feel new once again.

My joy when I was asked to host a recent *CW* Sail-a-Cat Adventure Charter was immediately replaced by trepidation when I was assigned to come up with a "Fat Evaluation" of the fleet, an analysis, if you will, in my own words about this type of sailing experience in company.

Needless to say, I was horrified. This sounded as if they expected competency from me, something I'd never indicated I was interested in, or capable of. Frankly, I hate being elevated to my level of idiocy, which, I must admit, doesn't take much elevation at all. But the job of being a starving writer is a difficult one. Hunger is compelling. I decided to soldier on.

The first person I met on Tortola was Peter King of King Charters. Peter and his wife, Carol, are partners with the magazine and conduct the trips. No words were minced. He came straight to the point.

"Your job," he said, "is to relax. Don't worry about anything. Do you think you can handle that?"

Already I was bending under the pressure to perform!

"I'll try," I said. "I make no promises, but I'll try. Is there anything I should know? Do? Are there any rules?"

"No, no and no," chimed in Carol with a smile.

Already I was beginning to like them.

Our weeklong flotilla—a respite from our circumnavigation and a return to our old stomping grounds—began with a party. It also ended with a party. And there were a *lot* of parties in between. But it was the first welcome party at Peg Legs Landing, at Nanny Cay Marina and Hotel, which I approached with butterflies of self-doubt: After all, I wouldn't get a second chance to make a first impression.

"How do we do this," asked Carolyn, my wife and co-host, as we climbed the stairs to the noisy, reggae-rocked restaurant and bar.

"I'm not sure," I said. "Let's start off with you distracting the men while I flirt shamelessly with their wives."

"So it's business as usual," she muttered as she slid off to mingle.

There was a crowd of rowdy people bellied up to the bar, many of them dressed in their distinctive purple *Cruising World* Adventure Charter T-shirts. I shook a few hands, patted a few backs, and was surprised to be accosted by one drunken fellow who proudly informed me he didn't read *Cruising World*, and he didn't care who I was. He was merely interested in the chartering.

Of course, I took it as a challenge. I turned on the charm. At first, he seemed immune. Luckily, after following him back to his table, I was able to dazzle a few of his crew.

I soon caught sight of Peter motioning at me from across the room but I didn't allow it to distract me, not when I finally had the whole table laughing at my sea yarns. I kept it up for almost an hour, until the whole gang of them were writhing on the floor, holding their laugh-cramped stomachs and pathetically demanding I stop telling them jokes.

Peter is a kind man. He's always smiling. "No purple," he laughed, and motioned to the distant table I'd just worked so hard. "Not one of ours!"

"Making your usual first-impression, are you?" Carolyn snickered as she floated by.

Luckily, I was rescued from turning beet red by Tim Miller, who was skippering *Dream Weaver,* a Fountaine Pajot Belize 43. A highly experienced sailor who teaches sailing at the Culver Military Academy, in Culver, Indiana, he was soon regaling us with riveting tales of square-riggers, wayward-but-willing cadets, and rough ocean passages in the Caribbean.

"This is my second charter with these folks," he told me, "And I'm already signed up for Thailand and Spain. I'd go on every one if I could!"

I would've liked to have talked boats with Tim more, but I was distracted by one of his crew, Ray Barsaloux, of Largo, Florida. Ray, a smiley, beaming fellow brimmed with good vibes. He was also an intelligent, insightful, straightforward occupational therapist who immediately proved it by joking, "Boy, are *you* in the wrong job, Fatty!"

His daughter "Grilled Cheese" Cheryl Barsaloux was with him. She had so much metal piercing her body I was thankful I didn't have a magnet. But her smile was amazing. And she quickly had all the island men panting after her. In fact, she got her chartering nickname the very first night when

one of her suitors said, "She so hot, mon, she like grilled cheese!"

Grilled Cheese always made me laugh. When I questioned her on her sailing experience, she wildly exaggerated it with, "Zero. Less, actually." A surgery-instrument technician, she finally admitted to being "on a cruise ship once or twice, sort of."

I learned an important lesson that first night: Charterers are a diverse lot with only two common denominators; a lust for adventure and willingness to try new things. Oh, yeah. And that Peter King was correct: My job was to relax.

"Damn it!" I yelled at Carolyn the following morning when I caught sight of *Sea Dream*, the Lagoon 500 we'd be spending the week aboard. "We forgot to bring the tennis rackets!"

It was that wide, that big.

Sea Dream, 51 feet long and 28 feet wide, is designed by Van Peteghem & Lauriot Prévost and displaced a whopping 45,000 pounds. It was built out of gleaming white dried snot... er, fiberglass. It didn't strike me as a boat so much as, say, a plastic pool toy on steroids.

"It has three refrigeration units and a large freezer," Carolyn oohed.

"How many units do you have aboard *Wild Card*?" asked Ruth LaBlonde, a trim, friendly real-estate broker from Arizona who'd twice chartered with the Kings in Africa.

"None," said Carolyn. "And every time I mention the subject of refrigeration Fatty asks me if I believe in reincarnation, as if that's my only hope! This boat has blenders, huge sinks, a giant oven, and a stern-rail barbeque. I'm in heaven. I'm *never* leaving this vessel, Fatty!"

I frowned. She liked it. A lot. Maybe doing this charter gig wasn't such a good idea.

"All four major staterooms have a head with shower," Carolyn continued. "There's air-con, a genset, and twin engines... I want one!"

I started to climb up to the flying bridge but had to stop to allow my ears to pop. "Hand me up a parachute or at least a bungy-jumping cord," I called down to Carolyn, "in case I fall over and want to survive the impact!"

It felt more like being on a small, white, fiberglass island than a yacht. It was about as far away from our modest, low-freeboard, 38-foot sloop *Wild Card*, as I could imagine.

"Oh, my gosh," squealed Carolyn. "There's even a small, intimate cockpit forward. How romantic!"

"That's not a cockpit," I said when I first laid eyes on it. "It's a passion pit."

"Yes!" she laughed as she dragged me down into it.

Ever the professional, I borrowed her drink napkin and quickly scribbled a note to myself— "Passion Pit: A+"— before tossing it aside for more important matters.

Alas, we were just getting into it, when we were interrupted by a hail from Morgoo the Magnificent. "Hey, bro!" he cried, dragged me to feet, and hugged me like an excited bear. "I'd like you to meet my wife, Beatrice."

Now I hate people calling me bro or brother, unless they really are. He was. He is. I'd named him Morgan myself, after the pirate. Like me, he, too, had been born aboard the schooner *Elizabeth*, and, yes, he'd recently informed me he'd met and married a German countess, but of course, I'd dismissed it as typical sibling rivalry.

Beatrice Chominsky turned out to be a good shipmate with a wonderful sense of humor. I immediately blurted, "Do you really have castles scattered all over Europe?"

"Well ...," she said, and I could sense she was attempting to wiggle out of it. "Large houses, some, perhaps, made of stone, would be more accurate."

I sighed, and slowly refocused on Carolyn. "No castles in your family?" I asked her accusingly. "None? What is your *problem*?"

"What's the shouting all about," asked Captain Mark Dubois. A South African, his voice is so melodious and rich it is like listening to Olivier do Shakespeare, even when he's talking trash. Basically, he was there—diplomatically and yet professionally—to restrain me from breaking the boat. He also conducted the daily navigation briefing. I immediately dubbed him our moral compass

"Ah," said Peter and Carol, as they strolled forward to complete our jolly *Sea Dream* crew. "All together, are we?"

I pointed to Morgan and said, "We're all here, but he's not together!"

"Does he always treat you like this," asked Beatrice with an arched eyebrow.

"Since I've been born," lamented Morgoo.

Our first stop was at Norman's Island. It wasn't easy for Peter to herd nine cats out of the harbor at approximately the same time. There was a tiny mix-up with the food: Some vessels had all the frozen chicken, while others contained the veggies. "No problem," said a grinning Peter, "we'll have great fun sorting it all out in tonight's anchorage!"

I was beginning to realize how Peter had managed to entertain 3,500 world-wide charter guests over the years, and retain almost every one as a friend. Nothing bothered the man, absolutely nothing. He correctly saw the big picture; we were in paradise, we shouldn't sweat the small stuff, it was all small stuff!

The sailing conditions on the first day were perfect: southeast trade winds at 22 knots with sunny skies and flat seas. Even better, the weather held that way for the entire week—fantastic sailing conditions, literally 24/7.

It was a wonderful first sail, a fast broad reach with the wind over our port quarter. The sea immediately worked its magic on me. I saw the sky and its puffy white clouds as only a sailor can. The water was an impossible blue. Gulls wheeled. Flying fish zigged. Porpoises zagged. Even the distant palm trees seemed to be waving welcome.

We managed to pick up a mooring at Norman's well known Bight well before dark. Some of the crew snorkeled the nearby caves, others shared Pina Coladas in the shade of the lofty flying bridge, and Carolyn and I retired to our stateroom for a nap. Later that evening we dined, all 55 of us, at Pirates Bight, a restaurant on the eastern side of the spacious anchorage

The following morning we visited *Sea of Love*, a Lagoon 440. The sailors were eating breakfast and immediately dealt us in. I was intrigued with the galley/cockpit arrangement: By sliding open the aft main cabin windows, food could easily be passed out to the large cockpit table. I wanted to see if it was really as convenient as it seemed. "More pancakes," I shouted. Carolyn helped with our informal vessel evaluation with, "More coffee too!"

Ah, there's nothing like hands-on testing when it comes to techno-nautical stuff. Needless to say, ever the professional, I jotted it all down on a borrowed syrup stained paper towel.

"Does the sliding window work well for passing around drinks? Snacks? Platters of lobsters, for instance?" Yes, indeed, the crew assured me—and we were soon passing dishes back and forth like Frisbees through the well-designed opening.

Of course, between long and elaborate charter meals we did manage to slip in an occasional sail. Actually, we stayed aboard *Sea of Love* for the entire day. Why not? We had no schedule. The food was good, the crew congenial. How much closer to paradise could we get?

Sea of Love was ably skippered by Larry Jaworski—a Hunter 29 owner who had also previously chartered with the group. His crew were especially warm and friendly, with professional dance instructor Linda Theiss and her sister Carol Karn waltzing nimbly around the galley, while Larry's daughter Lisa Miller, focused on napping her tan to perfection on the foredeck.

Today's destination was Cooper Island. The entire sail was dead to weather in brisk trades. Needless to say, we tucked a couple of reefs into the mainsail. The Lagoon 440 performed surprisingly well, once we got the hang of footing off for speed and paying attention to VMG—velocity made good—than to the apparent-wind angle.

Now, I have to tell something I thought I'd never say: I see why people like flying bridges, even sailing vessels with flying bridges. While the offshore sailor in me has always considered them landlubbing affectations, the inshore charterer within me now loves them. We were dry, completely dry, even beating hard to weather. We had perfect visibility. We were, literally, above the crowd.

Another area in which I was pleased was the Lagoon's ability to tack. As long as our sails were properly trimmed and we had good boat speed, she came about sure but slow, and there was no need to backwind the jib if our timing was good.

We anchored for a leisurely lunch off Peter Island. The afternoon sail was as thrilling as the morning: We literally didn't want to stop. First mate Gilbert Karn in particular had a nice touch on the helm. At one point we touched 10 knots in a smooth patch. It was great sailing. We tacked back and forth many times across Sir Francis Drake channel between Tortola and its string of southern islands, reveling in being afloat once again.

The wind was gusting to a refreshing 28 knots as crew members Rick and Mary Divelbiss picked up our evening's mooring off the Copper Island Beach Club, and Trisha Dougherty gathered us around the cockpit blender for the traditional Caribbean sundowner.

The following day was a 22-mile beam reach to reef-strewn Anegada. This is normally off-limits to bareboaters, but because of our guided group status, the visit was permitted. Carolyn and I sailed aboard another Lagoon 440, *Gato Del Sol*, with David Martino as captain, and Peter Gabbe as second in command.

Dave, who owns an apparel-design firm in Texas, has been sailing for more than 10 years, first on a Pearson 26 and now on a Gemini 105. There was an easy camaraderie about the boat: Dave and Peter are obviously good friends. It was a comfortable place to be.

Since the wind was slightly lighter than the previous day, yet expected to build, we elected to go with a single reef in the mainsail. We were slightly under-canvased initially and slightly over-canvased at the end—and darn-near perfect most of the time.

Also onboard were Canadians Ken and Rosanne Church. Ken wants to circumnavigate in a monohull, Rosanne leans more towards a year or two in the Caribbean aboard a large catamaran to test the waters. Thus, our entire day's sail was spent in a heated "cat-versus-mono" debate, with Rosanne wryly cautioning me, "Be careful what you say, Fatty. Ken ultimately makes up his mind fast—he might buy this thing before the hook's down!"

We led the nine-boat pack northward for a long time until Tim Miller on the Fountaine Pajot Belize 43 *Dream Weaver* came up behind us and tooted for the passing lane. This sent us into a flurry of sheet tweaking, as Peter Gabbe growled, "I'm not overly competitive, Fatty, but, on the other hand, *I hate to lose*!"

We made Tim work for it. You know what they say: Two boats on any ocean make a race. First Tim tried to pass just to leeward of us, but he failed. Next he worked up to windward of us, but pointing higher slowed him down, and he was unable to roll us. Finally he dove far below us and managed to punch through our lee without getting slowed by our dirty air.

"Damn," I said, my head hanging, when he eventually bested us. "Looks like we buy the first round!"

That evening was our Pirates and Mermaids costume party at Neptune's Treasure, on Anegada. I was bit skeptical, I must admit, but not to worry: When the Kings throw a party, they *throw a party*. And some of the costumes were incredibly elaborate. I was honored to be asked to award the Mermaid's prize and was going to give it to Rosanne Church—her minutely detailed costume (she's into quilting) was mind-boggling and beautiful—but my judgment was momentarily stunned by Valerie Peiser's giggling/jiggling coconuts. Yes, I'll admit it. Fairness went completely out the window. Valerie was just so *wanton* as she elevator-eyed me with a leer that made all rational thought leave my brain. Despite the chaos on the dance floor, I gave a brief after-dinner speech. The gist of my talk went: Carolyn and I are just regular folks. OK, a bit weird, sure, but really just regular people. We aren't particularly smart or brave, and yet we've sailed together for tens of thousands of ocean miles, for more than three decades, and we've circumnavigated. It ain't rocket science. If we can do it, so can you. Let's party! I brought my guitar ashore that night and many of us ended up howling at the moon. I have no idea when we returned to the boat.

We visited The Baths on Virgin Gorda on the fourth day. I love its shadowy grottos and how you can swim underwater and then emerge in a cave. I've never been anywhere in the world quite like these caves. It was wonderful to be back.

That afternoon, we cruised with the wild and crazy crew of *Castellina*, yet another Lagoon 440. Dale Flippo of Virginia was our skipper.

I'd been forewarned about these guys. Their 2004 *Freedonia* charter is somewhat infamous among Adventure Charterers, but I was pleasantly surprised to see that their sailing skills matched their party antics. The first night at the Peg Leg's party, crew member Amber Flippo, Dale's daughter, had somehow been hoisted into the air as a sensuous flying figurehead, and instantly set the stylistic tone of this year's charter. Oh, to be young again!

It is rather difficult to—how should I say?—keep your focus in the Caribbean. There are too many rum squalls and stationary drunk fronts that get in the way. So it is easy to get a bit lax, which is where Peter "Eagle Eye" King comes in. He's always on the job. He immediately spotted one of our flotilla's dinghies drifting away—and quickly tethered it astern of *Sea Dream*. Then he nonchalantly called each skipper of our flotilla on the VHF—and asked, offhandedly, "And, where is your dinghy now?" A long embarrassed pause revealed the culprit

"All's well that ends well," said a smiling Peter, who was gracious enough not to mention the $1,000 saved by his vigilant eye.

After spending a night tucked into the lee of Marina Cay, the next day we cruised to Jost Van Dyke after a snorkel stop at Monkey Point, off the south tip of Guana Island. We were aboard *Wind Dancer* with co-skippers Eric Boutiette and Sari Greene of Portland, Maine. They are so used to sailing in New England climes they actually brought their fleece jackets to the Virgins.

Since the boat was in such good hands, Carolyn and I were able to really relax and enjoy gamming with Todd Christian and Valerie Peiser, two fellow Virgin Islanders from St. Croix with whom we have much in common. Being Crucians, they knew our two local friends, multihull designer Roger Hatfield of Gold Coast Yachts and calypso-singer Llewellyn Westerman of the indomitable trimaran *Charis*.

But, as much as they both love Christiansted, Todd and Valerie have decided to move on and are currently in search of the perfect cruising vessel to "party around the world" aboard. There's little doubt in my mind they'll someday hail *Wild Card* in some exotic port with a cheery, "We told ya we'd do it!"

Jost Van Dyke is a truly magic place. While Carolyn headed off to see Tessa, the wife of calypso great Foxy Callwood, who owns Foxy's Restaurant, I went in search of Reuben, one of the most uniquely talented guitar players in the Caribbean, but I got hung up at Ivan's place, and then the Soggy Dollar bar. Yeah, Jost is just one great celebration after another.

The following day we sailed to Tortola aboard *Waypoint*, a Lagoon 410 with David Fenwick at the helm. I liked him. He had a keen sense of humor. On the personal detail sheet used by the Kings to match him up with compatible crewmates, he listed a couple of dozen hobbies, with "drinking" between every one. Under eating preferences, he put lobster with shrimp or shrimp with lobster preferred—that sounded reasonable to me!

A couple of early tacks aboard *Waypoint*, however, puzzled me. First it would seem that we didn't have enough boat speed and that we'd stall out or be caught in irons. Then, magically, we were fine and tacked on over. I just couldn't figure it out—until I remembered *Waypoint* was electrically powered: I couldn't hear the engine being bumped into forward for an instant to help us through the wind. ("Electric engines are A+ for cheating," my notes read.)

As we shot through the reef off Cane Garden Bay, we saw, in the crystal clear water below, a large expensive bareboat which had sunk the day before. This made all of our blood run cold for an instant—until someone jokingly offered me some snorkel gear and said, "Go get it, Fatty! The next *Wild Card* awaits!"

That evening was the mega-party aboard *Sea Dream* in Cane Garden Bay, on the northern side of Tortola. To say this party was a success is to make a vast understatement. It was an absolute ball. Despite our numbers, there was room to spare aboard *Sea Dream* for all 55 of us. Things got a little carried away. At one point, people were dropping through hatches like flies. Why, I've seen piranhas with better party manners than some of these ravenous, rum-fueled sailors. And getting rid of 'em was definitely not easy either. I thought for sure Peter King's "Time to go home now, folks!" would be subtle enough, but, alas, I still had to go around later (with an oar for a club) to chase Walter Ried and his entourage back into their dinghy.

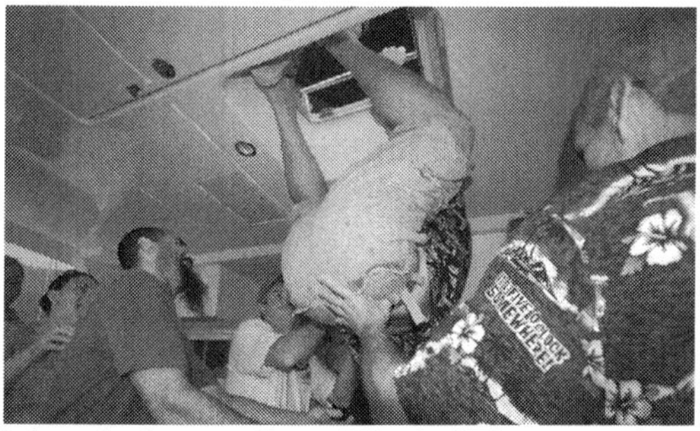

Next morning, we beam-reached down Tortola's north side to Soper's Hole, then, beat across Sir Francis Drake for the return to Norman. We practiced our morning jibes aboard *Dream Weaver* with Stanley Hornell at the helm, and I was amazed and delighted to see the progress Raymond Barsaloux had made as a sailor.

The first time I saw Raymond in a cockpit under sail, he looked like he was scared the sheet winches might bite. However, only six days later, he was nonchalantly trimming with the best of them, an amazing transformation in such a short time.

That afternoon, I studied my notes in the forward cockpit of *Sea*

Dream, attempting to arrange them in some logical, journalistic order, using soda cans as paper weights. One of the scribbled napkin notes actually mentioned how comfortable the cushions I was lounging on were—they were, indeed, comfy—and I must have dozed off while considering if this fact was important enough to mention in my article. (I'd decided not.) In midnap I awoke for a moment as a rainless squall came through, but immediately dozed off again. Finally I was awakened by a speedboat wake which made the soda cans noisily roll around the cockpit floor.

With a start, I peeled open a concerned eye. Damn it! I pivoted aft, hoping to see small, fluttering sheets of paper opportunely stuck to the cabin top. Nothing. None astern in the water either.

I sighed.

Just then Peter strolled by. "What's my job," I asked weakly.

"To relax, Fatty," he boomed good-naturedly. "Just relax!"

Moments later Carolyn came to visit.

"Wassup?" she asked.

"Just doing my job," I replied.

The final close reach back to Nanny Cay was aboard *Annie's Toy*, a Lagoon 380. This was the only vessel in our fleet with a solitary woman and four men aboard, but the arrangement worked out fine—sort of. Or, as Beverly Simmons put it, with a laugh, "The guys attempted to not be too gross and to act civilized... oh, for about the first five minutes."

This crew was perhaps the most technically oriented. They constantly badgered me with well-considered, intelligent questions and didn't give up until they completely understood the answers. We even hove to in midchannel so they could see how easy it was.

Walter Ried, in particular, seemed intent on learning as much as possible. "Why do you say that," he'd ask. "Back up!" he'd command in midstory. "Explain!" he'd inject.

I liked him. He had enthusiasm. He wasn't scared of learning, of asking questions. And he'd come on this charter to learn everything he could about catamarans, and that's exactly what he did.

Then we were back at Nanny Cay. It was a shock. Suddenly, the moment that no one wanted to think of all week was finally here. It was as if the air had gone out of a balloon. I felt sad. I wanted more. Reality was beginning to rear its ugly head, and I wasn't ready. I knew paradise was right outside the harbor. Why not continue on... forever?

"Get a grip," hissed Carolyn when she saw that look on my face.

So that was it. We hugged, we cried, we shouted our e-mail addresses from departing taxi cabs. No longer sailing mates, we were now mere dirt-dwelling civilians once again.

Coral-Lump Soup

It's not the tastiest dish at a cruiser's potluck, but it sure gets the party started.

Our Hughes 38, *Wild Card*, is a modest boat. She sails extremely well, but with 10-feet of beam, her interior's tiny. She's particularly ill-suited for entertaining: her tiller-swept cockpit is crowded with sail controls, you have to step directly on the main galley countertop to enter the cabin, and she doesn't even have a fixed dining table. Nor do we have refrigeration. The bottom line: *Wild Card* is a fine-sailing, two-person vessel aboard which three is truly a crowd.

But, despite the above, we have people aboard all the time. We average one major dinner party a week and a couple of spur-of-the-moment parties a month. Every time a local islander does something nice for us (about ten times a day in the South Pacific), we invite them out to the boat.

The reason we entertain so often is simple: everywhere we go, people treat us with kindness and respect. We feel obligated to return the favor. Cruising boats with a "no locals aboard" rule are, from our point-of-view, missing the best part of circumnavigating. The world isn't something we want to observe—it's something we want to partake of.

The trick is to not use the judgmental lenses of *your* culture to judge another culture. Example: back in the early 1980s an old wild-haired black man in dirty shorts circled *Wild Card* on a beat up, oft-patched old windsurfer in the Lesser Antilles. At first, I thought he was a bit of a nut, until I noticed how elegantly he handled his vessel and the merry twinkle in his penetrating eye. I waved him over and we had a nice chat. Turned out he was Sir James Fritz-Allen Mitchell, Prime Minister of St. Vincent and the Grenadines.

Another time, in India, I was shocked to discover the little grinning fella in the beige skirt on the dock who was volunteering to fix my SSB for free, was, in reality, Professor T. K. Mani, the inventor of the acoustical rain gauge, which measures rainfall at sea, who had just returned from addressing a large gathering of physicists in America.

The point I'm trying to make is: To travel is to learn. And the best, quickest, easiest way to learn a lot is through others.

This philosophy can lead to some unusual situations.

In my drinking days, I was nursing a beer in a waterfront dive in Cochin, Kerala, India, when a young man put down a bulky leather-and-pipe contraption on the stool next to me. I didn't really pay attention as I was admiring *Wild Card* anchored off in the shimmering distance. But I was puzzled why he made the bartender put one of his draft beers into a special plastic mug he carried. Just then, out the corner of my eye, I noticed some movement on the bar stool next to me,

The guy handed the beer to the contraption. A flapper hooked it. "Ah," the middle-aged American woman said as she twisted towards me and sipped her draft. "Hot today, eh?"

She had no legs, no arms, just sort of stump-flaps protruding from her hips and shoulders.

"Yeah," I said, as smoothly as I could. "India seems like an oven sometimes."

"She's been running me ragged," her boyfriend said as he glanced at her affectionately. "I'm like, 'Let's go back to the hotel for a nap' and she's like, 'Only one more shrine, please!'"

I liked her immediately. She even had a wicked sense of humor. "I like to travel," she said with a sardonic smile. "So I travel on the money I save on high heels!"

"She's been having fun mock pan-handling the local beggars," said her boyfriend, "She's like, 'You lucky bastards, cough up some rupees, please!'"

"Would you like to come out to my boat," I blurted, pointing at *Wild Card* in the distance. "My dinghy is nearby. There's some harbor chop but we'll be careful."

"Sure," she said without missing a beat. "I'd love to. I've never been aboard a sailing yacht. That would be *very* cool!"

She'd been born, exactly the way she was. Still, she enjoyed herself, and regaled us with story after story of the trouble she'd get herself into because of her "uniqueness." She was grateful for her life. She was alive. People loved her. Life was imperfect perhaps, but good.

The only sadness she expressed was when she spoke of how her financially strapped parents had borrowed money to take her to Lourdes. "I wasn't ashamed to be there or to be me," she said. "But I felt so sad for my well-meaning parents, standing there, waiting hopefully for a miracle I knew would never happen."

I realized immediately that this woman next to me was, in many ways, the finest human being I'd ever met. I also realized she couldn't swim. But it had come to me in a flash that she'd completely ignored her disability and, thus, so should I. So I blurted. And she was honored. Overjoyed. And loved having dinner and cocktails aboard *Wild Card.*

Practice "the blurt" and you'll seldom regret it. Take risks, not with your boat but with your heart. Don't restrict yourself with logic. Don't judge. Just blurt, "Why don't you come out to the boat?" whenever the mood strikes.

Which brings us, finally, to the actual subject of this rambling, demented column: the owners of a gleaming 50-foot catamaran I'll call *Splendid Isolation.* We'd both been anchored for a week or so off Pangaimotu, in Tonga, and yet we had never actually spotted them on deck. We knew someone was aboard: dinghies moved, generator's belched, and cabin lights glowed. But the crew remained shrouded in mystery.

Thus, on a spur-of-the-moment decision while ferrying people to and from *Wild Card* during an impromptu party, I just swung alongside *Splendid Isolation* and knocked. A silver-haired woman appeared inside the large sliding glass doors but didn't open them. Finally her husband showed up and tip-toed outside, carefully shutting the door behind him to keep in the air-conditioned cold. "Yes?" he asked, as if I was a door-to-door salesman.

"We're having a party on *Wild Card,*" I said and pointed. "Why don't you and the Missus come on over?"

"She doesn't like the heat," he said quietly

We were in the tropics—so I thought it best not to respond.

"What's the party *for,*" he finally asked.

"Nothing," I said. "Everything. I mean, the sun's gonna come up tomorrow, create some wind for our sails and charge the batteries, pretty special, eh?"

He looked at me as if was crazy. People do this to me a lot. I've gradually come to the conclusion that they do it because I'm crazy.

"Hey," I said, taking a different tack, "Booze! Boats! Broads! Music, why, my wife, Carolyn, is serving up some of her famous coral-lump soup right now. What do you say?"

I didn't think he was gonna go for it, but suddenly his face lit up. "What should I bring?" he asked.

"A bottle of something and, snacks? Dip? Crackers? Any cheese?"

His name sounded something weird like Penrod Pimpileston the Second so I introduced him as PeePee to the cockpit full of demented revelers aboard *Wild Card.* I gave him a quick boat tour— which required batting some of the local youngsters out of the Gameboy-cartridge-strewn nav area as I did so.

"Aren't you worried about them stealing?" he whispered to me as giggling Polynesian kids dropped in and out of the forehatch while playing pig pile in the forecastle.

"Not really," I said. "So now tell me, what's your story?"

"I was an attorney in Portland," he started in.

I couldn't resist inserting; "*Now* I'm nervous."

Actually, conversing wasn't easy. We had to shout. Somebody was playing my guitar on the foredeck, accompanied by a mis-timed, too-enthusiastic cabin-top drummer. Plus, some drunken fool was twanging the lifelines like a bass fiddle. And it sounded like a herd of elephants in the cockpit. Yes, *Wild Card* was bedlam.

Suddenly Ms Des, off *Skylark II,* thrust a drinking glass below. "More 'pagne!" she squealed, and I poured her another of her favorite Fizzy Tonics. As I passed it to her, I introduced her. "Des, this is PeePee," I told her. "PeePee, this is Des! Des is an expert at, what is it, Des, LSD? CPR?"

"I'm a certified CPA, Fatty," she said and gave me a playful swat. "It's nice to meet you, PeePee!"

Des is a wonderful woman. She was born in Sweden, worked, at Crook & Crook marine supply in the States and partied in Sint Maarten for a decade or so, where, on Orient Beach, the nude beach, she was famous as the woman whose lipstick always matched the single dethorned rose that she wore woven in her nether hair.

Today she skylarks around the world with Chris-the-Brit, the second luckiest man in the world.

Somebody else stuck their head down below as well, and slurred, "Darling, why do they call you PeePee—because you're a bed wetter or into golden showers?"

PeePee couldn't speak he was so aghast, and was just sort of desperately motioning to me for conversational help.

I didn't give him any. "Fess up," I said. "Which is it?"

"Don't be shy, we're all friends," somebody else added, and a roar went up from the crowd. "Be honest!" someone shouted, and another quipped, "If your kidneys aren't bashful, why should you be?"

The next time I spotted PeePee, he was in deep conversation with a beery-eyed Carolyn. "It ain't the boat or the preparation or the food, it's the people that make a party, PeePee! People like these, like you! And that 'coral lump soup' Fatty's always talking about? We just put a lump of dead coral in pot and set it a boilin'. Then row around the harbor and invite people. Once they're all aboard, we toss the boiling water and the lump overboard, and eat and drink whatever they've brought. The idea is to have a good time. You're having a good time, aren't you?"

Soon I was playing some nautical dirty ditties on the guitar, and it was a boat wide sing-along. PeePee's voice was surprisingly rich and he wasn't shy anymore.

Finally, well after midnight, I had to pull him away.

"Marvelous, Fatty, marvelous," he gushed on the dinghy ride home. "Do you really think the sun will come up again tomorrow?"

"Maybe," I said. "And it'll be another miracle, if it does."

I made sure he was safely aboard his catamaran. The spreader lights suddenly came on, indicated his wife was both awake and waiting.

"Quite a boat," I said, for lack of anything better to say. It seemed as wide as a tennis court.

"Yes," he said, "plenty of room for…entertaining."

Our combined silence said it all.

Finally, he grinned and asked, "Any chance you could write down the lyrics to 'Friggin' in the Riggin' for me?"

"Absolutely," I said.

Pactor Babe's Got Her Ears On

Whether sharing weather and news with a friend in a distant anchorage or monitoring a disaster, Carolyn Goodlander keeps Fatty in the know with her SSB radio.

I'm swimming upwards from deep, deep sleep and surface into the reality of my cozy, comfortable forepeak. My eyes snap open. I'm tired, very tired. It is still dark. My PDA is blinking and beeping insistently. I consider winging it through the open forehatch to hear a satisfying—but expensive—splash. Instead, I sigh and squint to see its screen. "Jim WX, 4 megs" it says. I rest my head back on the pillow and turn to look at Carolyn.

Her dark Italian hair frames an untroubled face. I look at her for a long time. I owe her. She was 15 years old when I first lured her into my cockpit. Now she is 55 and far lovelier on every level. I could not have become who I am without her.

"Hey," I say, and walk some calloused fingers down an alluringly exposed shoulder, "How's my Pactor Babe this fine morning?"

"Tired," she mutters, flops away from me, and snuggles her pillow, "I hate the America's Cup. Do it yourself."

Carolyn is my radio officer. We took our amateur radio license exams together. At the last moment, Carolyn snatched back her test paper and changed an answer. My score was perfect, 100%. She missed one. I happened to "let this slip" a couple of times so all the sailors in the Atlantic, Pacific and Indian Oceans knew. This infuriated her. Thus she continued her radio-theory studies to get her higher class license and, ultimately, to become a volunteer examiner for the Federal Communications Commission.

I didn't say anything for a long time but I could tell she was still awake. Finally I whispered, "This takes knowledge, skill and, well, some level of competency and technical expertise... which pretty much eliminates a macho techno-nerd like me. I'm just here to, well; act as a sort of pleasure-toy for the crew..."

"Ok," she said resignedly. "You win, Fatty. Do you want a GRS or NOGAP GRIB?"

"Both," I said, as I thought about the weather brief I'd put together for Jim, "and I wouldn't mind some NADI text too."

"You got it," she said and heaved her lovely self out of the bunk.

The reason we were both tired was because we'd roared ashore in the dinghy at 0200 to a fancy resort on a tiny island called Mala in the Vava'u group of Tonga, to watch the America's Cup, sort of. Actually, it was a live computer simulation of the Cup via the web, which was as close as we could get, technologically, to the action in Valencia. It was fun— but what a horrible groan went up at the bar full of rambunctious Kiwis when Team New Zealand ripped their chute and then wine-glassed its replacement during that fifth race.

I'd wisely preset the alarm for early so we could help out our buddy Jim Sublett and I could still get to writing at my normal time of 0800. The reason I was so being so stern with myself was because I'd been assigned a rather difficult article. Normally, I write exactly what I want and editors can lump it or leave it, but occasionally I'm so greedy that I take formal assignments—and I'd been asked to write a treatise about tribal communications in the Pacific.

Damn, it sounded boring even to me!

But first we had to help out a friend.

Our modest nav/communication station is opposite our small galley aboard our 38-foot sloop *Wild Card*, so as I brushed my teeth, I was able to watch Carolyn whirl her radio dials and punch her laptop keyboard.

First, she checked radio propagation via our bundled Airmail software. This allows us to determine, from any spot on earth at any moment, the best frequency to contact any other spot on earth. Next, she typed the commands that would let our computer tell someone else's computer just what it was we were looking for. Then, she fired up our ICOM 710 SSB radio along with our German-built Pactor digital modem, roamed for a clear station, and then hit "enter" with authority. Soon digital packets of information were whizzing back and forth between our vessel and the internet via an SSB shore station. Computer windows started popping open. These wind charts, text forecasts and razor-sharp digi-weather (known locally as "fleet codes," a holdover, strangely, from WWII) provided us with an astounding amount of cost-free location-specific "almost real-time" weather information at our digital fingertips.

"Yeah, that low-pressure system is sliding below us just like you predicted, Fatty," Carolyn mused as she perused the data, "and the northerly shift has already begun."

We traded places and soon, via a SSB voice transmission, I was conveying our morning weather analysis to Alaska Jim aboard *Bell Bird*, anchored 100 miles to the south of us off Ha'afeva in the Ha'apia group of Tonga.

"It looks like you should keep her in the barn for a couple more days until the wind backs into the southeast," I told him.

"Roger that, and give Miss Carolyn a hug for me!" he said as he signed off.

Sailors do stuff like this for each other all the time. We all give so we can eventually take. We regularly make deposits in the cosmic Karma Bank of Life. Nobody keeps score but everyone knows the score. Jim doesn't have a Pactor modem, so I give him the long-distance benefit of mine. I don't have a watermaker, and so I'm often invited aboard yachts that do—"for cocktails and bring your jugs"—during dry spells. (We catch most of our drinking water, but, alas, not all.) Basically, what goes around comes around. We all get the reputation we deserve. We sea gypsies are a small but global community. We reap what we sow. I remember one time being anchored in remote, population-less Chagos with ten other boats in the middle of the Indian Ocean, and there was enough technical expertise—computer designer, software engineer, outboard mechanic, fishing expert, playwright—to rule the entire world. *And* the wisdom not to!

Over a leisurely breakfast, Carolyn and I listened in to the infamous "Rag of the Air", our local southwest Pacific SSB cruising chat net. It meets every morning on 8173 at 1900 Zulu. This highly irreverent net is run by another sailor named Jim—Jim Bandy, an American ex-pat who swallowed the hook at Also Island off Fiji's north coast, and immediately invented his own informal talk show for sailors. The show reaches sailors in an area from Australia and New Zealand in the south to Tonga and Vanuatu in the north.

Basically, all the cruisers within 2,000 miles or so tune in every morning to check the small amount of weather info and large amount of gossip exchanged. The really weird day is Sunday, when the "Reverend Jim" seizes the microphone for his traditional 20-minute pseudo-sermon. Some of these homilies are so funny we're writhing on the cabin sole laughing. Others are decidedly not!

But Jim is a perfect reflection of the global marine community: half crazy, ever willing to help, generous to a fault, and totally "weird as a beard" as our daughter Roma would say.

That day, I tuned into the rag for a specific reason. A few days previously, I'd chatted with a happy-go-lucky Texan named Louis Honeycutt who sails *Elysium,* a 44-foot Cross-designed trimaran that was built in 1968. He was headed for Port Resolution, Tanna, in Vanuatu; a cruising destination Carolyn and I love dearly. We immediately told him how much we'd enjoyed our stay there and wished him luck. Unfortunately, the following day, Louis reported his recently repaired prop shaft had slipped aft of its coupling and the boat had nearly sunk before he'd been able to staunch the water flow. He was engineless, much of his electronics were down and he was now diverting to a harbor that would be easier to enter under sail. He didn't sound happy anymore.

Worse yet, the following day he didn't come up on the Rag, which was ominous.

On this morning, we hoped to hear that Louis and his three crew members aboard *Elysium* were in safe harbor and resting before attempting repairs. Instead, our friend Russ Cobb (KK4MT) on *Hygelig* surfaced on the frequency. Russ is an avid "ham" who is active on all bands. He often acts as a liaison between different nets, such as the very formal Pacific Seafarers net (14300, on 20 meters) and the laidback Rag.

"PacSea is reporting the 406 EPIRB registered to *Elysium* went off last night, right in our area. I mean, we know Louis had trouble, he isn't responding, and now his EPIRB has been activated. I think we should take this one seriously, guys!"

Immediately, all idle chatter ceased on the Rag. This is, after all, primarily why such cruising nets exist: to help. Suddenly dozens of people in dozens of countries—separated by a half-million square-miles of ocean—pooled their communication resources to help a fellow mariner in (at least potential) distress.

Jim Bandy, as net control, repeated *Elysium's* last reported position, and announced he'd act as Information Central. Vessels in Port Resolution (Tanna, Vanuatu) confirmed that *Elysium* hadn't arrived. Various SSB volunteers were dispatched to other marine nets on different frequencies to spread the word as accurately as possible, and to relay any pertinent info back to the Rag. To facilitate this, it was agreed to meet back on the same frequency in four hours, and four hours after that if needed.

Various people were able to help in different ways because of their specific technology. For instance, Randy Schneider, an American sailing a Gozzard 44, *Procyon,* used his satellite phone to contact the U.S. Coast Guard in both Hawai'i and San Diego. Ditto Captain Steve aboard *Aussie Oi*, who communicated with the Australian Coast Guard in Sydney. A passing New Zealand yacht in VHF-radio range of New Caledonia (which is the search-and-rescue base in this area) immediately brought the French up to speed on the situation. Other boaters contacted Louis' stateside family, and confirmed and expanded our known details. E-mails flew hither and yon. Carolyn queried Winlink to see how many boats with active ham radios were currently in the potential search area. (This technology to precisely locate a seagoing ham is so new it is rarely used, but it's *highly* valuable in SAR situations. Basically, we can always find out which of the boats around us equipped with ham radios are issuing position reports.)

That morning, there had been two ongoing incidents that the net had been following with interest; both were temporarily put on hold.

The first was a north-bound catamaran named *Holokai,* with Spike and Angela aboard, that was bound for Savusavu, in Fiji. It had broken its boom and ripped its mainsail during a welcome-to-the-tropics gale. Rick Walker on the catamaran *Endangered Species* volunteered to act as mission control on this non-life-threatening incident, taking the vessel's skipper off frequency to continue to closely monitor his condition without interfering with the main event. Another vessel was heading east from New Zealand in the distant South Pacific Ocean; the skipper had ended up taking an unplanned swim. My old Virgin Islands multihull friend Ted "Wood-Butcher" Cary on the much-modified Jim Brown trimaran *Seaquester,* decided to play good shepherd on this one.

Frequency-band conditions changed throughout the day, of course, as is common with SSB and Ham radios. This required frequency changes and lots of relays, where one yacht passes the "baton of information" onward to another, and thus vast miles of ocean are covered in seconds. Think of it as repeating smoke signals from mountaintop to mountaintop.

Yes, the modern world of marine communications is a truly wondrous thing. I never thought that a modest vessel like *Wild Card*, with our tiny cruising pocketbook, would be in almost continuous e-mail and radio contact with the rest of the world. Or that I'd be able to exchange text, pictures, software, MP3s, and graphics with other distant vessels, completely free of charge, thanks to our Pactor modem and free Easy Transfer software.

Wasn't it only yesterday that a whaler would convey news of a death aboard by painting a blue stripe around his vessel? Or fly a long red "homeward bound" pennant to signal his willingness to carry mail home? Why, a whaler's wife might be reading today's letter within the year!

If all this radio "busy-ness" wasn't enough, we also listened to the Pacific Report from distant Radio New Zealand for a comprehensive roundup of local Tonga/Fiji/Samoa news. Simultaneously—at one point we had three radios on at the same time—we checked into our local VHF Vava'u cruisers net on Channel 06 during its Treasures of the Bilge segment, hoping to trade our heavy 17.5-foot whisper pole for a lighter 14-footer; it's something we've been trying to do for, oh, five or six years now.

Mostly, while waiting for news of *Elysium*, we thought back on dozens of other "SSB rescues" we'd been involved with over the years.

Our SSB suddenly exploded with activity: Four sailors had swum ashore on the small island of Futuna, which lies just east of Tanna. It was officially confirmed: They'd been sighted on the beach by a French SAR plane. One crewmember was reported to have severe coral cuts, but the others were basically OK—rather shaken from their ordeal, sure, but OK. The boat, alas, was a total loss.

Carolyn and I didn't talk about it. Not then. It was too early. All the facts weren't in. And we hadn't fully processed it mentally. We've spent our whole watery lives a tack or two from catastrophe and don't relish hearing such hard-luck news about other sailors. Instead we shut off the cabin lights and crawled into our bunk.

I was dead-dog tired. Hell, I'd communicated with half the world even if I hadn't gotten off the boat. My mind was spinning. I could tell Carolyn was awake too: after 38 years in the same small, toe-touching V-berth, our sleepy consciousnesses have almost melded.

"You never got to your writing today," she mused into her pillow.

"*Manana's* fine," I yawed. "No problem."

"What's the writing assignment about?"

"Tribal communications," I said. "How certain groups of nomadic Pacific residents—specifically, we far-flung sea gypsies—communicate."

"So today you lived it," she began. And I concluded with, "And tomorrow I'll write it."

Neither of us said anything for a while. The tropic-night air felt delicious on our naked skin. There were a million/billion stars crowding the open forehatch above. Tiny waves lullabied our hull. Finally I whispered, "And how's my Pactor Babe?"

"Needy," she said.

The Cape of Good Hope: The Reluctant Way

When a war forces two humble equator-huggers around the tip of Africa, the key to survival is patience.

My wife, Carolyn, and I never intended to round the storm-tossed southern tip of Africa and the Cape of Good Hope. *Wild Card*, our Hughes 38, is a very modest production boat built in the 1970s. She, like her crew, intended full and well to spend her days in the benign tropics and their gentle trade winds. My motto, through 44 years of blissful living aboard and 100,000 miles of ocean cruising, has remained constant: "Be in the right ocean at the right time, stay near the tropics, and everything will be fine"

But as we set out from Thailand on the second half of our west-about circumnavigation, a war got in the way. Politics—not Mother Nature—was suddenly shaping our course homeward to the Caribbean. Instead of heading, as planned, up the Red Sea to Europe, we were forced to detour across the Indian Ocean, south through the Mozambique Channel, then around the southern tip of Africa. Thus it was, at the end of 2003, that we found ourselves in Richards Bay, on the eastern coast of South Africa, about to violate my own self-imposed rule: We were leaving the path of least resistance, dipping south in the Agulhas Current, and bound via the notorious Cape of Good Hope for Cape Town. And before the passage was over, we'd break yet another rule that had served us so well through the years.

Squash Zone

There are good reasons why the Cape of Good Hope is also known as the Cape of Storms. The first reason is the Agulhas Current. This major ocean current runs westward across the windy southern Indian Ocean and strikes South Africa just 50 miles north of Richards Bay. Once it hits the coast, it has no choice but to turn southward and squeeze around the southern tip of Africa. Offshore, the Agulhas is only moving at a couple of knots. But compressed along the outside edge of the 100 fathom line of continental Africa, it runs at up to six knots. Picture the Gulf Stream on steroids.

The second factor that makes rounding so difficult is the weather, which approaches from the opposite direction of the current. As lows run smack into the Cape, they tend to get compressed and forced southward around the tip. To further complicate matters, the gales stack up at the Cape, creating an area of compressed isobars, the dreaded coastal squash zones of the Cape of Storms.

Because the gales follow in close succession, sailors must wait a month or more before a two- or three-day weather window opens up with a fair northeast wind of less than 35 knots. And when the weather turns, it can turn quickly. It isn't unusual to be in fine weather, running southwest off the wind in 28 knots of northeasterly breeze, and in less than an hour be in a full gale from the southwest. So you have the worst of all worlds: a large, established northeast swell, a building squash-zone gale and a strong opposing current. The result, in the words of a South African weather forecast, is "abnormal waves of up to 20 meters (65 feet) in height." Oh, yeah—did I mention the fog?

It gets worse, safe harbors in South Africa are few and far between. The rounding of the Cape begins in earnest at Durban, about 100 miles south of Richards Bay. From Durban, the next safe harbor is East London, 288 miles away. Finally, officialdom adds its own nasty kink. You have to clear in and clear out of every port in South Africa, and you *must* leave within 48 hours of clearing out, or you have to repeat the entire day-long bureaucratic process.

As Carolyn puts it, "Every mile traveled in South Africa is a drama!" We had, alas, plenty of dramas.

Weather Gurus

We did have a few things in our favor. South African has one of the best meteorological bureaus on Earth as well as some of the nicest amateur routers. These hardworking men and women not only know where all the gales are, but also where they're going and how fast, often calling coastal wind shifts within minutes and wind velocities within a knot. During the transit months of December and January, they keep careful track of cruising boats in the region, shepherding over 80 boats around the Cape annually. South Africa requires you to file a float plan, so if you're late arriving at your next port, you'd best notify the authorities before they launch a search.

In short, rounding the Cape of Good Hope involves long periods of waiting for weather; followed by frantic rough water passages—mad coastal dashes, really—to reach port before the next gale. Our first taste mad dash came on December 3rd, when we cleared out of Richards Bay for Durban. There was a strong southwesterly gale blowing at the time. We went back to *Wild Card* and monitored the gale until our barometer topped out at 1020 millibars, then started making preparations to get underway. Thirty-six hours after we'd officially cleared out, we stuck our nose out of the harbor. Soon enough, we had a fair wind, though it was light. From sea buoy to sea buoy we sailed 100 miles in just over 12 hours, thanks largely to the current.

We enjoyed Durban, particularly the warm hospitality of the Royal Natal Yacht Club. We were tied up right downtown. It was an easy walk to the central city, the library, the maritime museum and the theater. The highlight of our stay was attending Alistair Campbell's famous annual party for cruisers, during which the amateur radio hams of Africa meet all the visiting sailors.

Tony Herrick, a local South African sailing writer of wide experience, told me pointedly, "This is one area where you have to have a lot of time. If you're trying to transit the Cape on a tight schedule, you're bound to run into a serious blow somewhere along the way."

"We have plenty of time," Carolyn assured him, "if not this year, then next!"

"That's the spirit," agreed Tony.

We left Durban just as we'd left Richards Bay, on a fading sou'westerly gale. We didn't turn southward at the breakwaters; instead we headed directly seaward to the 200-meter depth contour and the area of fastest current.

Our weather window was predicted to last 48 hours, and since I had the current, I wasn't too worried about making 260 miles before the next gale. Once we were in the current, we shut off the engine and sailed slowly southward in a dying breeze. This was a mistake. Along this coast, the prudent mariner moves as rapidly as possible, with absolutely no lollygagging. The other boats making the passage with us wisely kept powering at six knots instead of sailing at three. The wind was predicted to be 20 to 25 knots when we left, but that soon changed to "25 knots and gusting," then finally to "25 to 30 knots out of the northeast." Since the current and wind were heading in the same direction, I didn't think this would be a problem. But it was. The seas were somehow different, not steeper but breaking more often. And a number of waves were noticeably higher and steeper than their brothers. While we weren't in any danger, it wasn't exactly boring—particularly the last 25 miles.

The Longest Night

While the other boats in our group all reached the safe harbor of East London before nightfall on the following day, we were still cautiously stumbling along the African coast in the dark, in a building sea and veering wind, nervously racing an approaching gale.

"We can heave to until morning," I suggested to Carolyn, who has been my navigator for the last 35 years of cruising.

"No," she said firmly. "If we keep going, we should arrive at the breakwater just before midnight. The next southwest gale will rip through a couple of hours later. We'll have to go in. As you know, it's well-marked."

I'd studied the charts for weeks in preparation for this leg, and I knew every detail of the entrance to East London intimately. Still, I hate entering strange harbors at night, and I've made it a rule to avoid doing so at all costs. But every rule has its exceptions, and in this case, being in the Agulhas Current with an approaching gale, was the time to make one.

We decided to go for it.

There are two parts to entering a strange harbor at night that I don't like: When I'm not exactly sure of what I'm seeing—*and when I am.* I believe that nearly all the boats wrecked on breakwaters were driven by skippers who were "sure" they were right until they heard the breakers or felt the crunch.

First, we contacted one of the other boats in East London to confirm that the GPS coordinates agreed with our chart. Carolyn confirmed (for the third time) our carefully plotted GPS way-points, and both of us reviewed our detailed harbor-entrance chart, our guidebook and the Coast Pilot, particularly noting the bearings of the ranges and the entrance-light characteristics.

Once we actually started into the entrance, all idle chatter ceased. I was on deck, and I was careful to preserve my night vision. Carolyn was at the nav station with all her charts and books spread open before her and our electronic charting system blinking away at her side. In such situations, we both have to agree 100 percent on what is happening. If either of us gets confused or unsure, I'll immediately turn 180 degrees seaward, until we both agree on where we are or what course to take.

"I think I'm a little too far to starboard, too much north," I said. "I'm turning a tad to port."

"Fine," she said. A couple of minutes later, she said, "Does that look like the middle?"

"Yeah," I agreed. "Depth?"

"Eleven meters," she said, always reading it off to me in the measure of the charts we're using, whether it be in feet, fathoms or meters.

"I got the range in sight, just lining them up now. I'm turning."

"Excellent," she said. "Nice!"

In the end, we had no problem. The range was dead simple and we slipped in without a hitch.

"An idiot could come in here at night," mocked a sailor friend the following day.

"That's exactly what I was worried about," I said.

East London, South Africa's only river port, is at the mouth of the lovely Buffalo river.

Two days after we arrived in East London, another weather window opened and the eight-boat fleet with which we were traveling departed. But we decided to linger. I wanted to see as much of coastal South Africa as I could. The wait paid off with a near-perfect passage from East London to Port Elizabeth. We covered the 140 miles in less than 20 hours without problem. After some confusion over where we should settle for clear-in procedures, we anchored, with the Port Authorities knowledge, just outside the floating breakwater of the Port Elizabeth Marina.

A few days later, a 50-knot gale forced all the fishing boats, even the large offshore trawlers, to seek shelter. We were in the middle of a leisurely lunch listening to the gusts shake the rig when we heard the roar of a tug engine close to us. There was a sudden crash, and *Wild Card* tilted crazily until her starboard rail was momentarily underwater. All the wine and water glasses on the galley table shifted and slid, then shattered on the cabin sole.

"What the hell?" I shouted as I lurched back up and dashed out the companionway. It was broad day light and the Port Authority tug had backed right into our stern.

Luckily, the tug had struck us only a glancing blow. The major impact was on the port knuckle of our transom, where the fiberglass is particularly thick. True, the resin was crushed and raw glass exposed, but I could easily dab the area with epoxy for now, then fix it properly during our next haul out. The nicks in our topsides were minor and cosmetic. I could live with them, and we could continue our voyage. Though the port officials later apologized, the captain never did, and the encounter made us glad to leave Port Elizabeth in the next weather window.

We made the 180-miles run into lovely Mosselbai (Mossel Bay) without incident, and we were delighted to learn from our weather routers that the gale we were anticipating had unexpectedly jogged southward. Thus we had a brief, "calm wind" weather window into Cape Town if we wanted to leave straightaway. But first we needed fuel and it was Sunday morning at dawn. As luck would have it, a Good Samaritan sailor was up to the challenge. He piled me and my fuel jugs into his van and rushed me off to the only nearby fuel station open on Sunday.

We were at sea again within a half an hour of pulling into Mossel Bay.

It felt wonderful. The end was insight. We were going to pull this off. I began to relax.

One Last Thrash

Later that day, we saw one of the most amazing sights of our circumnavigation: a sheer 12-foot wave, more than twice the size of all the other waves around us, rolling abeam of us. But, what caught my attention were the birds, or at least that's what I thought they were a huge flock of 'em. But as the wave approached, I realized they weren't birds at all—they were dolphins, hundreds of them, surfing atop and shooting straight out of the nearly vertical face of the wave.

Around noon the next day, the Cape of Good Hope hove into view. It was a gorgeous sight, very dramatic and imposing. We only had 40 miles left to Cape Town. We were sailing along at five knots in a dying breeze. It was lovely, lovely, lovely.

"I never thought I'd see this." I said to Carolyn.

"Well, you'd better take a good, long look," she joked, "because I don't expect we'll be back anytime soon!"

I took her by the hand. There were no boats around. I twirled her experimentally in my sunburned arms, where she collapsed with a laugh. All was well in the world. All was as it should be.

About 20 minutes later, I returned on deck and noticed the wind had come up. I tucked a reef in the mainsail. Fifteen minutes later, I tucked in the second reef. Within the hour, I was nervously moving my genoa car forward to better trim my now partially furled jib. The Cape of Storms wasn't about to allow us to slip away without one more thrashing.

It was blowing 35 knots, and the sky to southwest looked awful. I flipped on the VHF radio and immediately heard a merry South African voice say, "The Doctor has arrived."

We were in for it, all right. The Doctor is a very strong, localized wind that regularly visits Cape Town.

"Watch out," the chuckling VHF voice added. "She's wearing her tablecloth!"

This means dense, cold clouds were being forced over nearby Table Mountain and are rapidly pouring into the valley below, with speeds of up to 45 knots. We needed a lee, and we needed it fast. Without hesitation, I steered for Slangkop Point, hoping to get behind it for protection from the building wind and sea. But I didn't find my lee there, nor further along at

Duiker Point. As we curved along the peninsula's southwestern shore, so did the wind. No protection. None.

I clawed down the triple-reefed mainsail—not an easy task at night with breaking waves regularly sweeping the boat. Soon we were down to a scrap of jib, and still I felt overpowered.

"What's our anemometer say," I yelled below to Carolyn.

"It's hitting 50 knots," she shouted back.

"Call Cape Town Port Authority, and ask them if they think this is going to last."

She did, and a couple of minutes later she reported that the weather was expected to be bad for at least 24 hours.

"Damn," I said. If we were going to stay out, we needed more sea room, but I was worried that once we were offshore, the Agulhas Current might sweep us right past Cape Town.

"It's your call, Fatty, but I think we should keep going in," said Carolyn. "It's only 25 miles or so."

They were the longest 25 miles of my life. The wild, rig-pumping gusts off Table Mountain were right off the scale. I expected the jib to explode at any second. I kept trying to work *Wild Card* shoreward to gain some shelter behind the looming Apostles Hills, but every time I turned our stern slightly so that it was no longer square to the face of the waves, one would break over us with a foam-smothering thunderclap. It was awful, but there was a strange and twisted beauty to it as well.

Africa is wild, wild, wild, and in that moment, I could see and feel and taste its wildness all around me. This was really happening. It was now. I was here. This was really, truly the Cape of Storms of my childhood dreams and nightmares. It was magnificently living up to its name. Everything seemed surreal, as if the world had suddenly turned "too true" to be believed. I blinked my eyes in wonder. The teeming metropolis of Cape Town was winking prettily before me. Gold and silver city lights sparkled against the backdrop of Table Mountain, silhouetted by the light of the rising moon behind it. Above the mountain's dark shape, the long, white "tablecloth" cloud gathered and then streamed down into its shrouded valley. The sight was more than mysterious; it was from another world.

I was jerked from my reverie by another boarding sea, bigger and louder than the others. As it hissed beneath the hull, Carolyn emerged with the latest update.

"The Port Authority says docking at the Royal Cape Yacht Club under these wind conditions might be tricky," said Carolyn. "They recommend anchoring at Granger Bay, just before the breakwater but well within the lee until the wind drops below 40 knots."

"Sounds fine to me," I told her. "I'll be happy to drop the hook anywhere I can."

It was past midnight, and we were virtually abreast of Victoria Harbor before the waves calmed down enough to think we might actually make it. Carolyn slid the main hatch back, and wearily stuck her beautiful head out, leaving the nav station and her computer somewhat exposed to the elements, a sure sign she believed the worst was over.

"I'll unlash the anchor," she was saying nonchalantly. "Just follow the waypoints I punched up." I saluted and she smiled. We were being silly with each other again, another sure indication that the danger was over. We'd made it. We were in the South Atlantic. The rough Indian Ocean and the dreaded Cape of Storms were behind us.

"OK, drop it," I shouted to Carolyn forward. I heard the chain pay out.

"Anchor down," she confirmed.

I was just popping the champagne cork when she came back into the cockpit.

"Champagne already?" she asked, but I could tell she was giddy with happiness.

The bottle was warm and the cheapest bubbles imaginable, but as we drank a toast with our arms intertwined, it tasted like Dom Pérignon.

"To us," said Carolyn.

To us, indeed.

South Atlantic Toddle

The Final Leg: From Cape Town to Reality

The longer I sail, the more I enjoy sailing long.

Let's put it another way: distance no longer intimidates me, mere miles mean nothing. So, three days out of Cape Town, I was a happy man. Almost six thousand miles of empty ocean lay ahead. I looked forward to the tranquility, the peace, the Zen of it. The vexations of shore would fade: My universe would shrink to me, my wife, and our vessel. God would be close: in every wave, behind every cloud, within each rainbow sighted. And I was doubly happy to have the Indian Ocean and the Cape of Good Hope finally behind me. I seemed lighter, happier and more carefree since rounding. I'd had no idea how heavy the weight of their dual challenge was, until I'd wrestled them on their own terms.

Cape Town was mega-fun. The Royal Cape Yacht Club is, perhaps, the most welcoming in the world. We toured the surrounding Cape vineyards, and dented their inventories as much as our wallets and livers would allow. The Victoria and Alfred Waterfront was delightful, as if all the exotic treasures of Africa had fallen down to its chilly southern tip.

Visually, Cape Town is absolutely stunning. Table Mountain majestically towers over the city—a kinetic, ever-changing feast for the eyes. It is this highly dramatic, flat-topped, straight-edged rock which makes the area so unique, especially when it wears its famous "table cloth" of dense, thick cloud.

I've never seen anything quite like it. I was fascinated. I watched it—hour after hour after hour, completely mesmerized. The clouds continuously get forced up and over its barren plateau, and pour down its steep slopes like sinking steam—silently boiling and tumbling and billowing and puffing. Picture dense smoke from an upside-down fire and you're close.

If the cloud manages to cat's-paw its way down Table Mountain so far that its hillside is almost entirely obscured; that's when "The Doctor" is really in, as the locals say.

That's the best part of cruising—the wild juxtapositions between shore, sea, and society. We'd just spent years in Asia, India, Chagos, and Madagascar and were enthralled to be suddenly thrust into the very heart of a modern, world-class city such as Cape Town.

Now we were ready for the final leg of our four year circumnavigation: the 6,000 mile "toddle" back to the Caribbean.

Of course, water-borne adventures can still beckon within the concrete canyons of the urban Cape Town. I'd always heard of how fanatical the racing sailors of Africa were, and

wanted to participate in one of the informal "Wednesday night races" that the club holds each week.

I thought I'd missed my chance; the "Doctor" visited Cape Town on that particular Wednesday, and it was blowing a steady 38 knots with gusts to 48 by late afternoon—good weather in which to lay ahull in the bar! But, no, the skipper of the Atlantic 44, I was invited to race aboard, showed up, didn't even mention the weather, and away we went.

It was strange. It was blowing so hard I was scared to even remove the sail cover. I mean, I didn't want to remove the compass *binnacle* cover without having my safety harness clipped on. And yet, we flew a full genoa and single-reefed mainsail during the *very* exciting start. There were 40-plus boats on the line and white-caps and blown-spume everywhere. Just as we were rounding the weather mark in severe, rail-dipping gusts of 45-plus knots, a South African crewman nonchalantly said, "Don't come about or jibe, skipper, we've lost the upper spreader on the leeward side!"

As we powered back to shore, we were requested by the very calm, very professional race committee to tow in another casualty, a J/24 that had lost its rudder. We were more than happy to do so, but it was difficult passing the towline, while avoiding several other distressed vessels drifting sideways through the fleet. Yes, South Africans like a lot of demolition derby with their yacht racing! Nobody seemed the least bit concerned that we'd just sailed our race boat to destruction. In fact, the only comment I heard was a typical, "Thank God we didn't lose the spreader when it was *really* blowing!"

How long did we stay in Cape Town? Why did we leave? Let's put it this way: We're sailors who care deeply about our cherished maritime traditions. Thus we spent our money like what we were—drunken sailors. So we headed out to sea with empty pockets and a hang-over. "Is it possible to go to sea without a headache?" my wife Carolyn, who has cruised offshore with me 35 years now, asked as she hoisted the mainsail, while I slacked the topping lift.

"I don't know," I told her truthfully. "I've never met anyone who has."

Wild Card, the ocean-weary Hughes 38 we'd salvaged off the bottom after hurricane Hugo in 1989, for a mere $3,000, seemed happy to be at sea again.

Robben Island, where Nelson Mandela was held prisoner for decades, slid by to port. We solemnly saluted it to honor the man. Not for all the pain and suffering he endured, but because he emerged with such a joyous, loving heart, completely without hate.

"Where to, Skip?" Carolyn asked. She does all our navigating now, since I've retired my father's World War II sextant to a display on our main bulkhead.

"Oh, I don't know," I said. "Up the middle of the South Atlantic, I guess. We might stop in St. Helena if the weather is settled. I understand there are 18-foot swells in the harbor when it's not!"

"Brazil?" she queried. "Devil's Island? The Five Apostles?"

"I doubt it," I replied. "I'm tired of putting the children of South American Customs officials through college. It's time to wrap up this Big Fat Circle. Why not rhumb line us straight to the Caribbean—non-stop!"

"That's close to 6,000 ocean miles," she said. "But who's counting?"

"Ah," I said, and yawned "A couple of months and we'll be there!"

It was easy, very easy, but not *quite* that easy!

As usual, we got off to a bumpy start. We'd hoped for a 72 hour weather window leaving Cape Town, but we'd sailed slightly slower than expected, and the approaching sou'westerly gale from the direction of Cape Horn had sped up a tad. Thus, we were severely pooped on our third night.

But it wasn't a problem, really. We ran off before it with only our jib-tongue showing (a yard or two the heavily reinforced clew of our strongest roller-furling jib) and thus had "no worries," as our Aussie sailing friends would say.

On the fourth day, we sailed into summer. One minute we had to be prudent, Indian Ocean-hardened seamen—and the next, it was Party-time in Paradise. The South Atlantic is the most benign ocean we've ever crossed. If you're ever going take an Optimist pram across an ocean, this is the one.

We opened up all our hatches and dried out the boat—and pretty much left them open for the next six weeks of ocean sailing.

The only major goof-up of the trip was entirely my fault. Here's the techno-nightmare: Despite my best, old-fashioned, low-tech intentions; more and more wires began to sprout from my Toshiba laptop to various shipboard electro-bits. I didn't plan on this—in fact, I guarded against it—but it happened nonetheless.

First, I hooked the GPS to the computer, then interfaced it with some way-cool electronic charts, popped in a little DOS program to upload my graphic chart positions back into my GPS, then I added a slick weather charting program, a marvelous star finder, some world-wide tide tables, a perpetual nautical almanac, some electronic guide books, and finally laced in a fine German Pactor III modem for SSB shipboard e-mail and inter-ship graphic exchange—and the next thing I knew my laptop was completely central to my nav station!

So, since my laptop computer was playing such an increasingly important role, I decided to water-proof it as much as possible before leaving Cape Town. Thus, I slightly elevated it so that any stray water or dampness could pass underneath, rubberized and sealed all its many connectors, and even made a special "splash" curtain so that, in the unlikely event of a rogue wave bounding below decks, the computer would be semi-protected.

About a week into the trip, on a perfectly nice sailing day, I was admiring said installation and mentally patting myself on the back for being such a clever and careful "prudent mariner." I leaned over the computer to observe its ultra-neat water-proofed and heat-shrunk back—and poured the entire contents of my steaming cup of very sugary coffee into the keyboard!

At first, I couldn't believe it. It wasn't possible. It hadn't happened. Nobody could be that stupid. Perhaps it was a visual hallucination? So I said aloud, "I didn't do that—couldn't have done that!"

Carolyn tossed aside the Harry Crews novel she was reading up in the cockpit, sighed heavily, and asked, "What now?"

Maybe it *had* been a hallucination! There was no puddle of coffee on the nav station. The computer screen was OK. The only problem was, my still-steaming coffee cup, which had been full just a couple of seconds ago, was now empty—and looking, well, accusingly at me.

"Gee, Carolyn," I said glumly, "I think I just really flubbed up— and drowned our computer."

She glanced over and started to say, "It's fine," but stopped as the screen got kinda wavery, then started bubbling, and finally blinked off forever.

There was a moment of silence during which Carolyn thought, "I've married an idiot" and I thought, "She's married an idiot." and then we both smiled sickly at each other.

I gently picked up the computer, tilted it, and watched coffee slosh out.

"That was an expensive cup of java," Carolyn said.

"Yeah," I agreed, "about two grand!"

To make matters even worst, we'd been posting our daily position on the internet (at shiptrak.org) via our SSB. Now our position would suddenly stop, and dozens of family and friends might think we were in trouble, when I was not actually in trouble but merely "extremely stupid," as Carolyn delicately put it.

Now this section of ocean between Cape Town and St. Helena isn't exactly teeming with discount computer outlets, but I'm the kinda guy who will grab at any straw. So I called around on my Icom 710 SSB, first on the marine frequencies, and then on the amateur ham bands, and was soon chatting up Paul and Susan Mitchell of *Elenoa* (N6HFC, N6HFD respectively), whom we'd met in Richards Bay, South Africa. (My call sign is W2FAT.)

Everything was fine with them, except both their masthead anchor light and their tricolor had stopped working. They, too, were in-transit and headed north to the Caribbean. They'd just "rushed through the Pacific and Indian Oceans in only a couple of decades of cruising," as they laughingly put it.

After a proper amount of chit-chat, I nonchalantly asked them if they had a back-up nav computer.

"Sure," said Paul, "but it's a very old IBM unit, ancient, like, well, kerosene-operated, and so slow it could barely chart continental drift."

"Are you planning to stop in St. Helena," I asked.

"Not really," he said.

"What?!?" I screamed into the microphone, "but you must! The harbor is like a millpond and I'll crank you up the mast so you can fix your masthead lights. I'll introduce you to what's left of Boney's old crew. And while I'm aboard your vessel, I'll take that useless, old, rust-stained, buggy, worm-infested computer off your hands and free up some valuable storage space on *Elenoa*—a real win-win situation, eh?"

"Er..." Paul said, his SSB signal raising and falling with the whims of oceanographic propagation, "Who is Boney?"

As a result, we both unexpectedly stopped in lonely, lovely St. Helena, and discovered one of the friendliest, least visited, seldom touched islands in the world.

We arrived on St. Helena after 14 days—the final ten days of which were spent in perfect 12-14 knot sou'easterly tradewinds. *Wild Card* seemed more like a magic carpet than a sailing yacht, clicking off 130-mile days, with open hatches, dry decks, and the cockpit table cluttered with books, snacks and small projects. It was lovely, utterly lovely, cruising—completely effortless. Yes, we could have gone faster. Ninety-five percent of the time we just "chicken-jibbed" it, with no mainsail despite the light winds. But why rush when you are exactly where you want to be?

St. Helena (latitude 16S, longitude 6W) is isolated, to put it mildly. It's over 1200 miles west of Africa and 1800 miles east of South America. This is just about as far away from anywhere as you can get on this planet. There is no airport, no harbor, and no commercial port—and thus, tourism is almost nonexistent. The result is that the Saints, which is what the 5000 residents modestly call themselves, are famous for their friendliness. Their only contact with the rest of the world is electronic, and a large, slow supply ship that sails from South Africa around ten times a year, unless it breaks down. It was being repaired in South African during our visit.

Since there is no place for freighters to tie up on St. Helena, all cargo must be lightered ashore aboard small vessels. Just before we arrived, six containers of large, land-based, "alternative energy" wind-generators arrived. The St. Helena longshoremen only dropped one tinsy-weensy container in the water—and that only very briefly—but, alas, it was the one with all the electronic controls in it. The twirling wind-generators have, alas, never worked quite right.

Even anchoring in St. Helena is a challenge. We first put our hook down in 127 feet of water, and dragged out during breakfast on the following day with 600 feet (three 200 foot rodes double-carricked together) of scope out. Hauling up this soggy, muddy mess with an ancient manual SL 555 windlass wasn't easy—especially in the six-foot swell.

We next re-anchored in a mere 65 feet. This time we had three anchors down and nearly 800 feet of line out. We held, but not with confidence. Basically, the chief amusement on St. Helena is watching a pristine international yacht anchor and see its proud, nattily-dressed crew arrive ashore—while said yacht slowly drags—actually, broad reaches under bare poles, while towing anchor weighted warps— westward into the setting sun.

Nothing is easy in St. Helena, even getting ashore. There is nowhere to safely land your dinghy on the iron-bound coast, so we used a local tire-clad "bum boat" to bring us in.

The procedure is this: The bum boat swings alongside and wipes off most of your gel-coat with the knuckle of their transom as you leap aboard. There is a square, flat area aft with a single strong stanchion made for just this purpose. If it's calm, they bring you alongside a stone quay with slimy, slippery, sea-weedy platforms at various tidal heights, and sort of toss you ashore.

Alas, on our first day it was a tad rough for that. Getting too close to the dock would be suicide for the bum boat. So the skipper hovered about eight feet off the dock while the port captain swung out a stout ship's hawser suspended from what looked like a very large, strong swing set bolted to the quay. Everyone yelled '*Now*!' on the crests.

At first I didn't get it. Why were large, heavy ropes swinging around my head? Then suddenly it dawned on me what I supposed to do. Thus, I waited for the proper moment, grabbed the line as it arced out to me, and swung ashore, like Tarzan, into the outstretched arms of waiting officials. I don't even want to *think* what would have happened if I'd lost my grip!

Wow, what a cool way for a sailor to make an island entrance. Later than night, in the pitch-black, with a snootful of gin and a large wet paper sack of spilling groceries, I was less enamored.

St. Helena is like a time-capsule. Except for the "One Big Event," not much has happened. Everyone looks amazingly like everyone else. If ever there ever was a place that is "one, big, happy family," it is St. Helena.

We immediately headed for *Anne's*, the local sailor's bar, and poured over her motley, but fascinating collection of signed logbooks which record nearly every yacht that has been there for decades.

Yes, the distant past is always quite close in St. Helena. We couldn't resist peeking into the living room of the little yellow house right next to *Anne's,* where Joshua Slocum regaled the locals with his now-famous sea yarns, when he passed through.

There is the "One Big Thing," of course, that St. Helena is famous for—being the death-place of exiled (1815-1821) Napoleon Bonaparte.

We got together with the crew of *Elenoa* and some other passing yachties, and hired an old farm truck to take us on an island tour. Our driver, a charming old duffer named Colin, explained the one local traffic rule: Uphill traffic has the right-of-way.

Yes, he admitted, his ancient green truck was a tad tired. He wasn't sure exactly how old it was, but his father had imported it to the island in 1929.

It was during that same day that we met up with noted local historian J. J. Smith, the "special friend" of the French envoy to St. Helena. He was kind enough to give us a detailed guided tour of Bonaparte's home at Longwood. The death bed is so tiny, it seems impossible that it once held the ruler of Europe.

While exploring the island, we vigorously "argued price" with the crew of *Elenoa.* This wasn't easy. They wanted to give us the computer; I demanded to pay $100. Finally I prevailed, but, gosh, dealing with such stubborn fellow cruisers can be tough.

As delightful as St. Helena was, the sea still beckoned. After a mere 72 hours, we were under sail again. Sometimes perfect places are so perfect—it's best to leave quickly.

Within hours, St. Helena was a mere smudge over our transom. In some ways, it seemed more dream than visit; always a good sign.

We'll be back.

There is a small island called Ascension 700 miles to the north. We didn't stop. A couple of weeks went by. We worked on our tans. I played guitar a lot. Carolyn sewed in the cockpit. We passed close enough to Brazil to hear the carnival music, but I could only think of Sir Peter Blake; such a sad, stupid end to such a wonderful, inspiring man.

We didn't stop in Brazil, either. We were almost out of drinking water when we hit the Intertropical Convergence Zone just north of the equator, and managed to top off our tanks under its many slow moving thunderstorms. We use PVC gutters on the edges of our cockpit bimini—crude but effective.

I guess we were almost a month out of South Africa, when Barbados slid passed. We were going to stop and visit Trudi, the German Weather Goddess, but our Caribbean friends were already gathering in St. Barts, French West Indies, for the first of dozens of Caribbean "coming home" parties scheduled. We wanted to get there before all the rum evaporated.

We were 33 days out of St. Helena—50 days and 6,000 sea miles sailed—from Cape Town when the Big Fat Red Line of our outboard track appeared on our tattered chart of the Lesser Antilles.

Carolyn, my navigator/wife/lover, sang out the numbers as we approached. "Only two more hours, Fatty," she said, then later, "four more miles, honey!" and finally, "five seconds, four seconds, three seconds..."

I thought of how far we'd come together; not just the last 50,000 ocean miles of this circumnavigation or the last 35 years of cruising offshore, but through life itself. As man and wife. As friend and lover. As ocean-kissed shipmates in every literal and literary sense.

I'd met her when she was 13 years old—the smartest, wildest, most free-thinking person I'd ever met. She had guts. She had vision. She had balls. And she didn't care what anyone thought; but me. And I, her.

"Two seconds, one sec... *there*!" she shouted with joy. "You did it, Fatty—just like you told me you would; so many, many years ago in Chicago, back at Gage Park High School!"

"We did it," I said, and turned away so she couldn't see my eyes brim. "We!"

The Downside of Circumnavigating

I'm shocked. Literally. No one warned me about the most dangerous part of circumnavigating. And I'm not prepared. I feel like I'm alone and friendless in uncharted waters. Even Carolyn, my wonderful wife, lover, and navigator of 35 years, can't seem to reach me. I'm drowning.

Let's start at the beginning: A decade or so ago, I was racing Lasers at the St. Thomas Yacht Club when it felt like an elephant stepped on my chest. The pain was so intense, that it jackknifed me off the boat and into the water. One foot tangled in my hiking strap, I was underwater. I couldn't breathe and my eyes were open. Time floated. Two thoughts danced slowly through my brain: One of them was, "I'm dying." The other was, "Damn, there goes my boat speed!"

I forced myself to relax. I calmed myself. I untangled foot, surfaced and crawled back on the boat. I stayed face down for a long, long time shaking like a leaf. I was terrified. But in all my life, I've never failed to finish a race. Finishing is important to me. I am goal oriented. I slowly sat up, sheeted in and continued on.

Back at the club, Henry Menin—who'll sit as a juror at the 2007 America's Cup in Spain— came up to me and asked, "Are you OK, Fatty?"

"Yeah, I had a little problem out there on the race course, but I think I'll be more competitive in the bar!"

Silly me. A few days later, I was evacuated by air to a cardiac unit in Puerto Rico. As they wheeled me down the corridor on a stretcher, I thought, "This can't be happening. I can't be dying. I haven't sailed around the world yet, and I haven't written the big book!"

I'd never realized it before, but those were the two givens in my life: I'd circumnavigate, and someday I'd write a book worth reading. (I've written five books but alas, only one, *Chasing the Horizon,* comes close.)

Things looked bleak at that point. For the first time in my life, my horizons were shrinking. But just before dawn is always the darkest time. The test results were surprisingly good: I hadn't had a major heart attack—just a severe cardiac wake-up call. I'd have to radically change my lifestyle, but with proper diet, regular exercise and the right medication, I'd survive.

"How are you?" Carolyn asked nervously as I tied up my dinghy painter to *Wild Card*, our 38-foot S&S-designed Hughes 38.

"I'm OK," I said, " and I want to sail around the world ASAP."

Confession: I am not a very good sailor. I'm not a very good ship's husband. Hell, I'm not much of a shoreside wager-earner, either. But I do have some small talents and abilities. Moving watercraft a couple of hundred miles downwind is one of them.

We left in the spring of 2000. I didn't hedge my bets and pretend that I wasn't sailing around the world—I was upfront and honest.

"I'm sailing around the world," I told people. "We're off on the Big Fat Circle!"

I'd even presumptuously "taken" my weekly St. Thomas radio show (broadcast on Radio One, WVWI-AM 1000) along with me and renamed it "The Circumnavigator's Report." (It's currently on its 15th year and I've never missed a show or been a nanosecond late.)

The moment we set off, I felt truly good. I had a goal, and it was clear, understandable, unambiguous. True, it was very complicated, but it was also achievable.

I'd keep the boat above the surface. I'd force enough money to dribble out of my pen to survive. And, occasionally, I'd pry *Wild Card* out of a harbor and drift downwind to a different locale.

"Check, check, check!" I laughed as I ticked them off my list.

Everything else faded, even the face of my mother. America dimmed. My daughter's e-mails seemed, well, interesting, but increasingly mundane. I'd listen to the news on the BBC and think, "They're all insane!"

We, however, were not insane. We were lit up. We were turned on, tuned in and had truly dropped out. We had finally becoming what I'd always hoped to be: sea gypsies. Citizens of the world. "Sailor sans frontiers," as the French say.

It is difficult to explain how each ocean mile traveled seemed to empower me. I was finally in tune with Mother Nature (or, more properly, Mother Ocean.) My home, my art, my profession, my transportation, my hobby and my sport had all melded into one 38-foot watery sphere. My diet of fish, rice, and beans agreed not only with me, but also my cardiologist.

The sky seemed so big, the ocean so blue, and Carolyn more beautiful than ever. I saw God on the face of every ocean wave. My rig hummed a celestial tune; its tattered halyards tattooed ancient, wind-borne rhythms. I surged with raw passion and gladly kissed each new day full-on-the-lips.

The Panama Canal flashed by. A blue-footed booby landed on our bow pulpit off the Galápagos. The waterfall in Fatu Hiva, Marquesas, was icy cold. A perfect pearl from the Tuamotus rolled aboard. I crashed-tacked in Bora Bora's inner lagoon—thinking the huge manta ray gliding beneath me was a reef. The 400-pound Tongan princess who served me kava was, after a few bowls, pretty cute. I asked a New Zealand farmer if he'd ever cheated on his wife, and he looked sheepish. Off Darwin, Australia, I altered course to avoid what I thought was a snarl of black poly rope in the water—as the large yellow eye of a nearly submerged saltwater croc winked at me.

Through it all, I kept all the circumnavigation balls up in the air: The boat still floated, its rig was up and the keel down, and our diesel auxiliary still cranked. My radio station unexpectedly e-mailed me—not to cancel my radio show but to give me a raise. I sold every story I wrote.

I could do no wrong.

Then came the Indian Ocean. Wow! I gulped it all in: the food of Thailand, the stench of India, the pristine state of the Maldives. Then Chagos: so empty of people and so full of life. It was everything I wanted—had ever wanted, really within a 50-mile radius of deep ocean. Everything I wanted and yet, thankfully, nothing more.

There was the madness of moody, spooky Madagascar, the awful racism of South Africa, lovely St. Helena, and then home.

I honestly thought crossing my wake and finally becoming a full-fledged, honest-to-God circumnavigator would be orgasmically cool. But it wasn't. It was just the beginning of a strange sort of emptiness.

There seemed to be a hole in my soul.

For four years there had been a sort of radar screen in my brain that constantly monitored the progress of the circumnavigation. I'd glance at it many times a day, often many times a minute. The challenge of circumnavigating, especially on a modest production boat with little money, was immense. I had to accomplish it in tiny bites, with a large series of cautious baby steps. It took a lot of planning, a lot of monitoring and many incremental, intermediate waypoints. And each mile traveled, each dollar earned, every boat-maintenance project completed brought us closer to our goal.

Now the radar screen was blank, just an irritating screech of white-noise where recently my life goal had glowed so magnificently. We'd just experienced the world's best vacation—and now I was suddenly and unexpectedly experiencing the world's worst case of post-vacation blues.

I could write a book about each place we'd stopped: how friendly the Polynesians are, how sweet the gentle Balinese, how gracious the smiling people of Thailand. How could I have ever been so foolish as to leave the Land of Smiles? How long would it take to sail back to Borneo and its orangutan-inhabited rain forests? To Madagascar and its leaping lemurs? To Africa and its naked, smiling drummers?

I'd felt so alive! As if life itself was a sensuous, delicious electricity caressing my body, as if my tiller wasn't merely a stick, but a magic wand connecting me directly to Mother Ocean. How can I explain what surfing atop the breaking crest of a 30-foot ocean wave feels like or watching a barometer finally tick upwards as a major gales passes overhead? Or how it feels to be snatched off your foredeck by a flailing Genoa sheet?

Even the worst moments of our circumnavigation were riveting: the pursuit by pirates in the Malacca Straits, hitting Australia's Great Barrier Reef, being surrounded—at night, on the dinghy dock—by violent thugs in Southeast Asia. I remember crying when we left India. Why? In many ways I hated India, but some of the people we met there were so wonderful and pure and spiritual that it was like saying good-bye to living angels.

But now, with a jolt, it was back to reality. I'm an American, for better or for worse, and here I was back on U.S. soil and surrounded by dirt dwellers, shore drones, bean counters and the dreaded suits in the executive suite.

I tuned in a local radio station. The national news came on, and I thought the lead story was a clever-but-crude parody of someone attempting to inflame anti-Islamic sentiment. I'd just spent two years being treated with dignity and respect in Islamic countries, and was horrified by some of the things I heard in "Fortress America" upon my return.

But it wasn't merely politics that turned me off. Consumerism seemed to have run amok while I was gone. All my friends were making massive amounts of money, but living impoverished lives on every level that mattered to me. There was noise everywhere. Video screens flicked from every doorway. Cars swooshed. Trucks roared. Everything seemed to be vibrating, as if a large unseen generator was about to blow a piston through its cylinder block. A Jimmy Buffet lyric ran crazily through my mind, "Where you gonna go, when the volcano blows?" I felt like a modern Flying Dutchmen, doomed to forever sail without touching the shores of my previous culture.

I went to bar and bought a cold beer. Snatches of conversation washed over me: "…John's new SUV has a DVD player in the back for the kids."

"…so I told him, 'I can't live on $35 an hour,' and he said, 'Well, if you factor in our health insurance...'"

"…don't the ragheads realize you can't rule the world without learning how to use toilet paper?"

I went back to Wild Card and sat in the cockpit. Carolyn could tell at a glance I was upset. I was thinking, "I'm forever changed. These last 50,000 ocean miles have ruined me!"

Carolyn sat next to me and didn't say anything. I felt confused, childlike and angry. Finally I blurted out. "I want to go."

"Go where?" she asked.

"Just go."

Afterword

The Future

Writing is the centerpiece of my professional life—and without economic freedom there is no personal freedom. So I want to continue writing for a living. And sailing.

I'd love to write a book a year, in addition to my duties at *Cruising World*. This book doesn't have to make a lot of money, but it does have to be profitable and allow me to speak my heart without censure.

Is there a secret to writing well? Yes. It is the truth. Whenever a paragraph sags, I simply ask myself, "What is the truth here, Fatty? What are you *really* trying to say?"

I'm extremely fortunate to have a life partner who believes in me. Carolyn is more than just my wonderful wife, my sensuous lover, and my best friend—she has helped, since the age of fifteen, to make me into who I am.

There have been times when we could not afford food, but I always had a ream of typing paper. Once, with a total of $18 in hand and a young baby at her breast, Carolyn convinced me to spend $12 on a used Olivetti portable typewriter. She's lugged tons of manuscripts to the post office and returned with tons of sharply worded rejection letters—with never a negative nor disparaging comment.

How can one man be so lucky?

Do I want to climb Mount Everest? Sail around the Horn? Make a million bucks? Not really.

What I *do* want to do, is to write another good sentence and to sleep in Carolyn's loving arms yet again. And I can. And I will.

Also available from Cap'n Fatty Goodlander:

Chasing the Horizon is a delightfully demented Celebration of A Way of Life. It is an outrageously funny, often touching, and continuously shocking tale of a modern sea gypsy.

Cap'n Fatty's story is too bizarre to be fiction. Father wears floral skirts; mother is a tad vague. Sister Carole isn't interested in her millionaire suitor; she's too busy smooching with the kid in the cesspool truck. Their strange live-aboard boat caravan includes Mort the Mortician, Backwards Bernie, Ruby Red the Conman, Barefoot Benny, Geeper Creeper, Para the Paranoid, Lusty Laura, Xlax, Shark Boy, the Pawtucket Pirate, Bait Broad, Scupper Lips, Bob the Broker, the Pirate Queen, Otto the Owner, the Twin Slaves of Green Slime—and even a terribly long-winded fellow named (Hurricane) Hugo. All seem hell-bent on avoiding the cops, the creeps, each other, and especially the Dreaded Dream Crushers.

Dive in!

The Collected Fat represents the very best writing from one of the most outrageous writers in the Caribbean. Cap'n Fatty will enthrall you with his rollicking tales of Lush Tropical Vegetables, Wonderful Waterfront Wackos, and Colorful Caribbean Characters.

A number of these stories will make you laugh. A few will touch your heart. One might change you, ever-so-slightly, forever. All will entertain, enlighten, and amuse.

Seadogs, Clowns, & Gypsies is more than just a book about the remarkable lifestyle of various Caribbean sailors. It is a Celebration of a Way of Life. The people who inhabit these salt-stained pages ("We're all here, because we're not all there!") have a true Lust for Living. They kiss life full on the lips, embrace each new day, welcome every fresh sensation. Yeah, they are louts and cads and drunkards and misfits and fools – and yet, somehow, they emerge from these yarns as a noble, vital people.

Order through our website at: **fattygoodlander.com**
or from **Amazon.com** (also available in Kindle editions)

If you have a favorite Cap'n Fatty story, let us know at:
www.fattygoodlander.com

CHASING
THE
HORIZON
The Life and Times of a Modern Sea Gypsy
By Cap'n Fatty Goodlander

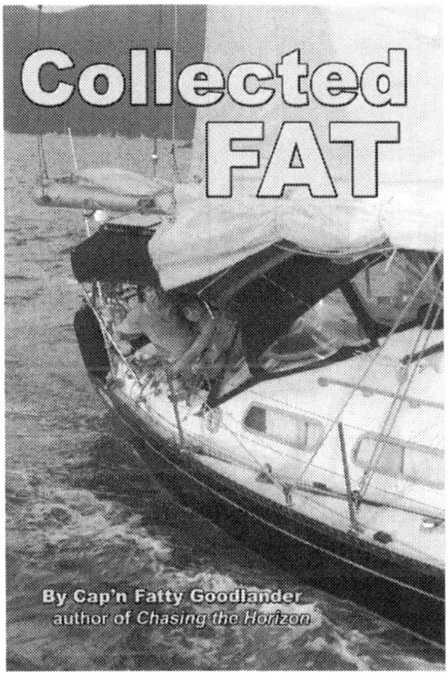
Collected
FAT
By Cap'n Fatty Goodlander
author of Chasing the Horizon

SEADOGS, CLOWNS,
& GYPSIES
By
Cap'n Fatty Goodlander
author of CHASING THE HORIZON
RUM
Twenty Modern Sea Stories about Colorful Caribbean Characters, Wonderful Waterfront Wackos, and Lush Tropical Vegetables

Cap'n Fatty Goodlander has lived aboard various sailing vessels for 48 of his 56 years. He has written numerous books—including his autobiographical comedy *Chasing The Horizon.* At various times, Fatty has been a professional actor, a radio broadcaster and a newspaper writer. He is currently on his second circumnavigation. His latest project was a series of summer travel spots for National Public Radio. For more info, see fattygoodlander.com. To purchase one of his books, go to amazon.com.

He and his wife Carolyn are currently anchored off the tiny rubber-tapping village of Ban Kho En, Phuket, Thailand.

He is an editor-at-large of Cruising World magazine.

68565832R00123

Made in the USA
Lexington, KY
14 October 2017